Praise for
Dismantling Mass Incarceration

"This book is a must-read for anyone fighting for justice, equality, and an end to mass incarceration."
—David Ayala, executive director of the Formerly Incarcerated, Convicted People and Families Movement (FICPFM)

"*Dismantling Mass Incarceration* is an urgently needed practical call to action on one of the defining issues of modern American history. The anthology is chock-full of big ideas from the big thinkers; it brings together a phenomenal collection of contributors, including fallen movement leaders, public intellectuals, scholars, formerly incarcerated artists, judges, lawyers, and more."
—Chesa Boudin, former district attorney of San Francisco and executive director of the Criminal Law and Justice Center at the University of California, Berkeley School of Law

"The injustices of mass incarceration have harshly affected my family for generations. I myself spent nearly thirty years cycling through the system. Today, as a state representative and lawyer, I devote my passion and expertise to reforming the criminal legal system. *Dismantling Mass Incarceration* is a brilliantly written tool for our national movement, and I am so thankful for the authors' gifts to all of us."
—Tarra Simmons, member of the Washington State House of Representatives for the Twenty-Third District

Premal Dharia by Prescott Loveland

James Forman Jr. by Harold Shapiro

Maria Hawilo courtesy of Loyola University Chicago School of Law

Dismantling Mass Incarceration

Edited by
Premal Dharia, James Forman Jr., and Maria Hawilo

Premal Dharia is the executive director of the Institute to End Mass Incarceration at Harvard Law School and the coeditor-in-chief of *Inquest*. She has written for *The Washington Post*, CNN, *Slate*, and other outlets.

James Forman Jr. is the J. Skelly Wright Professor of Law at Yale Law School and the faculty director of the Yale Law and Racial Justice Center. His book *Locking Up Our Own* won the 2018 Pulitzer Prize.

Maria Hawilo is a distinguished professor in residence at Loyola University Chicago School of Law. She has written for *The Appeal*, *Injustice Watch*, and other publications.

All three editors are former public defenders.

Dismantling
Mass Incarceration

Dismantling Mass Incarceration

A Handbook for Change

Edited by
PREMAL DHARIA,
JAMES FORMAN JR.,
and
MARIA HAWILO

FSG Originals
Farrar, Straus and Giroux
New York

FSG Originals
Farrar, Straus and Giroux
120 Broadway, New York 10271

Printed in the United States of America
First edition, 2024

Owing to limitations of space, permissions acknowledgments for individual texts
can be found on pages 465–468.

Title-page and part-opener design based on cover design by No Ideas.

Library of Congress Cataloging-in-Publication Data
Names: Dharia, Premal, editor. | Forman, James, 1967– editor. | Hawilo,
    Maria, editor.
Title: Dismantling mass incarceration : a handbook for change / edited by
    Premal Dharia, James Forman Jr., and Maria Hawilo.
Description: First edition. | New York : FSG Originals, [2024] | Includes
    bibliographical references.
Identifiers: LCCN 2023057424 | ISBN 9780374614485 (paperback)
Subjects: LCSH: Imprisonment—United States. | Alternatives to imprisonment—
    United States. | Criminal justice, Administration of—United States.
Classification: LCC HV9471 .D58 2024 | DDC 365/.70973—dc23/eng/20240214
LC record available at https://lccn.loc.gov/2023057424

Designed by Patrice Sheridan

Our books may be purchased in bulk for promotional, educational, or business
use. Please contact your local bookseller or the Macmillan Corporate and
Premium Sales Department at 1-800-221-7945, extension 5442, or by email at
MacmillanSpecialMarkets@macmillan.com.

www.fsgoriginals.com • www.fsgbooks.com
Follow us on social media at @fsgoriginals and @fsgbooks

10   9   8   7   6   5   4   3   2   1

To Arthur, who never gives up.
    —J.F.

To my loves, Mimi, Peter, Teo, and Konrad,
and to my parents, for everything.
    —M.H.

To my parents, my sister, and Chris.
But most of all, to Rohan.
    —P.D.

Contents

Contents

A Note from the Editors

Some of the selections in this reader have been edited for length and clarity. For ease of reading, we have generally not included brackets or ellipses to indicate deleted material.

Introduction

By Premal Dharia, James Forman Jr., and Maria Hawilo

Back when we started as public defenders, in the 1990s and early 2000s, the thing most people said about prisons was that we needed more of them. Legislators all over the country were passing laws to increase mandatory minimum sentences, jail children for life, and deny incarcerated people access to education and the courts. Prosecutors, judges, and sheriffs won elections by claiming they would lock up more people than their opponents, for longer, in the worst possible conditions. Police forced more people into the criminal system through aggressive surveillance tactics, including stop-and-frisk of pedestrians and pretext stops of drivers. The Department of Justice proudly issued reports with titles like *The Case for More Incarceration*.[1]

What did the American people think about these punitive policies? While there were some dissenters, mostly they cheered.

Much has changed since then. In the summer of 2020, more Americans than had ever marched before—on any issue—took to the streets to protest racism and police brutality. Our country's approach to incarceration, once overlooked even in the civil rights community, has become a central human rights and racial justice issue. Books like Michelle Alexander's *The New Jim Crow*, Bryan Stevenson's *Just Mercy*, Ta-Nehisi Coates's *Between the World and Me*, and Mariame Kaba's *We Do This 'Til We Free Us* have dominated bestseller lists and are required reading in high schools and colleges. In the law schools where we work, students once declined to become public defenders because they didn't want to represent "bad" people. Now, our students are more likely to avoid becoming prosecutors because they don't want to contribute to mass incarceration.

But the daily reality of our criminal system has not changed as much as the conversation surrounding it. America still incarcerates more people than any other country in the world. We still target Black people disproportionately. Though the racial disparity in incarceration rates has declined in recent years, Black adults are imprisoned at five times the rate of white adults.[2]

We jail hundreds of thousands of people only because they are too poor to post money bail. We imprison thousands more in solitary confinement conditions that the United Nations considers torture.[3] Once a person is released from prison, instead of welcoming them home, we stigmatize and exclude them by making it difficult for them to find a job or a place to live. And as some reforms are implemented, the system expands in new ways: cameras and monitors create a web of surveillance that can feel like its own sort of incarceration. All this policing and punishment requires an enormous bureaucracy: The 2.8 million people employed in our criminal justice system make up over 1.5 percent of the American workforce (by contrast, less than 1 percent of Americans are employed manufacturing cars).[4]

What will it take to make our approaches to crime, harm, and safety more humane? What can people who work within the system do to make their agencies more just? And most of all, what can ordinary people do to imagine and build structures that will truly make us all safer?

This book seeks to help answer these questions. We devote each part to a key stage of our criminal system, starting with police, where most criminal cases begin. We close by discussing the never-ending consequences of being entangled in the criminal process—restrictions on people's voting rights, housing eligibility, and employment that linger for so long that they merit the name "lifetime punishments." In between, we address the actors and institutions in the criminal process in the order they typically present themselves in real life: prosecutors, public defenders, judges, and prisons.

We organize the book this way because to understand how mass incarceration operates, we must break the system into its various pieces. A core truth about the criminal system is that it isn't a system at all. Instead, it is a series of largely disconnected actors, structures, and bureaucracies, each following their own incentives and logics.

One feature of our decentralized, disorganized non-system is that it resists accountability, allowing its disparate actors to shift blame. We've seen this in our own careers. We've presented judges with evidence of harsh sentencing and watched them nod sympathetically before lamenting, "If only prosecutors would change how they charge cases." We've spoken to prosecutors about racial disparities in incarceration rates and heard them acknowledge the issue before saying, "The real problem lies with police and who they arrest." We've met with police to discuss surveillance of Black teens and been told, "Parents need to do a better job of raising their kids." Since everybody can blame someone else, no one is forced to act.

The non-system also thwarts change by making it difficult for ordinary people to figure out who is responsible for particular injustices. We spend a lot of our time traveling around the country, giving lectures about the unnecessary damage caused by our current policies and their failure to keep us safe. At some point in the conversation, somebody invariably says, "If I want to make a difference, where should I focus my energy? Where should I start?" We wish we could tell everyone to call, write, and pressure the same person: the president, their governor, or their district attorney. But the truth is that there are thousands of possible places to start, and the best place for *you* to start will often depend on where you live, what issues you care about most, and who else is already organizing—and for what—in your community.

Though frustrating, this reality also presents an opening. Because our system is wrong and harmful in so many ways, it offers innumerable opportunities to make a difference.

That's where this book comes in. Over the past three years, we have scoured the literature, talked to experts, and debated with friends and each other, all with a single goal: to compile in one place some of the most useful, compelling, and provocative writing on how to dismantle mass incarceration. Our task turned out to be harder than we expected. While there has been an outpouring of writing about mass incarceration in the last decade, much of it is devoted to describing the problem, not the possible solutions.

This book fills that gap. To be sure, it does not provide concise solutions, because mass incarceration is not a concise problem. Rather, we take each portion of the criminal system in turn and share readings that span a spectrum of possibilities for intervention, reform, and disruption. We do this seeking to generate both discussion and action. When you finish Part I on policing, for example, you will be aware of a range of options for making policing less harmful. This book will also equip you with examples of communities that are implementing some of those changes—examples that we hope will inspire and guide you as you push for change where you live.

While the authors we have included here all agree that mass incarceration is an outrage, they often disagree about how—or even what it means—to dismantle it. In the parts on policing and prisons, for instance, tension exists between those seeking to abolish those institutions and those trying to reform them. In Part II on prosecutors, writers disagree on whether electing "progressive prosecutors" will produce meaningful changes or instead will absorb energy that is better directed elsewhere. Part III, on public defenders, offers a vigorous debate over whether improving our public defense system is a useful way to resist mass incarceration—or whether even hardworking public defenders necessarily legitimate the status quo.

We do not shy away from these disagreements. We present them because they raise questions that we struggle with ourselves. We hope you will struggle with them too—and that you'll emerge as a more effective advocate for whatever position you ultimately adopt.

We have included a wide range of responses to mass incarceration because we know no silver bullet will solve this crisis. In most cases, the writers in this book do not claim that a particular reform is *the* best or *the* most urgent but rather that it is one of many important things that should be done. Mass incarceration was built bit by bit, law by law, choice by choice, over generations, across our fifty states, Washington, D.C., the territories, and over three thousand counties. It will have to be dismantled the same way.

Some of you may devote your efforts to building libraries in prisons. Others of you will want to get police out of traffic enforcement, elect a reform-oriented prosecutor, establish a bail fund, organize to close a prison, or persuade your employer to be more open to hiring people with criminal convictions. In these pages, you will find stories of people pursuing all these ideas—and many more.

While most who pick up this book will be working outside the criminal system, others will have some role in it. If you are one of them, this volume also presents you with opportunities for action. Whether it is a police department diverting people using drugs away from jail, a prosecutor asking for less prison time, a panel of judges overturning a sentence tainted by racist assumptions, or a prison official making their own prison less isolating, this book presents real stories of changes led by actors within the system.

Some argue that the kind of action we include in this book will never, alone, end mass incarceration. Instead, they say, society must address the variety of social and economic conditions that foster it. We agree. We too believe that everyone deserves access to affordable housing, a guaranteed minimum income, quality health care, and drug and mental health treatment, and that these things would go a long way toward building safe, thriving communities. And we too believe that many of the forces that have created our system of punishment are far bigger than the system itself. Though we include a sampling of contributors making these arguments, we leave a more detailed discussion of those types of interventions for other books. We view them as complementary to the ones we delve into here.

The conversation surrounding the criminal system has changed dramatically over the past decade. It's a sign of progress that a book titled *Dismantling Mass Incarceration* can find a publisher—and, we hope, an audience ready to discuss and act on its lessons. But we concede that this book isn't for everyone. If you think—as some still do—that this country needs more prisons, you'll find little of interest here. If you think—as some still do—that police are unfairly constrained and need more leeway to do as they please, you will also be disappointed.

But if you are like the many people who approach us after we give talks at bookstores, universities, libraries, and houses of worship and ask, "How do we end this?" well, keep reading. You've come to the right place.

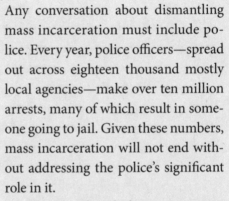

Part I

Police

Any conversation about dismantling mass incarceration must include police. Every year, police officers—spread out across eighteen thousand mostly local agencies—make over ten million arrests, many of which result in someone going to jail. Given these numbers, mass incarceration will not end without addressing the police's significant role in it.

The past decade has seen an avalanche of scholarship and activism studying and challenging what police do in the name of public safety. Police have injured—and killed—people engaged in almost every conceivable activity (and even non-activity): walking, running, driving, sitting, sleeping, and on and on. Police officers have often arrested people who would have been better served by shelter, mental health treatment, or addiction services. At times, this is because police don't seem to have any other options. But sometimes police arrest people even when they do have other options. The victims of policing's harms are disproportionately Black and often reside in marginalized communities.

During the 1990s and early 2000s, proposals to reform policing typically included calls to invest in community policing, empower civilian review boards, and diversify police forces. But as the abuses continue unabated, and with police culture seemingly impervious to reform, a new chorus of critics is asking different questions: Do we want police at all? And if so, what should police do?

The contributions in this part all revolve around these questions. We begin with the most provocative version: Can we imagine a society without armed guards patrolling its streets, hospitals, and schools? Derecka Purnell, a leading voice in the abolitionist movement, provides an answer in "How I Became a Police Abolitionist," Part I's opening essay. Purnell explains that police abolition initially repulsed her. She found it "white and utopic"; she'd seen too much violence in her life to conceive of a world without police. Purnell's perspective changed, however, as she studied abolitionist theory and practice alongside students, lawyers, and activists. She eventually came to believe that only abolition invited the questions she found most pressing: What investments will adequately address the root causes of violence? What alternative forms of accountability—including restorative and transformative justice—could replace the police-prison paradigm and offer true safety and healing? Purnell acknowledges that she lacks complete answers to these questions. But she urges us to live with uncertainty and discomfort, confident that the new world abolition seeks to create will be more just than our current one.

While Purnell grew up amidst widespread violence, Jill Leovy witnessed it during years of reporting on homicides for the *Los Angeles Times*.[1] In her conversation with *The Marshall Project*'s Bill Keller, Leovy points out that "[m]ore than half of the killers of black men go free in cities all over the country." In her view, law enforcement's failure to solve crimes and prosecute offenders is inexcusable: "Violence is not a problem for coaches and pastors to solve; the state must do its job." But Leovy doesn't call for the police to do more of what they already do. She argues that police spend an inordinate amount of time on tactics that damage the precise communities they are supposed to protect. As she tells Keller, "police need to annoy and alienate fewer non-offenders, and arrest more serious, violent offenders. Pull back from broken-windows-style saturation, targeting patches of geography, and stop-and-search tactics, and concentrate on ensuring judicial resolution of serious crimes."

Following the exchange between Leovy and Keller, we present another conversation, this one between criminologist Patrick Sharkey and journalist Rogé Karma. Like Purnell and Leovy, Sharkey has thought deeply about violence and how to reduce it. He points out that violence has fallen by roughly half in America since the 1990s. What caused the decline? According to his research, community-based actors and institutions deserve more credit than they've received. This insight leads to Sharkey's big idea: a demonstration project launching community-based anti-violence programs on an unprecedented scale. To be worth trying, Sharkey says, the project must be large-scale and sustained—guaranteeing each program the same level of funding that the local police receive, for at least ten years. Depending on a community's wishes, such a program could work in tandem with local police—or in lieu of them. It's an ambitious proposal, to be sure. But if the project worked, Sharkey argues, it could forever change how we respond to violence in American cities.[2]

Violence plays a lead role in most conversations about policing. But in fact, police are mainly occupied with issues other than violent crime. A recent study of 911 calls in nine American cities reveals that only 6 percent reported violent incidents; most were for traffic events, disorders, suspicious persons, follow-up service requests, and property crimes.[3] A study tracking how officers spend their time reached a similar conclusion. Examining police forces in New Orleans, Sacramento, and Montgomery County, Maryland, it found that about 4 percent of officer time was devoted to violent crime.[4]

Once we recognize how much of policing involves responding to nonviolent, nonemergency events, certain questions quickly arise: Do we need police for these tasks? Or could somebody else—with a different mandate, training, and culture—perform them with more compassion and less violence? These questions are prompting cities to experiment with new ways of responding to issues such as housing instability, mental illness, and substance use disorder. The next articles in this part argue for this approach, in which community-based groups, nonprofits, and social service agencies do more and police do less.

For example, in an editorial titled "Whom Can We Call for Help? Police Should Not Always Be the Only Option," the *Washington Post* Editorial Board asks us to consider cases like that of Daniel Prude, who died after police in Rochester, New York, forced his head into a hood and pushed his face into the ground while he was in the throes of a psychotic episode. The

Post asks, "What if instead of facing armed police officers while in the agony of a mental breakdown, Prude had been assisted by a crisis worker and a medic who were trained to de-escalate the situation and could connect him to mental health crisis services?" As the editorial documents, communities around the country are beginning to build a network of alternative providers who can offer people in crisis appropriate care instead of citations, fines, and jail.[5]

Building an alternative response network is extraordinarily complex, as Katherine Beckett, Forrest Stuart, and Monica Bell emphasize in "From Crisis to Care." While the authors embrace the urgency of efforts to create crisis teams that aren't led by police, they worry that current models have important limitations. They point out that many programs change the first response to the emergency call but don't offer follow-up services to the person in crisis. This isn't nothing—Daniel Prude would almost certainly still be alive if mental health workers had responded instead of police. But it also isn't enough. People who lack housing, mental health care, or addiction support need long-term assistance—a second, third, and fourth response as supportive as the first.

Such a program is underway in Seattle, write Beckett, Stuart, and Bell. Called JustCARE, it works with people living in unauthorized encampments and offers long-term, trauma-informed housing and care. Initial studies show that JustCARE participants are less likely to be re-arrested or imprisoned. Because it is robust, JustCARE isn't cheap. But, as the authors remind us, compared to prison it is both far less expensive and far more humane.

As more cities consider ways to redefine the role of police, traffic stops have become an obvious target. In 2018, traffic stops accounted for about 40 percent of all police contacts with ordinary people and over 80 percent of contacts initiated by police.[6] Too often, they turn deadly. According to *The Washington Post*, about 11 percent of fatal shootings by police begin with a traffic stop.[7] Even when traffic stops don't lead to death, they can be extraordinarily harmful. Many departments encourage officers to make what are called "pretext stops," using the pretext of a traffic violation to search a car for drugs or weapons. Black drivers are disproportionately subject to these stops, which makes them more likely to be cited, arrested, and charged. And because these drivers know they've been singled out for a pretext stop, they come to distrust police and legal institutions more broadly.[8]

Sarah Seo addresses this issue in "Police Officers Shouldn't Be the Ones to Enforce Traffic Laws." Seo understands the importance of traffic safety but argues that we can have both safer roads and fewer police encounters with drivers. She proposes technological solutions like automated speed and red-light cameras alongside those that can detect expired licenses and registrations. For situations that require human enforcement, Seo argues that unarmed traffic monitors could handle many of the stops currently conducted by police. Armed officers, in her view, should only get involved in cases involving serious crimes or threats to public safety. Because we have grown so accustomed to a blanket police presence in traffic enforcement, some of Seo's suggestions might seem far-fetched. But various jurisdictions—including Philadelphia, Pittsburgh, San Francisco, Berkeley, and the state of Virginia—have recently taken steps to prevent police from stopping drivers for low-level violations.[9]

In addition to using traffic stops as a pretext for searches, police often use them to make money, subjecting drivers to fines and fees that help fund local governments. This turns policing on its head: rather than a public service, it becomes a tax. And not just any tax, but a highly regressive one. Because police disproportionately stop Black drivers and those in low-income neighborhoods, this tax is borne by a community's poorest residents. How to challenge this predatory relationship? The next selection, "Fines, Fees, and Police Divestment: Statement and Policy Recommendations," by the Fines and Fees Justice Center, offers a series of ideas. Among them: prohibit municipalities and law enforcement agencies from receiving any of the money police generate from traffic stops, misdemeanor arrests, and property forfeiture. Under this proposal, local governments would no longer have a financial incentive to subject marginalized communities to policing and plunder.[10]

One of this book's central themes is that ordinary citizens can intervene in the criminal system where they live. But can people really change policing—an institution that has long resisted democratic accountability?[11] Residents of New Orleans—and a growing number of other places—have said yes to trying. In "She Wants to Fix One of Louisiana's Deadliest Jails. She Needs to Beat the Sheriff First," Jessica Pishko chronicles the grassroots campaign to elect one of the country's first reform-oriented sheriffs.[12] Although the responsibilities assigned to sheriffs vary—some run the local jail, others act as police officers, and many do both—they all wield substantial authority. Yet they have typically flown under the radar in conversations about how mass incarceration came to be—and how to dismantle it. That is changing. While individual sheriffs elected on progressive platforms may not always enact all of the promised reforms, they do hold real power in these roles. We lift up this piece in the hope of furthering a conversation about the role sheriffs play in the criminal system, and to highlight the organizing efforts involved in one race—efforts that will out-last any one candidate.[13]

Victories like these are important but insufficient, argues Marie Gottschalk. Questioning—or changing—the role of po-lice also requires us to dig deeper; if we can reduce crime, harm, and disorder itself, we can more easily downsize policing. In this part's final essay, "Bring It On: The Future of Penal Reform, the Carceral State, and American Politics," Gottschalk reminds us that structural inequality is a dominant contributor to mass incarceration. Like Derecka Purnell, Gottschalk argues that to prevent crime, we must invest in social programs that provide housing, health care, education, and employment.

None of these transformations are easy. Community action and policy reforms may take years to implement. Laws can't change culture quickly. But these readings demonstrate that the conversation around policing has already changed. They call on us to continue challenging current approaches to public safety, and they point the way toward promising alternatives.

How I Became a
Police Abolitionist*

Derecka Purnell
2020

We called 911 for almost everything except snitching.

Nosebleeds, gunshot wounds, asthma attacks, allergic reactions. Police accompanied the paramedics.

Our neighborhood made us sick. A Praxair industrial gas-storage facility was at one end of my block. A junkyard with exposed military airplane and helicopter parts was at the other. The fish-seasoning plant in our backyard did not smell as bad as the yeast from the Budweiser factory nearby. Car honks and fumes from Interstate 64 crept through my childhood bedroom window, where, if I stood on my toes, I could see the St. Louis arch.

Environmental toxins degraded our health, and often conspired with other violence that pervaded our neighborhood. Employment opportunities were rare, and my friends and I turned to making money under the table. I was scared of selling

---

* Derecka Purnell, "How I Became a Police Abolitionist," *The Atlantic*, July 6, 2020.

drugs, so I gambled. Brown-skinned boys I liked aged out of recreational activities, and, without alternatives, into blue bandanas. Their territorial disputes led to violence and 911 calls. Grown-ups fought too, stressed from working hard yet never having enough bill money or gas money or food money or daycare money. Call 911.

When people dismiss abolitionists for not caring about victims or safety, they tend to forget that we are those victims, those survivors of violence.

The first shooting I witnessed was by a uniformed security guard. I was 13. I remember that the guard was angry that his cousin skipped a sign-in sheet at my neighborhood recreation center; the victim told police it had started as an argument over "something stupid." I was teaching my sister how to shoot free throws when the guard stormed in alongside the court, drew his weapon, and shot the boy in the arm. My sister and I hid in the locker room for hours afterward. The guard was back at work the following week.

Like the boy at the rec center who was shot by the guard, most victims of police violence survive. No hashtags or protests or fires for the wounded, assaulted, and intimidated. I often wonder, *What if Derek Chauvin had kneeled on George Floyd's neck for seven minutes and forty-six seconds instead of eight?* Maybe Floyd would have lived to be arrested, prosecuted, and imprisoned for allegedly attempting to use a counterfeit $20 bill. Is that justice? This, for me, is why we need police abolition. Police manage inequality by keeping the dispossessed from the owners, the Black from the white, the homeless from the housed, the beggars from the employed. Reforms make police polite managers of inequality. Abolition makes police and inequality obsolete.

"Police abolition" initially repulsed me. The idea seemed white and utopic. I'd seen too much sexual violence and buried too many friends to consider getting rid of police in St. Louis, let alone the nation. But in reality, the police were a placebo. Calling them felt like *something*, as the legal scholar Michelle Alexander explains, and something feels like everything when your other option is nothing.

Police couldn't do what we really needed. They could not heal relationships or provide jobs. We were afraid every time we called. When the cops arrived, I was silenced, threatened with detention, or removed from my home. Fifteen years later, my old neighborhood still lacks quality food, employment, schools, health care, and air—all of which increases the risk of violence and the reliance on police. Yet I feared letting go; I thought we needed them.

Until the Ferguson, Missouri, cop Darren Wilson killed Michael Brown. Brown had a funeral. Wilson had a wedding. Most police officers just continue to live their lives after filling the streets with blood and bone.

I drove from Ferguson to law-school orientation two weeks after Brown's death. I met, studied, and struggled alongside students and movement lawyers who explained the power and the purpose of the prison-industrial complex through an abolitionist framework. Black abolitionists have condemned the role of prisons and police for centuries, even before W. E. B. Du Bois's *Black Reconstruction*. They imagined and built responses to harm rooted in community and accountability. In recent decades, abolitionists have developed alternatives to 911, created support systems for victims of domestic violence, prevented new jail construction, reduced police budgets, and shielded undocumented immigrants from deportation. Abolition, I learned, was a bigger idea than firing cops and closing prisons; it included eliminating the reasons people think they need cops and prisons in the first place.

We never should have had police. Policing is among the vestiges of slavery, tailored in America to suppress slave revolts, catch runaways, and repress labor organizing. After slavery, police imprisoned Black people and immigrants under a convict-leasing system for plantation and business owners. During the Jim Crow era, cops enforced segregation and joined lynch mobs that grew strange fruit from southern trees. During the civil-rights movement, police beat the hell out of Black preachers, activists, and students who marched for equality wearing their Sunday best. Cops were the foot soldiers for Richard Nixon's War on Drugs and Joe Biden's 1994 crime bill. Police departments pepper-sprayed Occupy Wall Street protesters without provocation and indiscriminately tear-gassed Black Lives Matter activists for years—including me, twice. Black people I know trust police; they trust them to be exactly what they always have been.

After each video of a police killing goes viral, popular reforms go on tour: banning choke holds, investing in community policing, diversifying departments—none of which would have saved Floyd or most other police victims. The Princeton professor Naomi Murakawa wrote to me in an email:

> At best, these reforms discourage certain techniques of killing, but they don't condemn the fact of police killing. "Ban the chokehold!" But allow murder with guns and tasers and police vans? The analogy here is to death-penalty reformers who improved the noose with the electric chair, and then improved the electric chair with chemical cocktails.
>
> But the technique of murder doesn't comfort the dead. It

comforts the executioners—and all their supportive onlook-
ers. Like so much reform to address racism, all this legal fine
print is meant to salve the conscience of moderates who want
salvation on the cheap, without any real change to the material life-and-death realities for Black people.

When Donald Trump was elected president, many liberals
feared the end of consent decrees, legal agreements between
the Department of Justice and police departments, intended to
spur real change. After law school, I worked for the Advancement Project, which supported community organizers in Ferguson on the decree that was negotiated in the aftermath of
Brown's death. Millions of dollars went toward an investigation, publicity, and a lawsuit to rid the Ferguson Police Department of "bad apples" and transform its culture. After a year of
militaristic ambush on the community, the consent decree provided members of the police department with mental-health
services to cope with the unrest, but no treatment or restitution for the residents who were teargassed, shot with rubber
bullets, and traumatized by the tanks at the edge of their drive-
ways. The Obama administration's DOJ objected to dismissing
thousands of old cases that were the result of unconstitutional
policing, and protected the police department from criticisms
that community organizers shared with the judge in court.

Constitutional policing is a problem too. As the legal scholar
Paul Butler explains, the overwhelming majority of police violence is constitutional. Reforms cannot fix a policing system
that is not broken.

Still, many Americans believe that most police officers do
the right thing. Perhaps there are bad apples. But even the best
apples surveil, arrest, and detain millions of people every year
whose primary "crime" is that they are poor or homeless, or

have a disability. Cops escalate violence disproportionately against people with disabilities and in mental-health crises, even the ones who call 911 for help. The police officers who are doing the "right thing" maintain the systems of inequality and ableism in black communities. The right thing is *wrong*.

Policing cannot even fix the harms of our nightmares. People often ask me, "What will we do with murderers and rapists?" Which ones? The police kill more than a thousand people every year, and assault hundreds of thousands more. After excessive force, sexual misconduct is the second-most-common complaint against cops. Many people are afraid to call the police when they suffer these harms, because they fear that the police will hurt them. Thousands of rape survivors refuse to call the police, worried about not being believed or about being re-assaulted, or concerned that their rape kit would sit unexamined for years. In three major cities, less than 4 percent of calls to the police are for "violent crimes." Currently, police departments are getting worse at solving murders and frequently arrest and force confessions out of the wrong people.

So if we abolish the police, what's the alternative? Who do we call? As someone who grew up calling 911, I also shared this concern. I learned this: Just because I did not know an answer didn't mean that one did not exist. I had to study and join an organization, not just ask questions on social media. I read Rachel Herzing, a co-director of the Center for Political Education, who explains that creating small networks of support for different types of emergencies can make us safer than we are now, and reduce our reliance on police. The Oakland Power Projects trains residents to build alternatives to police by helping residents prevent and respond to harm. San Francisco Mayor London Breed just announced that trained, unarmed professionals will respond to many emergency calls, and Los

Angeles city-council members are demanding a similar model. This is the right idea. Rather than thinking of abolition as just getting rid of police, I think about it as an invitation to create and support lots of different answers to the problem of harm in society, and, most exciting, as an opportunity to reduce and eliminate harm in the first place.

Defunding the police is one step on a broad stairway toward abolition. Cities can reduce the size and scope of police and thus limit their opportunities to come into contact with civilians. There should be as much support for the anti-criminalization organizer Mariame Kaba's call to cut law enforcement by half as there has been to cut the prison population by half. Communities can demand hiring and budget freezes, budget cuts, and participatory budgeting opportunities to ensure that police will not be refunded in the future. States should stop the construction of new prisons and begin closing remaining ones by freeing the people inside. No new police academies should be established. These are only a few suggestions from a broader set of abolitionist demands.

More important, society must spend money and time reducing the root causes of violence. If we want to reduce sexual violence immediately, we should expand restorative and transformative processes for accountability. If we are committed to eliminating this harm long-term, then society must offer quality housing, food, day care, transit, employment, debt cancellation, and free college so that people will not be stuck in unhealthy relationships because they need food, money, health insurance, or a place to live.

If we care about reducing neighborhood killings, we must invest in street-violence interruption models such as the one that the feminist organization Taller Salud uses, which minimizes violence through community development and peace programs. These likely would have reduced killings and re-taliation in my neighborhood without police. I wouldn't have hid in the locker room for hours because of a shooting, and maybe my sister would have a better jump shot. We can re-duce and eliminate shootings long-term if we provide the most dispossessed communities with opportunities to thrive, and choose comprehensive gun reform over police occupation of our schools, places of worship, and neighborhoods.

Slavery abolition required resistance, risk, and experimen-tation. Black people rebelled, ran away, and built an under-ground railroad. Abolitionists wrote and orated against the "peculiar institution." Allies funded campaigns, passed legis-lation, and changed the Constitution. Of course, people then felt a range of anxieties about abolition. Slave owners worried about their plantations and the profits that the labor camps wrought. White overseers feared joblessness. Both feared the loss of superiority. Some Black people had reservations about how they'd sustain themselves without the steady, yet violent, protection of their owners. Police abolition triggers similar anxieties today—moral, economic, and otherwise.

But if abolitionists waited to convince every single person that liberation was worth the pursuit, Black people might still be on plantations. Slavery's violence and repression was riskier than Black people's plans, imagination, and will to be free. So they held the uncertainty in their bellies and started running.

Rather than waiting for comforting answers to every po-tential harm ahead of us, let's run. And continue to organize, imagine, and transform this country toward freedom and justice without police and violence. Let's run.

And never look back.

Ghettoside Author Jill Leovy on What We Have Learned Since Rodney King: Not Nearly Enough, She Says*

Jill Leovy, in Conversation with The Marshall Project's Bill Keller

2016

Keller: Your book covers the scourge of black homicides in South Los Angeles, and by extension many other urban communities across the country. To oversimplify a bit, *Ghettoside* points out that, while much attention has been focused on recent cases of police excesses, African-Americans also

* Jill Leovy, in conversation with *The Marshall Project*'s Bill Keller, "*Ghettoside* Author Jill Leovy on What We Have Learned Since Rodney King: Not Nearly Enough, She Says," *The Marshall Project*, March 3, 2016.

are victims of police indifference—and, by the way, media indifference—in the face of an epidemic of black homicides. The alienation in many black communities is as much a result of under-policing as over-policing.

Leovy: I think of homicide, not as a social or cultural problem, but as a material one—an absence of effective law. We can't see law. We can't touch it. And yet, when it works, it swaths us from birth to death in safety like a bulletproof shield. Just as widespread vaccination comes of well-developed public-health bureaucracies, freedom from personal violence comes of fully-realized state legitimacy, manifest in a functioning legal system.

The safe take safety for granted. They assume that they are safe because safety is a state of nature, and that violence is an aberration. They fail to realize that, historically, it's the safe people who are the strange ones. The wealthy suburbs of, say, the San Fernando Valley, where *The Brady Bunch* was filmed, are relatively crime-free, not because they are normally functioning "communities"—another loaded and unexamined term—but because their inhabitants are the inheritors of centuries-long legal, bureaucratic, and political processes that have manufactured high levels of personal safety. They don't have to negotiate with killers. Their neighbors don't coerce them. Their living rooms are not firebombed if they break ranks with the community. They are the beneficiaries of institutional progress that has shifted the burden of conflict resolution from individuals, families, clans, or sects to a highly developed criminal justice system, rooted in democratic processes, controlled by an independent judiciary, and governed by the rule of law. They don't know how lucky they are. Not seeing this, both the political right and left treat violence as exceptional, and thus, as pathological and anti-social in origin. It follows that the problem of urban violence must proceed from some kind of exotic misfire—some psychological, social, or cultural wrong turn. The phrase "senseless violence," that chestnut of police press conferences, reflects this mistaken framework for understanding homicide.

Mostly, violence among black men in places like Watts and Compton is anything but senseless. It is, in fact, extremely useful—"instrumental," as the academics would say—and insofar as it produces results and can be used with impunity, it represents a crushingly decisive application of sense. Those who wield it stand to gain. Nor is violence anti-social. Far from it. Many urban homicides are inherently social acts, arising from close social contact, interdependence, and communal ties. Violence is a means of regulating social relations—specifically, conflicts—and it's terrifically effective. This is why homicides stem most often from arguments. When there is no other means available to regulate conflict—to put an argument to bed, as it were, once and for all—that's when the chance of a violent resolution soars. I don't think this notion of violence is especially original. Many historians and international scholars conceptualize violence as a consequence of legal development, or the lack of it. I'm reading a terrific nineteenth-century history book, *Eternity Street*, by the historian John Mack Faragher, about bandits, brigands, and lynching in frontier Los Angeles. "Most violent crime went unpunished," he writes. "In the absence of formal justice, lethal violence runs rampant and outlaw justice prevails." Well, yes.

Somehow, the importance of a functioning formal justice system is taken as self-evident when talking of the American frontier or of various failed states around the world.

But when it comes to contemporary black inner cities, with their very similar patterns of violence, the notion flies out the window.

So before we talk of addressing legitimacy, we have to be clear about the problem we are trying to fix. The real problem is that formal justice is materially lacking among populations that suffer high rates of violence. It's missing, and it must be supplied. That means no amount of warm and fuzzy talk will fill the bill. More than half of killers of black men go free in cities all over the country. The unincorporated areas of Los Angeles County posted solve rates for homicide in the thirty-percent range through some of the most violent periods of the eighties and nineties. This translates to thousands of killers operating with impunity over decades in America's poorest urban enclaves—dozens per square mile in South Los Angeles over just a few years. And that's just a glimpse of the uncharted depths of the impunity problem, a statistical dark zone, where no good information exists on the frequency of non-lethal crimes, assaults, and threats. The resulting lawlessness is a cruel form of deprivation afflicting tens of thousands of mostly poor, minority residents of America's inner cities, who get roughed up, robbed, and raped with appalling frequency and live in daily fear that their sons might be killed. Its remedy must be to supply official justice, not just engage in "dialogue." Violence is not a problem for coaches and pastors to solve; the state must do its job.

Keller: You're a reporter, not a prescriber, but did you emerge from this work with any sense of how to go about repairing trust between police and minority neighborhoods?

Leovy: What is so strange and interesting is that the political back and forth over policing has been so consistent, for so long, with the same durable themes and complaints sounded on both sides, not just since Rodney King and the millions of dollars spent on police reforms after the L.A. riots, but since long before, back to the 1960s, even the thirties and forties. Much has changed and yet nothing has. We are chasing each other around a box. Self-styled progressives, especially, often talk as if legitimacy-building were merely a matter of creating "improved relations" between police officers and minority residents of urban neighborhoods. If police were just nicer, more sensitive, had a better understanding of civilians, or vice versa, things would improve. This is as hollow, in its way, as conservative talk of self-generated cultural and moral renewal in black neighborhoods. Legitimacy will not be built solely of community meetings, youth programs, skillful official propaganda, or artful expressions of empathy. They may have value, but as a cure for lawlessness I think they miss the core point, and in some cases risk deputizing civilians to assume conflict-resolution functions that rightly belong to the state.

The state's job is to intervene in conflicts—yes, even between people of the same color—and it must do so unequivocally and consistently. So, police need to annoy and alienate fewer non-offenders, and arrest more serious, violent offenders. Pull back from broken-windows-style saturation, targeting patches of geography, and stop-and-search tactics, and concentrate on ensuring judicial resolution of serious crimes. Broken windows sprang from the premise that police were too focused on violence at the expense of quality-of-life crimes. But the premise is based on error. American criminal justice has *never* been very effective at investigating and prosecuting violence, especially in black communities; the reported statistics that claim otherwise are flawed. Violent crime in America today, as in generations past, begs for more systematically thorough and effective investigation, and clean, vigorous prosecution. A mother who grieves for a son lost to an unsolved homicide should not go years without hearing from police about new investigative efforts. A witness who testifies in spite of threats should not be abandoned to deal alone with the long-term consequences. Homicide units in high-crime areas should be solving nearly all murders, not half or less. The system will build legitimacy through its constitutionally constrained yet vigorous response to people who are hurt, violated, and bereaved by violence. The criminal justice system must *deliver.* I'm not arguing for a hammer. Tensions between police power and civil liberties are real and involve high stakes; their resolution need not tilt toward law-enforcement. But those who claim the mantle of civil rights should not forget that crime victims—not just defendants—are disproportionately black, and that they suffer unspeakably. My newspaper just reported the killing of a one-year-old baby, Autumn Johnson, in Compton. The mother of this black child said: "I feel like my life is over. I wish it would have been me instead of her." I don't assert black crime victims are the only constituency that matters. But they deserve more somber, respectful consideration than they get, and they belong at the center of any serious discussion of police reform. Very often, these victims want and need their attackers to be caught and prosecuted. Omit their names, elide over their sufferings, relegate them to footnotes—as is the case in so many popular criminal justice critiques today—and you lose the claim to humane advocacy. There's a long list of potential remedies detailed in *Ghettoside*—better witness protection, better detective training and selection, improved coordination between police functions to solve crimes, etc. Better minds than mine have recommended more radical steps. But I think the first task is getting oriented about what the problem is—getting our heads straight about how essential formal criminal justice is to basic well-being. People need law, that's why we have it.

Keller: Some defenders of the police use the alarming numbers of what they call "black-on-black" violence as a rebuke to the media and the Black Lives Matter movement, as if to say, "Why are you paying so much attention to Michael Brown and Eric Garner and Walter Scott when this other problem looms so much larger." How do you feel about that argument?

Leovy: Both sides are talking past the issue, for different reasons. There exists an inarguably anomalous homicide problem among black Americans, and it is both poorly understood, and a source of truly immense human suffering. We are in desperate need of serious, detached, and in-depth research aimed at understanding homicide dynamics among black Americans, and conducted with an eye to improving people's safety, especially black men's safety, since they are statistically the most vulnerable of all Americans. Neither talk of blame on the one hand, nor defensive minimizing, would seem to have much relevance to this task.

We face extremely difficult questions of why outsized American homicide rates have endured for so long, why black Americans suffer with such devastating frequency, and how we can reduce this mortality. Homicides by police are a small but significant share of overall homicides; anyone serious about the topic of homicides considers them both, especially since police homicides tend somewhat to mirror trends in overall violence. It is as if both forms of homicide were measures of the same unseen aggregate levels of conflict and diffusion of violence to individuals. I think it's significant, for example, that police homicides, killings of police officers, and overall murder rates have all tended historically to be highest in the South, which reinforces some of the assertions I make in *Ghettoside* about the links between personal violence, state legitimacy, and the long after-effects of civil war and insurgency. But there remain many questions, particularly in the area of historic trends and attendant conditions. We know that both killings of suspects by police and killings of police officers by suspects are far below the levels of previous eras. I would like to know much more about these changes, how they happened, when, where, as a result of what, and what related circumstances altered with them. I would also like to see more comparative studies of policing and homicide internationally.

Obviously, I don't think black Americans generally ignore black-on-black homicide. That has not been my experience. Especially those living in high-crime neighborhoods do talk about the problem of homicide, all the time. In fact, they agonize over it—it's just that no one is listening to them. One of the most poignant events I have ever attended was a march through South Los Angeles organized by employees of local mortuaries—embalmers, funeral directors, all of them black—who were tired of burying so many young homicide victims. And there certainly should be no rebuking of ordinary black residents of urban neighborhoods on the grounds of their high homicide rate. It is not their fault. They can't do anything about it and shouldn't be expected to.

Homicide is not a collective moral failing—or if it is, it's a collective moral failing of human beings universally, since it flares across cultures and throughout history. With us since Cain and Abel. Nor do I think the usual social explanations hold up especially well, for all that they are parroted as gospel.

As for more heavy-handed policing being the cure, well, see above. Smarter policing, yes, but figuring how to do that is a devilishly difficult task, and we are nowhere near there yet. At the same time, I understand why many police officers perceive a double standard in those who claim to speak for the poor, yet in many cases appear unwilling to acknowledge the almost daily ravaging of poor neighborhoods by shootings, stabbings, and beatings.

Cops feel moral outrage, too. They are not racist for feeling so—they are human. A detective I know got a Christmas card every year, sent from a man whose brother, an older black man, was the victim in one of his homicide cases. The killing had gotten no press at all, and the detective failed to solve the case. The man sent him a card every year anyway, the tone forgiving and kind—but also saturated with unceasing pain. I happened to be present one day when the card arrived. Guilt and sadness engulfed the detective's face; he slumped. For those exposed daily to urban homicide, the emotions are visceral. The maimed and bloody bodies and unrestrained weeping are real, and those who haven't experienced this world first-hand can't know what it's like. The hardest part to handle for any frontline worker is the public indifference. That is the part that can make you crazy—much harder to handle than the sight of blood.

Victims get no press coverage, no protests. I beg to differ with those who assert otherwise—I have been to the scene of hundreds of homicides, and closely tracked their aftermath over many years, and the lack of press coverage and public outrage is conspicuous. It feels like no one cares. And on some days, coming home and flipping on the TV news can feel like rank mockery. I understand why cops are resentful. I've been there. It is not to be dismissed.

There is also a lot of just plain muddy thinking and silly assertions far too casually thrown about for an issue of such crushing weight. The blind faith of police and their supporters in the broken windows dogma is puzzling. On the other side, you see breathtaking distortions resulting from dubious math. Yes, blacks are the victims of police shootings at a rate far out of proportion to the percentage of blacks in the population. But black neighborhoods are far more densely policed than white ones, as they should be, because they have more crime. Higher deployment in black neighborhoods is one of the important reasons why police on average, have disproportionate contact, and hence force incidents, with black people. Similarly, to suggest a police officer with a gun pointed at him or her should expend seconds thoughtfully weighing how to respond in a non-lethal manner is silly. One thing I know for sure is that we don't possess deep understanding of our problems with policing, legitimacy, and violence. These are mysterious and multi-faceted problems—very, very challenging. What bothers me most, on both sides, is those who behave as if we have all the answers. We don't.

How Cities Can Tackle Violent Crime Without Relying on Police*

Patrick Sharkey, in Conversation with Rogé Karma

2020

One of the most robust findings in criminology is that putting more police officers on the streets leads to less violent crime. Yet, as recent police killings and violence against protesters have reminded us, policing also produces staggering costs that many communities are no longer willing to bear. These seemingly incongruous views represent a tension at the core of any efforts to reform, defund, or abolish policing.

Few scholars have wrestled with this tension as rigorously as Princeton University sociologist Patrick Sharkey. In his 2018 book, *Uneasy Peace: The Great Crime Decline, the Renewal of City Life, and the Next War on Violence*, Sharkey makes the case that the decline in violent crime in America over the past

---

* Patrick Sharkey, in Conversation with Rogé Karma, "How Cities Can Tackle Violent Crime Without Relying on Police," *Vox*, August 7, 2020.

three decades is one of the most important social transformations of our time. At the same time, he argues the US's chosen methods for responding to violence have become far too
destructive, and offers an alternative vision for public safety
that relies primarily on communities and residents, not law
enforcement.

We are currently being forced to confront a question that
has animated Sharkey's work for years: How can we continue
to reduce violence, but do so using a model that relies far less
on police and prisons? That's a much harder question than
simply asking whether some of the jobs police currently perform can be replaced—and it demands an even more rigorous
answer, especially considering the extent to which high levels
of violence can devastate disadvantaged communities.

I spoke to Sharkey about what's causing the uptick in gun
violence in big U.S. cities, whether there is an inevitable trade-
off between reducing police presence and reducing violence,
his vision for a community-driven approach to public safety
(and the evidence base behind that vision), what he thinks
the "defund the police" campaign gets right (and wrong), and
more.

Karma: Can you describe the "uneasy peace" that we are currently living through?

Sharkey: Since the 1990s, violence has fallen by roughly half
across the country. In a number of cities like New York,
Los Angeles, Washington, D.C., Dallas, San Diego, and San
Francisco, violence has fallen by 70 or 80 percent. Even
places we still think of as violent—Chicago, Philadelphia,
Oakland—have seen violence fall by between a third and
a half.

These changes have transformed city life as we know

it. As violence falls, public life starts to return. Parents let their kids play outside, libraries fill up, shopping districts become more lively. Academic performance rises; young people are less likely to drop out. Families invest in neighborhoods as they become safe, and businesses return.

There's causal evidence that children growing up in cities where violence is declining are more likely to rise up in the income distribution when they reach adulthood and move out of poverty. In short, when violence falls, cities start to return to life, and the greatest benefits are experienced by the most disadvantaged segments of the population.

But the paradox is that the methods we've relied on to deal with violence—primarily aggressive policing and mass incarceration—have had staggering costs. They have left millions of Americans enmeshed in the prison system with consequences that affect not only the people who are involved in the system but also their families and the next generation.

For several decades now, we've asked police departments to dominate public spaces through any means necessary. The police violence that has become so visible recently is a function of that task; the controversy, the attention, the unrest, the anger toward policing is a response to a strategy to reduce violence that has been intact for several decades now.

That's what I mean when I'm talking about the peace being uneasy: Violence has fallen, but we need a new method to address it going forward.

Karma: That's a good segue into our current moment. Multiple cities are currently experiencing a sharp uptick in shootings and homicides—some of which is being blamed on efforts to delegitimize police authority and reduce police presence. So I'm wondering: Is that the trade-off we face? If we try to scale back policing, is rising violence the inevitable byproduct?

Sharkey: It's not an inevitable trade-off.

To be clear, there is a pattern of violence rising in the aftermath of these kinds of high-profile protests against police brutality. This happened after Freddie Gray in Baltimore, after Michael Brown in Ferguson, and it's clearly happening now. But that doesn't mean that protests against police *cause* violence to rise. It also doesn't mean police are the only institution capable of confronting violence. It means that when we rely primarily on police to respond to all forms of violence and then police stop playing that role, neighborhoods become destabilized.

That happens for a few different reasons. One is that police make a conscious decision to step back from their role in being the primary institution responsible for public safety. That might happen due to increased scrutiny on policing. It might happen due to shifts in policy, like the fact that the NYPD dismantled their plainclothes anti-crime units that respond to many serious forms of violent crime. It also may happen because law enforcement is slowing down intentionally to make a statement.

A second piece is that residents may be less likely to work with the police, defer to the police, or cooperate with investigations. Young people may come to the conclusion that this city doesn't care about me—I'm not playing by the rules anymore. People obey the law when they believe it's legitimate; when the belief in the legitimacy of this institution is undermined, that can result in a rise of violence.

None of this implies people should stop protesting police brutality. It means that the methods we've historically used to reduce violence are unsustainable, and we need to start thinking of a strategy for confronting violence that relies a lot less on those methods.

Karma: Let's talk about that strategy. Can you paint me a picture of what an alternative model of public safety would look like that didn't rely so heavily on police?

Sharkey: There's a basic conclusion from the research on what creates safe neighborhoods: Police are effective at reducing violence, but they aren't the only ones who are effective.

There's lots of evidence telling us that other core institutions in a community—institutions that are driven by residents and local organizations—can play a central role in controlling violence. But we've never thought of these organizations and residents as the central actors responsible for creating safe streets, so we've never given them the same commitment and the same resources that we give to law enforcement and the criminal legal system. When we talk about how to respond to violence, the default response in the U.S. is always to focus on the police and the prison.

The next model should be one driven primarily by residents and local organizations as the central actors. Police still certainly have a role to play, but responding to violent crime takes up only a tiny fraction of police officers' time. So the idea here is that we can rely on residents and local organizations to take over most of the duties that [officers] currently handle and make sure neighborhoods are safe.

Karma: The critique you'll often hear on this is that the evidence base for some of these community-based methods for reducing violent crime is not nearly as robust as the evidence base behind policing as a way to reduce violent crime. How do you respond to that?

Sharkey: I agree that the research on the effectiveness of policing on crime is strong. But the motivation for developing a new model for how to deal with violence is the observation that while police may have been effective in controlling violence, that has come with significant costs, which aren't accounted for in any of those studies. It's come with the type of aggressive, and sometimes violent, policing that I think most of the country is no longer willing to tolerate. Policing as a method to confront violence is now seen as unacceptable by a large chunk of the population.

I would also dispute that the evidence base for the alternative approach focused on community actors and institutions is not as strong. We now have a pretty well-established base of evidence telling us that residents and local organizations are at least as effective as the police in controlling violence.

The programs run out of the Crime Lab at the University of Chicago, all of which are run as randomized controlled trials, are extraordinarily effective. The Becoming a Man and Choose to Change programs, which rely on a combination of mentoring and cognitive behavioral therapy (CBT), reduce participants' involvement in violence by about 50 percent. Summer jobs programs have led to over 40 percent decreases in violence.

The READI program, which provides adults most at risk of becoming a victim or perpetrator of gun violence with transitional employment and CBT, is currently under evaluation, but the early results have shown extraordinary potential. Community-based programs that redesigned randomized abandoned lots in Philadelphia to become public spaces reduced violence in and around those lots by around 30 percent.

The Cure Violence programs, which have been cited as

if they always work, do have a more mixed evidence base. I think it is important to be very transparent about that— they don't work every single time. Still, this can be a very effective model. Programs in New York, Baltimore, and elsewhere have been rigorously evaluated and shown to be extremely effective at reducing violence.

There's also national data on this. I carried out a study on the role that the expansion of the nonprofit sector played in contributing to the crime drop. What we found was that in a given city with a hundred thousand people, every new organization formed to confront violence and build stronger neighborhoods led to about a 1 percent drop in violent crime and murder. So the expansion of nonprofits focused on building stronger communities and working against violence played a big role in contributing to the crime drop.

The evidence base for a community response to violence is at least as strong as the evidence base for policing. That's why I don't really think it's about the evidence base—I think it's about a mindset. In America, policy discussions about violence focus so intently on the police and the prison as the default responses. We've been investing in these methods for so long, it's all we know—it's hard to even imagine a different response to violence.

Karma: I want to talk about that mindset. In *Uneasy Peace*, you talk about our historic approach to issues like violence, poverty, and inequality as one of "punishment and abandonment" and warn that if we focus on only addressing the "punishment" side of things but ignore making investments in abandoned communities, then reform efforts will ultimately fail.

I think this framework applies to conversations around "defunding the police." If the goal is to just reduce the injustices that come with policing, then slashing police budgets works great. But it strikes me that this strategy could also lead to an uptick in overall violence levels if it's not paired with investments in alternative mechanisms for reducing violence.

Can you walk us through that broader framework and how it may apply today?

Sharkey: Calls to defund or dismantle the police are really about how we deal with an institution that is seen as racist and anti-democratic; what I've argued for is to shift the focus toward how we can most effectively create safe and strong communities. When we make that shift, it forces us to think about not just how to scale back police shootings but what active steps need to be taken to make sure that communities are safe and everyone is welcomed.

For the past fifty years, our model of responding to concentrated urban poverty has been abandonment and punishment. We've ignored the challenges of urban inequality and responded by scaling up the policing and prison systems. Over time, there has been a recognition of the injustice of those systems, so we've moved toward a model that is trying to gradually scale them back. That means we have moved away from a focus on punishment and toward a focus on justice. But if we just focus solely on justice, then we're going to end up with a situation where communities don't have the basic investments that they need to be strong, stable, and safe.

That's my motivation for a different approach: to focus not only on justice but also on the investments that are needed to create safe neighborhoods. I agree entirely that just scaling back the budgets of police departments is going to leave us with neighborhoods that are more vulnerable to a rise in violence. That's why I make the case for investments in a different set of institutions driven by residents and local organizations that can play a central role in creating safe streets and strong communities.

That's the step we haven't taken. We started the conversation about scaling back the excesses of law enforcement and the criminal legal system. But we haven't had the conversations about the investments that are needed to make sure neighborhoods are safe and no one falls through the cracks.

Karma: Let's have that conversation. You've called for "a demonstration project that is both more cautious and more radical than the call to defund the police." Can you outline that for me?

Sharkey: Instead of calling for a rapid change where we dismantle police departments and immediately shift all police responses to other entities, the idea here is to try to maintain stability in communities at a time when violence is rising, but also start to plan for what an alternative model for dealing with violence might look like.

There are a few steps. Begin with a community within a city where the police are not seen as a legitimate institution—where residents are looking for an alternative to law enforcement. There has to be buy-in from the community where this is implemented and it has to be driven by members of that community. Second, establish a "community quarterback": a single coalition of organizations that are brought together and see it as their responsibility to make sure all public spaces are safe in their community.

Third, provide funding to that organization equal to what law enforcement would be provided in that precinct. For instance, each of Washington, D.C.'s fifty-plus police service areas receives, on average, about $10 million per year to fund a workforce of roughly eighty full-time employees for a population of around twelve thousand. That's the kind of commitment I'm asking for: the same level of commitment that we give law enforcement. For far too long, we've asked community groups to mobilize to respond to violence on the cheap, often without any resources or compensation.

Then allow this new organization to decide how it wants to hire, train, and deploy its resources to deal with all of the incidents that police departments currently deal with: mental health crises, young people dealing drugs, small-scale altercations that occur outside bars or other hot spots, drug addiction.

Lastly, make a long-term commitment to this new coalition; I'm calling for a ten-year commitment. Give it a chance to fail. Give it a chance to go through scandals and mishaps and bumps along the way, and know that it's still going to be there in ten years. There's no easy way to respond to every challenge in a community. There's gonna be problems along the way. So it's really a mayor and a funder that have to be willing to go through these challenges and stick with an organization.

Now, communities may decide that there are places where armed responders are still necessary, like gun violence, and could choose what kind of relationship they want with the local police department accordingly. But in those places, we could imagine a model where even for situations where police are first to respond, they would need to respond with a member of this community coalition with them. Then, for all other 99 percent of incidents, the members of this coalition would be the first to respond to incidents in public space.

That's the proposal: Give an alternative coalition of residents and organizations a chance to play a central role in creating a safe community and give them the resources that we devote to law enforcement. I just have to believe that, based on the evidence we have, that coalition would be at least as effective as law enforcement, and would come without the costs of law enforcement.

Whom Can We Call for Help? Police Should Not Always Be the Only Option*

The Washington Post
Editorial Board
2021

Rayshard Brooks was killed by a police officer in Atlanta after Wendy's employees called the cops to complain that a man, asleep in his car, was blocking the drive-through lane.

Daniel T. Prude died in Rochester, NY, after police officers forced him into a hood and then pushed his face to the ground while he was in the throes of a psychotic episode. His brother had called 911, later saying, "I placed a phone call for my brother to get help. Not for my brother to get lynched."

Kenneth Shultz has been homeless for more than nine years and has been charged with trespassing ninety-six times. As

---

* Editorial Board, "Whom Can We Call for Help? Police Should Not Always Be the Only Option," *The Washington Post*, March 16, 2021.

ABC News has reported, Mr. Shultz has spent one out of every three nights of the past nine years in jail and has more than $40,000 of debt from court costs, fines, and fees.

In each of these instances, was law enforcement really the best public safety tool?

What if, instead of the police, the Wendy's staff had been able to call an unarmed community patrol worker—perhaps a neighbor who knew Brooks—to drive him home or to a sober-up station for the night?

What if instead of facing armed police officers while in the agony of a mental breakdown, Prude had been assisted by a crisis worker and a medic who were trained to de-escalate the situation and could connect him to mental health crisis services?

What if instead of being repeatedly arrested for trespassing, people without homes such as Mr. Shultz were given the medical care they so often need and offered transport to a shelter?

Brooks, Prude, Mr. Shultz, and countless other Americans are failed by a system of public safety that defaults to the police at the expense of developing serious alternatives. It's not just that law enforcement is ill-equipped to help people in crisis and that other organizations could do better.

In some cases, police cause unnecessary harm. In many cases, communities and law enforcement would support police functions being reassigned to trained civilians.

Incident response is an obvious candidate. Noting that a disturbing number of killings by police originate in a 911 call, jurisdictions around the country are questioning whether an armed police officer is really the best response to most calls for help. Philadelphia, Dallas, Denver, and Atlanta are among the growing number of cities experimenting with new, unarmed response teams to better respond to crisis calls, particularly where mental health is involved.

Atlanta's Policing Alternatives and Diversion Initiative (PAD) was born in 2017 out of frustration over the frequency with which police arrest people for crimes of homelessness and poverty, such as public urination. By intervening before arrest, PAD can keep vulnerable community members out of jail for minor offenses and instead offer them support. Today, program participants are referred either by police officers, who can call PAD instead of making an arrest, or by community members, who can call 311 for a non-police, support-driven response.

Not all such programs are new. For three decades, Crisis Assistance Helping Out on the Streets (CAHOOTS) in Eugene, Oregon, has sent a medic and a crisis worker in response to 911 calls that involve a nonviolent emergency. According to the White Bird Clinic, which runs the program, CAHOOTS costs about $2.1 million a year. Based on the Eugene Police Department's estimated cost of $800 per police response, the clinic estimates that CAHOOTS saves the city about $8.5 million in public safety spending per year.

But beyond saving money, reimagining incident response could give people in crisis the help they need—it could keep Mr. Shultz from another night in jail and possibly prevent deadly, unnecessary escalations of the sort that killed Brooks and Prude.

There will always be emergency calls that warrant a responder who can use force, but they are surprisingly rare. In 2020, calls about violent crime—homicide, rape, robbery, and aggravated assault—made up only about 1 percent of police calls for service in many city police departments, including Baltimore, Cincinnati, New Orleans, and Seattle.

There will also always be murkier situations in which the presence of someone authorized to use force could prevent harm by de-escalating conflict but might also lethally escalate the situation.

Even then, jurisdictions could experiment with a blended response in which civilians and law enforcement work together.

Civilian responders including medics, crisis workers, and others with rigorous de-escalation training could try to resolve crises while law enforcement waits nearby, out of sight. If civilian responders aren't able to resolve the situation, they could call for backup. That capability could save lives, but again might be needed in surprisingly few cases: In 2019, out of 24,000 calls the CAHOOTS team received, police backup was requested only 150 times.

Overhauling incident response is not a panacea. The police can't solve complex social problems, but neither can civilian responders. Connecting homeless people with medical or social services is obviously more humane and helpful than arresting them for trespassing, but neither will address the toxic web of abuse, affordable-housing shortages, and addiction that contributes to homelessness in the first place. Incident response reform must be just the first step.

Still, cities around the country are realizing that this first step is crucial—that they can offer people help they really need while minimizing the chance that a lethal escalation will make a person's most vulnerable moments their last. Our current system wasn't designed consciously to answer the question "What would be the best response to emergencies that flow from homelessness, mental health crises, and addiction?" By considering that question more thoughtfully, we can build systems that help where today's systems hurt.

From Crisis to Care*

Katherine Beckett, Forrest Stuart, and Monica Bell
2021

Daniel Prude. Nicolas Chavez. Linden Cameron. All of them were either severely injured or killed by police. All of them suffered from mental illness. They represent but a fraction of people in crisis who are harmed by the police. One out of four fatal police encounters involve people suffering from mental illness, and that's not counting a broad spectrum of harmful, nonfatal encounters that rarely, if ever, make national headlines.

The importance of reducing police interactions with people experiencing such crises cannot be overstated. In this time of increasing attention to police violence and the need for change, alternative crisis response initiatives that authorize civilians to respond to 911 calls involving people in crisis are receiving significant attention and acclaim. Regardless of where one stands on the role or existence of police in our society, many

* Katherine Beckett, Forrest Stuart, and Monica Bell, "From Crisis to Care," *Inquest*, September 2, 2021.

people support the idea of having civilians address noncriminal situations that involve mental health crises.

There is much to commend in these initiatives. Alternative crisis response frameworks address a very real problem—namely, over-reliance on police. They reflect and help realize a more holistic understanding of what public safety entails and what it requires. And they are clearly superior to many of the inhumane and utterly pointless tactics—including arrests, sweeps, and banishment—that have been used in the past. New ways of responding to vulnerable people who are experiencing mental health crises are clearly needed.

At the same time, some current models have a number of limitations that are worth considering. We explore these limits here not because we are opposed to the current popular approach—we are not—but rather because we believe we should, and can, do *more* to respond to people in crisis (some of whom commit crimes or inflict harm, and some of whom do not) over longer periods of time.

One of our main concerns with some current models is that many alternative crisis response programs are limited to calls for service that do not involve any allegation of crime or danger. Most alternative crisis response initiatives focus on calls that are coded as "mental health crises" and "mental health disturbances" that do not involve weapons; some also prioritize other non-criminal issues such as public intoxication and syringe disposal. This separation of crisis and crime—and the treatment of the latter as largely off-limits for civilian first responders—creates a limiting framework for those who are truly seeking lasting change outside of the criminal legal system.

In our work, we aim to bridge this gap—while proposing a new course forward that merges the best of what current

models have to offer while also being careful to avoid repro-
ducing old patterns. Here, we'll identify some of the current
limitations and argue that alternative first response initiatives
should be accompanied by new ways of responding to people
and situations that *do* involve allegations of crime, while providing ongoing support to people who are experiencing chronic
crises. In short, we need to not only imagine and develop alternative first responses to acute crises, but also "second responses" designed to address the deep social marginalization
at the root of those crises.

Many alternative crisis response initiatives in the United
States and Canada are based on the CAHOOTS, or Crisis Assistance Helping Out on the Streets, model that was pioneered
in Eugene, Oregon. CAHOOTS is not new, but the deepening
of the national conversation around police violence has drawn
attention to it. Originally developed in 1968 as a volunteer-
run mobile crisis unit aimed at reducing police interactions
with vulnerable people, the erstwhile "bummer squad" that
later became known as CAHOOTS responded to certain calls
alongside the police, evolving in the 1980s to become a civilian
mobile crisis unit dispatched through the 911 system.

Fast-forward to the summer of 2020, and CAHOOTS had
310 outstanding requests for information from communities
across the country. A seemingly endless list of cities—among
them Oakland, Rochester, Portland, San Francisco, Denver,
Dallas, New York, and Toronto—have recently announced the
development of new initiatives based on CAHOOTS. And the
recent expansion of federal Medicaid funding for such initiatives means that this model is likely to continue to spread.

As sociologists, we have studied policing, homelessness, and
related issues for decades, observing and interviewing officers,
organizations, and community members in places as diverse

as Washington, Ohio, and California. We have been struck by the rapid growth and rising popularity of CAHOOTS, and yet are concerned that some of the models' structural limitations are being overlooked.

Although the original CAHOOTS units in Eugene and Springfield, Oregon, are housed in and are partially funded by their respective police departments, they're commonly described as an alternative to police. In one sense, this is accurate. Many CAHOOTS-inspired initiatives are aimed at reducing police involvement in non-emergency and non-criminal situations involving mental health issues. The Rapid Integrated Group Health Care Team (RIGHT CARE) in Dallas, for example, seeks to "shift the focus of mental health crisis response to paramedics and health systems in order to create a health-based response to mental health crises." Similarly, San Francisco's Street Crisis Response Teams (SCRT) "provide rapid, trauma-informed response to calls for service to people experiencing crisis in public spaces in order to reduce law enforcement encounters." CAHOOTS itself reports mainly dealing with calls involving mental health, suicide threats, welfare checks, and family disputes. Roughly three-fourths of the calls they respond to involve people who live unsheltered.

This focus on the intersection of mental health, substance use, and poverty makes good sense. People experiencing homelessness, mental health disabilities, or unmanaged substance use disorders are the subject of many 911 calls and often cycle repeatedly in and out of jail. In San Francisco, the police receive roughly one hundred thousand 911 calls about homelessness each year. Portlanders call the police about people they deem unwanted—homeless individuals and others combating behavioral health issues—once every fifteen minutes. And a growing number of studies document the myriad harms caused by police to vulnerable populations. Reducing the likelihood of death is a primary concern: one-third to a half of all people killed by police are disabled, while one in four people killed by police suffers from a mental illness. Moreover, half of all police killings of unarmed civilians originated in a 911 call. Less-than-lethal forms of police violence, to say nothing of harassment, stops, stress, and the dignitary costs of needless police interactions, are also common and CAHOOTS-type interventions may make these less common.

But there are important implications of this model that must not be overlooked. First, if situations involving perceived criminal law violations—including minor offenses such as trespass, drug possession, theft, and illegal camping—are out-of-bounds for these non-police interventions, the capacity of these initiatives to facilitate decriminalization or decarceration will be dramatically reduced. These situations, thus, will continue to be handled by the criminal legal system, where racial inequities persist. Research on implicit bias suggests that reliance on 911 callers and dispatchers to identify situations that involve crises but *not* crime or weapons raises the very real possibility that calls involving white people in crisis are more likely to be deemed eligible for an alternative response than those involving people of color. Beyond creating disparities in alternative responses, this dynamic perpetuates the long-standing practice of white residents who weaponize 911 against people of color they personally deem too loud, suspicious, or out of place in parks and other public venues.

Second, approaches based on CAHOOTS do not invite widespread reconsideration of our collective reliance on 911 to address issues and behaviors that are currently defined as crimes. In addition to important systemic changes, any real transformation regarding the role of police in our society will be impossible without a broader cultural shift toward valuing the expertise of people who are *not* police officers. This kind of cultural transformation begins by reassessing our reliance on 911 and working together to develop non-punitive, community-based responses to non-emergency situations. The fact that some residents, especially people of color, are reluctant to call 911 further underscores the need for non-police response models that do not rely on 911. Fortunately, such initiatives have been developed in some cities. Alternative crisis response initiatives in Rochester and Atlanta, for example, encourage people to call a non-emergency number rather than 911. These shifts are a move in the right direction, but the primary referral mechanism for most alternative crisis programs remains 911.

There's the added complication that CAHOOTS initiatives are often housed in, and funded by, police departments. For example, CAHOOTS itself and Olympia's Crisis Response Units are housed within their city police departments. Other initiatives are jointly housed in municipal police and fire departments. (Some CAHOOTS-type initiatives are administratively housed in non-profit organizations, but this appears to be less common.) To the extent that these initiatives are housed in, and funded by, police departments, they do not truly shift resources and control away from the police. Moreover, many initiatives are touted as a way to save police departments money. But what this often means in practice is that the programs simply pay civilian first responders significantly less than police officers. This wage disparity, of course, makes staffing challenging and creates significant turnover, leaving CAHOOTS-like initiatives worse off than their parent police departments.

Finally, as people directly involved with CAHOOTS point

out, the program does not entail ongoing support for the people they assist or any significant reallocation of resources. As a result, outreach responders who work for CAHOOTS-type programs often end up interacting with the same people over and over again. As one CAHOOTS case manager put it, "All these other cities are really looking to CAHOOTS right now as this Band-Aid, right, because they want to have that thing that looks good and says, look, police aren't responding to these situations. But we're still going to end up being part of that same machine of oppression . . . if there aren't other resources to get folks connected to." Some alternative response initiatives are hiring staff who provide follow-up support to people who are the subject of repeated 911 calls. Still, the modal encounter generated by most alternative response models is short-term by design.

FROM SHORT-TERM CRISES TO LONG-TERM CARE

Although it has clearly captured the imagination of policymakers, funders, and advocates, the CAHOOTS model is not the only non-police option for responding to situations that involve untreated mental health issues, substance use, and extreme poverty. JustCARE, a holistic and collaborative initiative that involves numerous programs and organizations, emerged in Seattle, Washington, in 2020 and provides a useful contrast. If CAHOOTS offers an alternative first response to *acute* crises, JustCARE can be understood as a second response aimed at offering a longer-term response to *chronic* crises—and low-level criminal behavior. Together, they form a more holistic strategy for cementing deeper transformations and reducing the reach and impact of the criminal legal system.

JustCARE enables people living in unauthorized encampments to move into non-congregate, supportive interim lodging where they receive trauma-informed care guided by harm reduction principles, with the goal of securing permanent housing and meeting other goals participants identify as important to them. To begin, JustCARE partners conduct outreach in encampments that generate significant concern—and many 911 calls—in order to better understand residents' situations and needs. JustCARE staff also work closely with people who live and work in affected neighborhoods and address their concerns as well. Most camp residents are then offered, and accept, the opportunity to move into safe, private, and supportive housing and to work closely with case managers, many of whom have relevant lived experience that enables them to build trust with participants. Once safely housed, people receive on-site medical services and intensive case management support. Dedicated staff and dedicated safety teams use de-escalation and other harm reduction techniques to ensure that participants and staff are safe and to avoid reliance on 911.

The findings from a recent developmental evaluation of JustCARE's first six months of operations (which one of us co-authored) are encouraging. In interviews, JustCARE participants reported significant improvements in their emotional well-being after securing housing that offers safety and privacy and establishing positive relationships with case managers. The availability of on-site medical providers means that many are also able to address long-standing health challenges. Nearly all of the participants who acknowledged having previously relied on illicit survival strategies such as theft and drug sales reported ceasing or curtailing those activities once housed and supported. Some are able to secure permanent housing with the support of case managers—though increased investments in affordable permanent housing, expanding access to housing

vouchers, and improvements in mental health care and substance abuse treatment remain vital.

The JustCARE model addresses many of the limitations
of the CAHOOTS framework. First, JustCARE providers intentionally focus on situations (i.e., unauthorized encampments) that involve residents who sometimes rely on illicit
survival strategies and commit other low-level crimes. In fact,
84 percent of the campers screened by JustCARE outreach responders in its first month of operation reported regularly using drugs, mainly methamphetamine and heroin. Many also
relied extensively on illicit survival strategies. By responding to
people and situations that involve criminalized behaviors, Just-
CARE has the potential to reduce not only potentially harmful
police encounters, but also criminal legal system involvement
more generally. And by specifically engaging residents of encampments that mainly include campers of color, JustCARE
may also reduce racial inequities in the criminal legal system.

Second, rather than responding to redirected 911 calls, Just-
CARE works with community members to address their concerns and identify areas of need. In the process, JustCARE staff
are engaging in deep cultural and relational work in affected
neighborhoods, taking neighbors' concerns seriously while
also inviting community members to reevaluate their tendency
to rely on 911 to address non-emergency situations. In this
sense, JustCARE is doing the cultural work that reducing the
"policeability" of mental health issues, poverty, and drug use
will require in the medium and long term. JustCARE's focus
on heavily impacted neighborhoods means that it can provide
tangible improvements that are then deeply felt by people who
live and work in those neighborhoods—people who have generated many 911 calls in the past.

Finally, as noted previously, JustCARE provides interim

supportive lodging with the goal of supporting participants in, among other things, securing affordable permanent housing. Alternative first-response models are simply not designed to do this. Of course, this intensive case management (and the provision of interim lodging) means that JustCARE is comparatively expensive. Over the long term, bringing JustCARE to scale may necessitate progressive tax reform and/or reallocation of funds currently allocated to law enforcement, which adds an element of unpredictability to the enterprise. And of course, continued federal funding for local housing initiatives and expanding access to permanent affordable housing is essential. The available evidence suggests that such investments would likely pay handsome dividends.

Although quite different, these two types of interventions are, in theory, compatible. And CAHOOTS-based initiatives can do some things that JustCARE cannot. For example, because of its focus on targeted encampments, JustCARE is not in a position to respond to calls for service pertaining to particular individuals who live outside of targeted areas but generate many 911 calls. In this way, frameworks such as JustCARE might benefit from the existence of alternative crisis responders who can refer people with long-term needs to ensure that they receive the housing and support they need.

While it remains unclear how the co-existence and collaboration of these two approaches might play out, it is evident that a meaningful and transformative response to homelessness, mental health, and substance use will require responding to both acute and chronic crises. Alternative first-response models have an important role to play, but they alone cannot bear the weight of the policing and housing crises that are unfolding in cities across the United States. Together, the CAHOOTS and JustCARE models provide a glimpse of how cities might begin to reimagine our collective response to homelessness, substance use disorders, and mental health issues without relying on either the police or the criminal legal system. Doing so will require significant financial and social investment in housing and in our most vulnerable residents, increasing community well-being in the long term. Indeed, the alternatives—abandonment, sweeps, crackdowns, and mass incarceration—are far costlier in every way.

Ed. Note: The authors have updated the original piece for publication in this anthology.

Police Officers Shouldn't Be the Ones to Enforce Traffic Laws*

Sarah A. Seo
2021

When Daunte Wright was fatally shot by an officer during a traffic stop near Minneapolis this week, he joined a long list of people who have died at the hands of the police after being pulled over for a traffic violation. Traffic stops should not be harrowing or dangerous experiences, but too often they are for people of color.

One way to address this problem is to reduce the number of encounters that drivers have with police officers. At the same time, any responsible reform must account for the fact that accidents involving motor vehicles are a leading cause of death for Americans under the age of fifty-four. Road safety is itself

* Sarah A. Seo, "Police Officers Shouldn't Be the Ones to Enforce Traffic Laws," *The New York Times*, April 15, 2021.

a serious problem, one that requires laws and regulations that must be enforced.

How can we reduce traffic stops without undermining public safety? The solution is to decrease our reliance on human enforcement. Having police officers implement traffic laws is not the only way to promote road safety. Indeed, the evidence suggests that it is not even the optimal way to do so.

Automated speed cameras and red-light cameras, for example, have proved to be effective in decreasing traffic accidents, injuries, and fatalities, precisely because they're more consistent than human oversight. They also don't selectively—or discriminatorily—choose to pull over violators. Automating citations for speeding, a major cause of accidents, could significantly reduce police encounters. In New York State, for example, speeding accounts for nearly 20 percent of all traffic citations, according to recent data.

Similar technology could be used to check for expired licenses and registrations—common infractions that disproportionately ensnare the poor and people of color. (Expired registration was the reason the police gave for stopping Mr. Wright.) Many police departments already use automated license-plate readers. Instead of having human officers issue citations for this violation, license-plate readers could be used to send notice by mail that a license or registration has expired or is about to.

As with any technological solution, we would need to be mindful of individuals' privacy rights. Without sufficient protections in place, the police could cull a great deal of data from traffic cameras and license-plate scanners and misuse that information.

Decreasing our reliance on human enforcement of traffic laws does not always mean switching to automated enforcement. Better design of streets and highways can protect lives too.

The legal scholar James Willard Hurst once remarked that the people who figured out how to draw a line down the middle of the road did more to enforce the keep-to-the-right rule than anything the police could do. Raised medians can help keep bikers safe from cars (and even beautify the streets), which regulations on separate lanes can't do. Let's think about speed bumps as well as speed limits.

Of course, some human enforcement of traffic laws will always be necessary. But the traffic police do not need to be weaponized officers trained to approach stops with a heightened expectation of conflict; unarmed traffic monitors could be used instead. The police would still pursue criminal violations, and they could provide assistance when requested by traffic monitors. But an armed response would be a last resort, not routine.

This makes statistical sense: Available evidence shows that a negligible percentage of routine traffic stops result in serious injury or death to officers. That number is just a fraction of a percent in Florida, where a bill is pending to create a public safety department with traffic monitors who would enforce moving infractions. Transferring enforcement of civil traffic laws to a nonpolice agency can decrease police encounters on the road and still protect drivers and pedestrians.

These ideas are not entirely new. The father of modern policing, August Vollmer, who was the police chief in Berkeley, California, from 1909 to 1932, argued that traffic enforcement distracted the police from their main job: fighting crime. His insight was soon forgotten, however, as American society became a car society and as the getaway car often accompanied the commission of crime. Law enforcement came to depend on investigatory stops—that is, traffic stops conducted primarily for the purpose of looking into criminal activity.

The strategy of investigatory stops has not affected crime rates, according to a recent study by the Policing Project at New York University's School of Law. But it has served to alienate and harm those unjustifiably targeted for inspection. Mr. Vollmer was right that traffic duty is a distraction from the goal of solving crime. What he didn't know was that—in terrible, tragic ways—police enforcement of traffic laws would also come to undermine the primary purpose of traffic stops: public safety.

Fines, Fees, and Police Divestment: Statement and Policy Recommendations*

Fines and Fees Justice Center
2020

Across the country, people are demanding that the government divest from law enforcement and invest in communities of color that have been over-policed and under-served. Any discussion of shrinking the criminal legal system and investing in low-income communities of color must include fines and fees. When state and local policymakers use police and the criminal legal system to raise revenue, they systematically extract wealth from Black and Brown people—who not only are disproportionately stopped, cited, and arrested, but are more likely to face potentially violent encounters with law enforcement.

---

* Fines and Fees Justice Center, "Fines, Fees and Police Divestment: Statement and Policy Recommendations," August 4, 2020.

The Fines and Fees Justice Center supports efforts to redirect police funding to human and social services that better protect public safety and health. The current economic crisis, as well as community demands for reform, are forcing state and local governments to revisit and reassess their law enforcement budgets. Decisions made in the next few months will have long-lasting impacts.

Fines and fees serve as a common, yet counterproductive, revenue source. Eighty percent of convictions are punishable by fines, and every conviction carries additional fees—often hundreds of dollars and often exceeding the underlying fine. Due to over-policing in Black and Brown communities, these families are most likely to get trapped in a cycle of debt and criminalization simply because they can't afford something as minor as a traffic ticket.

Aggressive collection practices—like the widespread suspension of driver's licenses for nonpayment—increase police-civilian encounters and make it harder for people to pay what they owe. Reliance on this unreliable and inefficient source of government revenue is bad economic policy that can cost more money than it even generates.

To reduce policing, we ultimately must end reliance on fines and fees to raise revenue. Fines and fees are harmful, regressive taxes, imposed on the communities least able to afford them. Eliminating fees and making fines equitable would result in millions of dollars remaining in the communities that are demanding public investment. This would allow more individuals and families to meet their basic needs, while increasing economic prosperity for everyone.

Since the 2008 recession, state and local governments have increasingly used fines and fees to fill their budget shortfalls.

Too often, police are incentivized to issue citations for traffic, municipal code, and other low-level violations instead of focusing on public safety. Policing-for-profit has no place in our communities. Government can, and must, do better.

Below are some recommendations for advocates and policymakers considering working toward defunding law enforcement and reinvesting in the communities most harmed by mass criminalization, racial injustice, and economic inequality.

1. State and local jurisdictions should stop assessing all court fees, surcharges, and other costs, while ensuring that all fines are equitably imposed and enforced.

2. When jurisdictions do impose fines, they should identify ways to reduce enforcement that can lead to savings without harming public safety. Policymakers must take into account the full costs of collections and enforcement, as well as the long-term financial harms to individuals, families, and businesses.

3. Defund law enforcement that's geared toward revenue raising, while reinvesting that money in communities. Law enforcement should never impose a quota system requiring or suggesting that officers should write a set number of tickets, nor should police performance be evaluated based on the number of tickets an officer writes. Policing should never be tied to raising revenue because it creates perverse incentives.

4. Provide data transparency to disincentivize pretextual stops and policing-for-profit. Data on traffic stops would allow us to evaluate how police are being deployed and whether they are addressing serious public safety issues or merely raising revenue. Such data should detail

where traffic stops occur, against whom, and for which violations. This data should also be publicly accessible.

5. No revenue from fines and fees should go directly or indirectly to law enforcement. If fines are imposed, the revenue should flow to general funding and not be required for government budgets to break even.

She Wants to Fix One of Louisiana's Deadliest Jails. She Needs to Beat the Sheriff First.*

Jessica Pishko

2021

For a stretch of time last year, the deaths seemed to keep coming in the Orleans Justice Center, New Orleans's jail. In August, forty-six-year-old Robert Rettman died from what the coroner's office called "asphyxia due to hanging." Before Rettman, there were thirty-five-year-old Christian Freeman and twenty-seven-year-old Desmond Guild, both of whom collapsed suddenly in their cells, were rushed to the hospital, and died. Freeman had fentanyl and a veterinary-grade sedative in his system; he also tested positive for Covid-19. Guild appears to have died from a blood clot.

---

* Jessica Pishko, "She Wants to Fix One of Louisiana's Deadliest Jails. She Needs to Beat the Sheriff First." *Politico*, November 10, 2021.

These men are not alone. This month, Incarceration Transparency, a project out of the Loyola University New Orleans law school, released a database documenting fifteen deaths at the Orleans Justice Center between 2014 and 2019. Only two other Louisiana jail facilities, both of which have larger incarcerated populations, had higher death counts. Almost all the Orleans Justice Center's inmates are pre-trial, and many are jailed for nonviolent charges. "The fact is, so many people go in for traffic tickets, and don't come out," says Ursula Price, a longtime criminal justice reformer now serving as executive director of the New Orleans Workers' Center for Racial Justice.

These deaths add to long-standing concerns about the safety of the approximately nine hundred people housed in the Orleans Justice Center (once called the Orleans Parish Prison), which falls under the control of New Orleans Sheriff Marlin Gusman. Gusman, who has held his seat since 2004, has long faced criticism from prison reform advocates, starting with his oversight of the facility during Hurricane Katrina. In 2008, the jail ranked among the deadliest in the nation. The next year, the Justice Department issued a report on what it said were unconstitutional and dangerous conditions inside the jail. In 2012, Gusman was sued, and the jail was placed under a consent decree, subjecting it to federal monitoring until it can bring confinement conditions up to legal standards.

Through it all, Gusman kept getting reelected, largely with support from New Orleans's political establishment. Now, though, for the first time since 2014, he has a serious electoral challenger: progressive candidate Susan Hutson, who hopes to oust Gusman in the election this coming weekend with support from criminal justice reform groups around the city.

An attorney with a background in activism, Hutson served

for more than a decade as the independent monitor for the New Orleans Police Department, which has been under its own consent decree since 2012. In that capacity, she pushed to reform a department long accused of misconduct in its policing, and the department saw modest improvements. As sheriff, Hutson wants to bring the jail into compliance with its consent decree and ultimately decrease the jail's population. Taking a cue from the calls for reform that emerged after the death of George Floyd, she also hopes to work with local groups to push city leaders to invest more resources in the community and scale back the footprint of the police force.

Beyond the stakes for New Orleans, the election represents one of the first big national tests of whether the criminal justice movement can make an impact on sheriffs' offices, which so far have remained largely impervious to reform, even as progressives and grassroots groups have had success in electing district attorneys and pushing modest local and state police reforms. Still, sheriffs present a uniquely challenging office to overhaul, particularly at a time when federal police reform efforts have failed, reform-minded prosecutors are facing recall elections, and crime rates are ticking upward. The job of the sheriff has always had a strong tough-on-crime culture, and to date few progressive candidates have been willing to take on the challenge of reforming a system that touches everything from immigration to policing to jails. Because most sheriffs are elected at the county level, they also must appeal to a wide swath of voters, while left-leaning mayors in big cities can appoint their police chiefs and interview candidates from across the country.

For the past decade, criminal justice reformers have taken to the ballot box to elect progressive-minded prosecutors and judges who vow to reduce penalties—or dismiss charges altogether—for low-level crimes, avoid excessive sentences, and right the injustices of the past by reviewing questionable cases. More than two dozen progressive-minded prosecutors have managed to win elections in that time, including Kim Foxx in Cook County, Illinois (home to Chicago); Rachael Rollins in Boston; Larry Krasner in Philadelphia; and Chesa Boudin in San Francisco. Although these prosecutors have faced challenges once in office, their elections alone signaled a change. Because sheriffs, like prosecutors, are elected officials, advocacy groups have been inspired to attempt a similar strategy to elect progressive sheriffs. But the results have been mixed at best, especially when it comes to reforming jails.

There have been recent successes, many related to immigration reforms. In 2016, after decades of organizing, Latino activists in Maricopa County, Arizona, ousted Joe Arpaio, the county's fiercely anti-immigrant sheriff. (Liberal megadonor George Soros contributed $2 million to the effort, which probably helped.) In 2018, North Carolina voters elected a slate of reform-minded sheriffs in Mecklenburg, Durham, and Wake counties, each of whom agreed to withdraw from a federal program that enables sheriffs to assist Immigration and Customs Enforcement in deporting jail inmates. And in 2020, Cobb County, Georgia, and Charleston County, South Carolina, both elected sheriffs who ran on reform platforms. Still, none of these candidates explicitly argued for downsizing their budgets or their jail populations—a core goal of many criminal justice reformers. "I think there is a movement across the country of people who are fighting for something different," says Max Rose, executive director of Sheriffs for Trusting Communities, a nonprofit that supports grassroots organizers in sheriffs' campaigns. "Elections are an important and limited tool in that fight."

Almost all these new sheriffs are Black (Kristin Graziano, the new sheriff in Charleston County, is white and an out lesbian), which is significant because sheriffs have historically been predominately white and male, while the populations most affected by sheriffs' work are disproportionately Black and Latino. A 2020 report by the Reflective Democracy Campaign found that 90 percent of the nation's sheriffs are white men, while fewer than 3 percent are women.

There are signs that this pattern is changing. In Fort Bend County, Texas, a suburb of Houston, voters in 2020 elected the first Black sheriff since Reconstruction. In the recent sheriff's election in Erie County, New York, Kimberly Beaty, a former deputy commissioner of the Buffalo Police Department, ran against Republican John Garcia. Beaty would be the first Black woman to hold that office; the election has come down to absentee ballots, which are still being counted. If elected, Hutson would be the first woman to serve as New Orleans sheriff, and the first Black woman.

Still, the barriers to electing progressive sheriffs remain high. Most sheriffs hold office for multiple terms, stretching to decades, often because of a mix of institutional entropy and a lack of public awareness about the office. Michael Zoorob, a postdoctoral researcher at Northeastern University, found in an analysis that sheriffs have an incumbency advantage that "far exceeds that of other local offices" such as city councilor, state representative, or mayor. Much of this advantage, Zoorob wrote, comes from a sheriff's nearly unchecked discretion, which can include the ability to hire and fire employees at will, award contracts, initiate investigations, and block oversight. Plus, sheriffs' elections, as compared with other city races, tend to hinge on more suburban and rural voters who are more likely to lean conservative on criminal justice issues.

The sheriff's race in New Orleans would be another milestone for criminal justice reform. Hutson sees herself as part of the broader movement to change the office of the sheriff; she says she is inspired by women like Graziano who have been elected on reform platforms, and she likes to talk about "Black girl magic." But she also recognizes that, even if she wins, she will have a lot of work to do to overcome the history of abuses in the New Orleans jail.

Louisiana has a long history of high incarceration rates and heavy-handed sheriffs. In the nineteenth century, the state's sheriffs assisted in a practice known as convict leasing—the renting out of incarcerated people's labor. Today, sheriffs can operate work-release programs, in which they keep the bulk of the incarcerated workers' wages, and they can incarcerate people on behalf of state and federal agencies, for which they receive per diem pay from the government. The state also gives wide latitude to sheriffs to hire deputies and run their jails, including contracting with private health care providers. And the state sheriffs' association holds significant political power, often lobbying to block criminal justice reforms. "Why would I want to be governor when I can be king?" one Louisiana sheriff once asked. (He is memorialized in a fourteen-foot statue in Metairie.)

New Orleans has long struggled with accountability in its justice system. In the 2012 suit against Gusman, a group of people housed in the Orleans Justice Center alleged horrific conditions: "Rapes, sexual assaults, and beatings are commonplace throughout the facility. Violence regularly occurs at the hands of sheriffs' deputies, as well as other prisoners. The facility is full of homemade knives, or 'shanks.' People living with serious mental illnesses languish without treatment, left vulnerable to physical and sexual abuse," the lawsuit read.

Gusman challenged the lawsuit, and said the city wasn't adequately funding the jail. After the federal government joined the suit, DOJ sought its consent decree, which was approved by a judge in 2013. In his ruling, the judge found that the conditions at the jail had become "an indelible stain on the community." Since then, the jail has been under a federal monitor who oversees the jail's mandated efforts to protect individuals from physical and sexual assault, provide adequate medical and mental health care, prevent suicides, and ensure adequate sanitation.

In her campaign, Hutson is drawing on her activist background to highlight how she would approach the job differently. Before she was born, her grandfather was shot and killed by a sheriff's deputy in East Texas, an incident she says inspired her to fight racism in the criminal justice system. As a college student at the University of Pennsylvania, she protested South African apartheid and agitated for change after the 1985 MOVE bombing, when the Philadelphia Police bombed a Black neighborhood, killing eleven people. After law school, she worked as a prosecutor and police overseer in Austin, Texas, and Los Angeles before landing in New Orleans.

As the independent police monitor, a position created by the city to oversee the police department, Hutson made advisory opinions, including reviewing use-of-force incidents, complaints, and disciplinary procedures, as well as helping the department improve community relations. But she did not have the ability to implement reform herself. "You use your bully pulpit, but you're not the actual decision-maker," she explains. Still, serious use-of-force incidents in the New Orleans police went from thirteen in 2013 to one in 2018, and, in polls, residents have cited more positive attitudes toward the police. (The New Orleans Police Department declined to comment on Hutson or "any candidates for public office.") Before she stepped down to run for sheriff, Huston was president of the National Association for Citizen Oversight of Law Enforcement and was cited around the country for her expertise on police oversight.

Ahead of the election, Hutson has been campaigning around the city, trying to make sure voters know her name and talking up her commitment to what she calls the "three c's" of correction: care, custody, and control. Her platform is ambitious. She wants to end the jail's contract with Wellpath, the private company that provides health care to people inside the Justice Center, replacing it with health professionals the sheriff's office can hire and control. She also wants to avoid increasing the jail population; encourage people inside the jail to vote and engage in rehabilitative programs; and, in her words, "comply with the consent decree and implement strict financial controls" over the jail's budget and expenditures. Most important, she says, is to "listen to what our community is saying." For Hutson, that means taking seriously grassroots demands for decarceration and working with the city to try to shift funding to community care, which is not something a sheriff would typically do. "I want to be a part of changing the system to be closer to the point where we may not need [jails] anymore," she says. "Is it going to happen in my lifetime? I don't know. But I definitely want to do my part."

Still, even some of her supporters admit to having questions about how much a progressive sheriff can actually change the system if elected. In Los Angeles, Democratic voters elected Alex Villanueva as sheriff in 2018 based on his promises of reform, but he has found himself fighting with the Civilian Oversight Commission that monitors the sheriff's department, the county board of supervisors, the D.A., and pretty much everyone else who stands in his way. In Mecklenburg County, Sheriff Garry McFadden, elected in 2018 on a reform platform, has had to answer to a slate of jail deaths and protests.

Those who work on progressive sheriff campaigns are not naïve to the challenges. "I do not believe a single candidate can be our salvation," says Sade Dumas, executive director of the Orleans Parish Prison Reform Coalition, one of the groups that opposes the New Orleans jail expansion. "But I believe a progressive sheriff can make things less bad by refusing to enact regressive, harmful practices."

Ed. Note: Susan Hutson was elected the first Black female sheriff of Orleans Parish after winning the general election on December 11, 2021. She assumed the leadership position on May 2, 2022. Since her election, federal jail monitors—appointed to monitor and ensure compliance with a long-standing federal consent decree—released a report addressing jail conditions. The report, issued on July 3, 2023, noted some improvements since Hutson became sheriff, including the formation of an independent compliance unit that would continue to monitor and investigate issues. For years, federal monitors had encouraged the previous sheriff to establish a compliance unit, but he never did. The report also highlighted continued concerns over serious violent incidents, deaths of people held in custody, and disputes related to transparency.

Bring It On: The Future of Penal Reform, the Carceral State, and American Politics*

Marie Gottschalk

2015

The findings of decades of research on what explains variations in violent crime, especially homicide rates, are remarkably robust. Certain structural factors consistently predict higher rates of homicide: larger and denser populations, geographic location in the South, a higher proportion of divorced males, and higher rates of poverty and income inequality. Two other key structural factors that are related to income inequality— residential segregation and pervasive economic discrimination against certain groups—are likely consequential as well.

Over time, the relative weight of these factors has shifted,

* Marie Gottschalk, "Bring It On: The Future of Penal Reform, the Carceral State, and American Politics," *Ohio State Journal of Criminal Law* 12, no. 2 (Spring 2015): 559–603.

with structural economic factors related to poverty and income inequality now accounting for a greater proportion of
the variance. Differences in policing resources and strategies
also likely explain variations in rates of violent crime, though
experts do not agree on just how much to credit the police for
sustained drops in rates of homicide and violent crime.

If the United States is serious about addressing these high
levels of concentrated violence then it has to be serious about
addressing the country's high levels of inequality and concentrated poverty. The only way out is to develop a new social and
economic agenda that designates the alleviation of the uncon-
scionably high rates of hunger, poverty, and joblessness that
vex these communities as a top priority, not a public policy
afterthought. This would necessitate an infusion of resources
and new policies and programs to address persistent residential segregation, inadequate investments in good housing, and
disparate access to equitable residential loans and quality public education.

It also would entail a renewed commitment to government
intervention to bring down the unemployment rate and to
foster the revitalization of organized labor and collective bargaining. All the hand-wringing and fatalism today about the
government's purported impotency when it comes to creating
jobs obscures the fact that the expansion of the public sector
beginning in the 1960s was a key factor in the sizable reductions in the poverty rate for blacks. Penal and social policies
have long been two sides of the same coin in governing social
marginality. Increasingly, penal policy has become the policy
of first resort to address the massive economic and social dislo-
cations of the last half century and the related crime problem.

The main emphasis has been on the need for more police
and new policing strategies to enhance public safety, most

notably Compstat and "hot spots" policing. This has fomented a technicist approach that "depoliticizes crime prevention, by reducing it to the purely neutral scientific task of identifying 'best practice.'" Such an approach is inattentive to the important political and symbolic dimensions of crime prevention and penal policy more generally.

Policing enthusiasts contend that policing strategies based on the proven deterrent effects of swift and certain apprehension and punishment are the key to lowering crime rates. They have a point. It is "surely . . . better to prevent people from committing crime through a visible police presence than to wait for them to commit it and then put them behind bars," concedes sociologist Elliott Currie. But it "is one thing to prevent crime by improving social conditions or by making people more capable and productive," explains Currie. It is another thing altogether to prevent crime "by frightening unproductive, desperate, and alienated people with the threat of arrest and incarceration if they break the law."

In recent decades, the resources available to many police departments and law enforcement agencies escalated. This occurred largely without a commensurate increase in police accountability to the communities they serve. Police and their political benefactors have stridently resisted creating independent civilian review boards with real teeth to monitor and discipline their activities. Many prosecutors have been loath to aggressively pursue charges of police brutality and other criminal activities by police officers. Thanks to lucrative and highly permissive forfeiture laws and other measures, police departments have expanded their paramilitary operations, their anti-drug task forces, and other controversial operations. The police have also been the main foot soldiers in the war on drugs and in carrying out massive stop-and-frisk campaigns in certain neighborhoods. Additionally, they have become important players in the local enforcement of federal immigration policies in some communities. As a consequence, the police are widely viewed in many inner-city neighborhoods and elsewhere in the country as an occupying army unaccountable to the local citizens.

The uproar following the death of Michael Brown, an unarmed black teenager shot to death by a white police officer in Ferguson, Missouri, in August 2014, brought national and international attention to this issue.

Crime prevention policies have followed strikingly different trajectories in Europe compared to the United States. In Europe, they have been inextricably "bound up with concerns about social exclusion and urban renewal in disadvantaged communities." The countries of the European Union have many more police per capita than the United States, but they also have more expansive social welfare programs that seek to reduce crime by ameliorating poverty and inequality.

For decades, conservatives have brazenly dismissed the claim that social welfare spending reduces crime. Indeed, many have argued the exact reverse. Although the relationship between crime and spending on social welfare has been a hotly debated topic, research in this area is surprisingly sparse. The limited research available suggests that certain types of social welfare spending and programs reduce crime.

What we do know conclusively is that states and countries that spend more on social welfare tend to have lower incarceration rates; moreover, high rates of inequality are associated with higher rates of imprisonment and crime.

The unequal distribution of crime and the persistence of extraordinarily high levels of violent crime in certain urban neighborhoods is a major inequality that needs to be addressed.

However, as discussed earlier, in addressing the crime problem, we must be careful not to conflate it with the problem of the carceral state. The United States needs a visionary agenda aimed at ameliorating the root causes of crime and other persistent and gaping inequalities in high-crime communities. In the meantime, there is no excuse for keeping so many of the residents of these communities locked up or otherwise ensnared in the carceral state.

Part II

Prosecutors

In the popular imagination, lawyers argue each side of an issue, while the judge or jury makes the decision. But when we worked as public defenders, we learned that prosecutors were often the true power brokers: They chose what charges to bring, how much discovery material to provide, and whether to offer a plea bargain. And we believed they often used their authority for ill, standing as barriers between our clients and justice.

What we were seeing was just one small part of a national phenomenon, as criminologist John F. Pfaff explores in *Locked In: The True Causes of Mass Incarceration and How to Achieve Real Reform*. Pfaff calls attention to the vast, unchecked discretion that prosecutors enjoy in our criminal system.

After police make an arrest, prosecutors decide whether to file charges—and courts have repeatedly held that judges lack the power to second-guess this decision.[1]

Legislatures have been complicit, largely outsourcing the question of punishment to prosecutors. They've done so by criminalizing a wide array of overlapping conduct—a single armed robbery often allows a prosecutor to charge not only armed robbery but also aggravated assault, theft, unlawful possession of a weapon, and so on. One event can thus give rise to dozens of charges, any of which the prosecutor can choose to bring or not. Because the maximum penalties for each offense are often severe, prosecutors can use them as cudgels to force a guilty plea: Instead of going to trial and risking a draconian sentence, defendants feel tremendous pressure to plead guilty to a lesser offense. And plead they do: Recent data show that 98 percent of people charged in federal court pled guilty in 2020, with the percentages in state court not far below.[2]

What does the Supreme Court think of this? In *Bordenkircher v. Hayes* (1978), it essentially gave prosecutors free rein to wield their discretion as they see fit. In *Bordenkircher*, Paul Hayes was indicted for forgery amounting to $88.30. The prosecutor offered Hayes a five-year prison sentence if he pled guilty. But if Hayes refused, the prosecutor threatened to charge him as a habitual offender, which carried a possible term of life imprisonment. Hayes rejected the deal, was convicted at trial, and was sentenced to life in prison. On appeal, the Supreme Court denied that the prosecutor's threat of life imprisonment was "vindictive" and approved the arm-twisting that resulted in Hayes's life sentence. This "trial penalty," where prosecutors seek higher sentences at trial to deter people from demanding one in the first place, has become commonplace.[3] Indeed, sentences imposed at trial are 64 percent longer than those imposed through pleas.[4]

Finally, prosecutors are rarely held accountable by voters. This may come as a surprise, since head prosecutors—unlike chief public defenders, many judges, and police officials—are largely elected officials in the United States. In fact, we are the only country that elects them. Yet many of these elections are uncontested. Between 2012 and 2017, of the more than 2,300 jurisdictions that elect their prosecutor, fewer than 700 presented voters with more than one candidate.[5] This lack of choice was even more extreme when the incumbent prosecutor ran for reelection—incumbents ran unopposed 75 percent of the time.[6]

This noncompetitive electoral system has produced a homogeneous set of prosecutors. A 2019 study by the Reflective Democracy Campaign revealed that 95 percent of our country's prosecutors are white and 76 percent of them are male.[7] When viewed in the context of who is being prosecuted, these numbers illustrate devastating, foundational truths about our criminal legal system: Black Americans are incarcerated in state prisons at nearly five times the rate of white Americans, and in twelve states, more than half the prison population is Black.[8] A study of Manhattan criminal cases from 2010 to 2011 also found that Black people were 19 percent more likely to be offered plea deals that included jail time.[9]

This description of prosecutors—powerful, punitive, unchecked—has been true for so long that many people felt it would never change. Writing as recently as 2017, Pfaff lamented, "For all their power, prosecutors are almost completely ignored by reformers."

Then things started to shift. In 2016, insurgent candidates

in a diverse set of cities and counties—including Denver, Chicago, and St. Louis—challenged incumbent prosecutors. Rejecting the typical punishment-first rhetoric that had long dominated such races, they campaigned on promises to charge fewer children as adults, not to prosecute certain drug cases, and to rarely (or never) seek the death penalty. These long-shot candidates attracted little national attention—until the votes were counted. Once they were, it was clear that a new movement had launched: "progressive prosecution."

The definitive book on this topic is Emily Bazelon's *Charged: The New Movement to Transform American Prosecution and End Mass Incarceration*. Bazelon tells the story of U.S. Supreme Court Justice Sonia Sotomayor, who grew up in a housing project in the Bronx and began her legal career in the Manhattan district attorney's office.

While she loved her five years as a prosecutor, Sotomayor came away from the work thinking that, as she put it, the criminal justice system "accomplishes nothing we think of as its purpose." Although Sotomayor practiced in an earlier era, she learned some of the same lessons that animate today's progressive prosecutors. Bazelon calls the movement to elect such prosecutors "the most promising means of reform I see on the political landscape."

Law professor Angela J. Davis chronicles the emergence of this strategy in "Reimagining Prosecution: A Growing Progressive Movement." She links its origins to the Black Lives Matter movement, explaining that "the police killings of unarmed black men in recent years served to educate the public about the power of prosecutors and their central role in the criminal process." When prosecutors refused to bring charges against police officers in these cases, voters gained a new understanding of the biases so many prosecutors brought to their roles. As a result, they were motivated to elect prosecutors who shared their values.

While she embraces the progressive prosecutor movement, Davis also recognizes that it can be difficult to determine what makes a prosecutor "progressive." At a minimum, she says, such prosecutors must be "committed to reducing mass incarceration and racial disparities in the criminal justice system." But Davis rejects a strict litmus test. She argues that we must recognize that a "District Attorney attempting to implement criminal justice reform in Columbus, Mississippi, cannot run on the same platform as a District Attorney in Philadelphia, Pennsylvania, because Mississippi is much more conservative and the electorate would likely not be as receptive to radical changes."

Still, the readings in this part invite us to consider the potential for real democratic intervention in this field. Across the country in the last few years, some prosecutors have established policies eliminating or limiting the use of cash bail, refusing to charge sentencing enhancements that increase prison time, reopening old cases for "second looks" and exonerations, refusing to seek the death penalty, investigating police misconduct, and reducing incarceration rates. While these reforms do not turn the function of prosecution on its head, they are meaningful steps by actors uniquely positioned to take them.

For a concrete example of a prosecutor seeking change, we highlight the policy memorandum that Philadelphia district attorney Larry Krasner issued upon taking office in 2018. The memo opens with this remarkable statement by a chief prosecutor: "These policies are an effort to end mass incarceration and bring balance back to sentencing." The memo then identifies concrete measures to achieve that goal, such as requiring courtroom prosecutors to explain—on the record and in every case—how much a prison sentence will cost taxpayers and why they believe that cost is justified. Requiring prosecutors to defend the cost of a prison sentence is so striking because, in our experience, prison is taken for granted in most sentencing hearings. It never has to prove its worth. Forcing it to do so, as Krasner does, has the potential to permanently alter sentencing narratives.

Since the release of Krasner's memo, the conversation about how progressive prosecutors should combat mass incarceration has only attracted more voices, not all of them supportive. Reform-minded prosecutors have been met with resistance by other system actors—including some within their own offices—wedded to our current system of prosecution and punishment.[10] Pennsylvania legislators circumvented Krasner's office by empowering the attorney general to prosecute gun cases in Philadelphia.[11] In San Francisco, the police union spent over $650,000 on ads opposing reformer Chesa Boudin's election—and in 2022 he was recalled by city voters.[12]

Black women have encountered especially fierce resistance from the rest of the system.[13] For example, the Florida legislature slashed $1.3 million from the budget of Orlando's reform prosecutor, Aramis Ayala, when she refused to seek the death penalty.[14] In Chicago, Cook County state's attorney Kim Foxx announced that she would not seek a third term after spending her first two working to free the wrongfully convicted and shrinking prosecutions of minor offenses.[15] A local judge there had appointed a special prosecutor to review her decision-making in one high-profile case; she also faced persistent criticism by law enforcement for her reform efforts.[16] And in St. Louis, Kim Gardner resigned in the wake of a proposed bill in the Missouri state legislature that would allow a special prosecutor to be appointed in lieu of her office in any case involving a "threat to public safety."[17] All of these prosecutors also experienced racist and sexist harassment, including death threats.[18]

This blowback against reform-minded prosecutors hasn't been universal, however. Indeed, the women above were all voted into office, some for more than one term. In 2020, voters reelected Krasner in the Democratic primary with even higher margins than before. Communities facing high rates of gun violence overwhelmingly supported his campaign.

In 2021, ACLU attorneys Taylor Pendergrass and Somil Trivedi published an article arguing that change-making prosecutors should jettison the mantle "progressive" in favor of "transformational." In their view, transformational prosecutors should pledge to decarcerate, adopt a stance of radical transparency with respect to their data and charging policies, and champion legislative reforms that advance decarceration. We excerpt a portion of their article in which they argue that prosecutors should commit to shrinking the legal system—including the role of the prosecutor itself.

Very few prosecutors have done what Pendergrass and Trivedi suggest. Even progressive prosecutors have avoided going before a legislative body to request a smaller budget. Few have supported laws requiring prosecutors to open their files to the defense. But such steps are required if reform-minded prosecutors hope to make lasting change, argues Rachel Barkow in "Can Prosecutors End Mass Incarceration?" It's not good enough, says Barkow, for a prosecutor to say, "Give me more money, I'll use it for diversion programs and other alternatives to prison." After all, even if their intentions are pure, once they leave office, they are powerless to stop their successor from using those funds to lock up more people.

Along with readings that are broadly supportive (though often with caveats) of the progressive prosecutor movement, we have included two pieces that are more critical. Both raise doubts about whether progressive prosecutors deserve to be featured at all in the fight against mass incarceration. "Abolitionist Principles and Campaign Strategies for Prosecutor Organizing," a guide published by a group of contributors including Community Justice Exchange, argues that some reform-minded prosecutors have begun to develop cults of personality. By claiming credit for all meaningful changes in a community's justice system, these prosecutors end up reinforcing the view that prosecutors must remain central to reform efforts. In response, the authors call for a careful analysis of policies to see whether prosecutors are actually decriminalizing, decarcerating, and working to reduce their own role and power in the system. We include the guide along with a new reflection from its authors on the four years that have passed since its drafting.

The final critique comes from Paul D. Butler, who addresses a question that many of our students ask us as they contemplate their careers: If a young lawyer seeks to make our criminal system more just, should they work in a prosecutor's office? In "Should Good People Be Prosecutors?," Butler, a former prosecutor himself, does not hedge in his answer: a resounding no. At the end of the day, he argues, a prosecutor's main function is to criminalize, prosecute, and punish. As he puts it,

> Becoming a prosecutor to help resolve unfairness in the criminal justice system is like enlisting in the army because you are opposed to the current war. It's like working as an oil refiner because you want to help the environment. Yes, you get to choose the toxic chemicals. True, the boss might allow you to leave one or two pristine bays untouched. Maybe, if

you do really good work as a low-level polluter, they might make you the head polluter. But rather than calling yourself an "environmentalist," you should think of yourself as a polluter with a conscience.

Year after year, nearly thirty thousand prosecutors across America spend $6 billion to convict people in over two million felony cases.[19] The contributors to this part invite us to ask whether those people and resources are being put to good use. They also raise fundamental questions about the infrastructure of our criminal legal system, identify points of possible intervention, and assess the risks and rewards of certain reforms. Is addressing the role of prosecutors among the most effective means of dismantling mass incarceration? If so, is electing reform-minded prosecutors a productive path or does it merely entrench and legitimize the system that produced the problem in the first place? Instead of elevating and supporting progressive prosecutors, should we work to limit the power of prosecutors altogether? Or can we pursue multiple paths at once? We hope that these different perspectives will create a rich foundation for your own conversations—and action.

From *Locked In: The True Causes of Mass Incarceration and How to Achieve Real Reform**

John F. Pfaff

2017

Few people in the criminal justice system are as powerful, or as central to prison growth, as the prosecutor. Recall that over the 1990s and 2000s, crime fell, arrests fell, and time spent in prison remained fairly steady. But even as the number of arrests declined, the number of felony cases filed in state courts rose sharply. In the end, the probability that a prosecutor would file felony charges against an arrestee basically doubled, and that change pushed prison populations up even as crime dropped.

Yet here's the remarkable thing. For all their power, prosecutors are almost completely ignored by reformers. No major

* John F. Pfaff, From *Locked In: The True Causes of Mass Incarceration and How to Achieve Real Reform* (New York: Basic Books, 2017).

piece of state-level reform legislation has directly challenged prosecutorial power (although some reforms do in fact impede it), and other than a few, generally local exceptions, their power is rarely a topic in the national debate over criminal justice reform. They are essentially invisible.

Perhaps the most revealing example of this invisibility comes from a report by the National Research Council on the causes of prison growth. The NRC is the branch of the prestigious National Academy of Sciences tasked with producing expert reports on important public policy issues. Yet when called on to explain the causes of soaring incarceration rates, it barely discussed the role of prosecutors at all. In this part I confront this startling blind spot in our national conversation on prison reform.

Two features of the modern prosecutor's office demand particular attention. The first is that the number of line prosecutors (those who actually try cases) has grown significantly over the past forty years, but in a somewhat peculiar way. From 1970 to 1990, the number of prosecutors rose by three thousand, from seventeen thousand to twenty thousand. From 1990 to 2007 (the last year of reliable data), the number of line prosecutors grew more than three times as fast, to thirty thousand. This is the opposite of what one would expect. Between 1970 and 1990, violent crime rates rose by 100 percent, property crime rates by 40 percent, and the number of line prosecutors by 17 percent. From 1990 to 2007, violent and property crime rates both fell by 35 percent, but the number of line prosecutors rose by 50 percent—a faster rate of growth than during the crime boom.

The second is the magnitude of the discretion they wield. For example, prosecutors have the unreviewable ability to decide whether to file charges against someone who has been arrested, and they face almost no oversight about what charges to file if they decide to move ahead with a case. The U.S. Supreme Court has made it clear that it will not regulate these sorts of decisions: in 1985, the Court said this bluntly in *Wayte v. United States*, calling the "decision to prosecute" something "particularly ill-suited to judicial review." So while this power is not new—public prosecutors have had substantial discretion since their offices were founded—prosecutors appear to be using it in increasingly aggressive ways these days.

Over the years, legislators have expanded this discretion by giving prosecutors a growing array of often-overlapping charges from which to choose. For example, the Model Penal Code, drafted by the prestigious American Law Institute in 1962 as a framework to help states modernize their criminal codes, included exactly two degrees of assault: simple assault (for "bodily injury") and aggravated assault (for "serious bodily injury"). New York State, however, now has twenty-three or so assault offenses, many of which overlap. Take "Assault on a Judge," which is simply "Second Degree Assault" with the additional fact that the victim is a judge trying to perform his official duties. Second Degree Assault is a Class D felony; on a judge, Class C. A prosecutor in New York facing a case that qualifies for Assault on a Judge can nonetheless charge the case as Second Degree Assault if he wishes. No one can review this, and the difference matters. The statutory maximum for a Class D felony is seven years, compared to fifteen for a Class C. By the choice of charge, the prosecutor can more than double the potential sentence a defendant faces.

This is a tremendous amount of power for one official to have, and it is made all the more powerful by the fact that prosecutors generally wield it out of public view. Nearly 95 percent of the cases that prosecutors decide to prosecute end up with the defendant pleading guilty. For all the courtroom drama we see on *Law and Order*, nearly everyone in prison ended up there by signing a piece of paper in a dingy conference room in a county office building, or in a dingier room in a local jail.

This lack of a public record actually makes it easy for prosecutors to look less aggressive than they are. A striking example comes from the federal system, where a single criminal act can implicate numerous overlapping statutes, some of which carry vicious mandatory minimums while others do not. Congress has recently set about trying to roll back some of these mandatory minimums, but the lobbying organization for federal trial lawyers, the National Association of Assistant United States Attorneys, has pushed back strongly. One of the NAAUSA's arguments is that the mandatory minimums should not be repealed because they are almost never used, but instead are saved only for the worst of the worst defendants. At a simple level, the NAAUSA's argument appears correct, since few federal inmates have been sentenced to these mandatory minimums. But federal prosecutors often wield the threat of the mandatory minimum to persuade a defendant to plead guilty to a charge that doesn't carry such a stiff sentence. Using a gun during a drug deal can result in a mandatory minimum of up to thirty years under a particular statute. A prosecutor, however, can tell a defendant that if he pleads guilty to just the drug charge, the prosecutor will make the gun disappear. The threat of thirty years is enough to terrify most defendants into agreeing. So even if the mandatory minimum is rarely imposed, it is *used* much more often. But thanks to the plea process, the public almost never sees how prosecutors actually deploy it. If the public were able to observe how often federal prosecutors threaten relatively minor defendants with these mandatory sentences, there would (perhaps) be a backlash.

Plea bargaining not only shields prosecutors from account-ability, it also makes them more powerful by allowing them to process more cases per year. Pleas can be resolved in a matter of days, compared to the weeks or months that would go into a trial. Most commentators admit that the criminal justice sys-tem in the United States would grind to a halt if plea bargaining were banned. The handful of jurisdictions that have attempted to abolish plea bargaining have quickly given up, if they ever really stopped it at all. Furthermore, plea bargains help prose-cutors work around weaknesses in their cases. Even if the main case is weak, a prosecutor can come up with a set of charges and sentences that are more appealing to the defendant than the risk of something worse at trial. Given that defendants have almost no constitutional right to discovery during the plea process, prosecutors are often able to convincingly bluff with weak hands, especially given the sorts of threats that *Borden-kircher* allows and harsh sentencing laws facilitate.

Taken together, these attributes and tools make prosecutors the most powerful actors in the criminal justice system. While the police determine who "enters" the criminal justice process, prosecutors have complete control over which cases they file and which ones they dismiss. If prosecutors decide to move a case forward, their choice of what charges to bring is limited solely by what they think they can prove—or what they think they can convince defendants they can prove. These charges in turn often place significant limitations on the sentences that judges can impose. Prosecutors are free to threaten whatever severe sanctions legislators have passed, and legislators have been happy to enact tougher and tougher laws. It's true that judges are required to sign off on pleas and can thus reject those they find unsatisfactory, but in general, they will acquiesce to the deals struck by the prosecutors and defense attorneys.

Prosecutors, as we've noted, have used this power to drive up prison populations even as crime has declined over the past twenty or so years. To date, however, no state- or federal-level proposal aimed at cutting prison populations has sought to explicitly regulate this power. Everyone else in the criminal justice system currently faces reforms, such as efforts to change interactions between civilians and police, or to amend sentencing laws and parole policies. But prosecutors have remained untouched.

Bordenkircher v. Hayes*

Justice Potter Stewart
1978

The question in this case is whether the Due Process Clause of the Fourteenth Amendment is violated when a state prosecutor carries out a threat made during plea negotiations to reindict the accused on more serious charges if he does not plead guilty to the offense with which he was originally charged.

The respondent, Paul Lewis Hayes, was indicted by a Fayette County, Kentucky, grand jury on a charge of uttering a forged instrument in the amount of $88.30, an offense then punishable by a term of two to ten years in prison. After arraignment, Hayes, his retained counsel, and the Commonwealth's Attorney met in the presence of the Clerk of the Court to discuss a possible plea agreement. During these conferences the prosecutor offered to recommend a sentence of five years in prison if Hayes would plead guilty to the indictment. He also said that if Hayes did not plead guilty and "save the court the inconve-

* *Bordenkircher v. Hayes*, 434 U.S. 357 (1978).

nience and necessity of a trial," he would return to the grand jury to seek an indictment under the Kentucky Habitual Criminal Act, which would subject Hayes to a mandatory sentence of life imprisonment by reason of his two prior felony convictions. Hayes chose not to plead guilty, and the prosecutor did obtain an indictment charging him under the Habitual Criminal Act. It is not disputed that the recidivist charge was fully justified by the evidence, that the prosecutor was in possession of this evidence at the time of the original indictment, and that Hayes's refusal to plead guilty to the original charge was what led to his indictment under the habitual criminal statute.

A jury found Hayes guilty on the principal charge of uttering a forged instrument and, in a separate proceeding, further found that he had twice before been convicted of felonies. As required by the habitual offender statute, he was sentenced to a life term in the penitentiary. The Kentucky Court of Appeals rejected Hayes's constitutional objections to the enhanced sentence, holding in an unpublished opinion that imprisonment for life with the possibility of parole was constitutionally permissible in light of the previous felonies of which Hayes had been convicted, and that the prosecutor's decision to indict him as a habitual offender was a legitimate use of available leverage in the plea-bargaining process.

We granted certiorari to consider a constitutional question of importance in the administration of criminal justice.

We have recently had occasion to observe: "Whatever might be the situation in an ideal world, the fact is that the guilty plea and the often concomitant plea bargain are important components of this country's criminal justice system. Properly administered, they can benefit all concerned." The open acknowledgment of this previously clandestine practice has led this Court to recognize the importance of counsel during plea negotiations, the need for a public record indicating that a plea was knowingly and voluntarily made, and the requirement that a prosecutor's plea-bargaining promise must be kept. The decision of the Court of Appeals in the present case, however, did not deal with considerations such as these, but held that the substance of the plea offer itself violated the limitations imposed by the Due Process Clause of the Fourteenth Amendment. For the reasons that follow, we have concluded that the Court of Appeals was mistaken in so ruling.

While confronting a defendant with the risk of more severe punishment clearly may have a "discouraging effect on the defendant's assertion of his trial rights, the imposition of these difficult choices [is] an inevitable"—and permissible— "attribute of any legitimate system which tolerates and encourages the negotiation of pleas." It follows that, by tolerating and encouraging the negotiation of pleas, this Court has necessarily accepted as constitutionally legitimate the simple reality that the prosecutor's interest at the bargaining table is to persuade the defendant to forgo his right to plead not guilty.

It is not disputed here that Hayes was properly chargeable under the recidivist statute, since he had in fact been convicted of two previous felonies. In our system, so long as the prosecutor has probable cause to believe that the accused committed an offense defined by statute, the decision whether or not to prosecute, and what charge to file or bring before a grand jury, generally rests entirely in his discretion. Within the limits set by the legislature's constitutionally valid definition of chargeable offenses, "the conscious exercise of some selectivity in enforcement is not in itself a federal constitutional violation" so long as "the selection was [not] deliberately based upon an unjustifiable standard such as race, religion, or other arbitrary classification." To hold that the prosecutor's desire to induce a guilty plea is an "unjustifiable standard," which, like race or religion, may play no part in his charging decision, would contradict the very premises that underlie the concept of plea bargaining itself. Moreover, a rigid constitutional rule that would prohibit a prosecutor from acting forthrightly in his dealings with the defense could only invite unhealthy subterfuge that would drive the practice of plea bargaining back into the shadows from which it has so recently emerged.

There is no doubt that the breadth of discretion that our country's legal system vests in prosecuting attorneys carries with it the potential for both individual and institutional abuse. And broad though that discretion may be, there are undoubtedly constitutional limits upon its exercise. We hold only that the course of conduct engaged in by the prosecutor in this case, which no more than openly presented the defendant with the unpleasant alternatives of forgoing trial or facing charges on which he was plainly subject to prosecution, did not violate the Due Process Clause of the Fourteenth Amendment.

Accordingly, the judgment of the Court of Appeals is *Reversed*.

Tipping the Scales: Challengers Take On the Old Boys' Club of Elected Prosecutors*

Reflective Democracy Campaign

2019

White control of prosecutor seats holds fast at 95%

Despite some notable victories by candidates of color in cities such as Chicago, Baltimore, Boston, and Ferguson, prosecutors nationwide are as overwhelmingly white as they were in 2015.

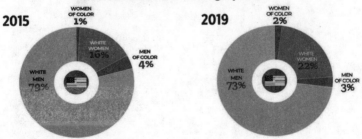

Elected Prosecutor Demographics

2015
- WOMEN OF COLOR 1%
- WHITE WOMEN 16%
- MEN OF COLOR 4%
- WHITE MEN 79%

2019
- WOMEN OF COLOR 2%
- WHITE WOMEN 22%
- MEN OF COLOR 3%
- WHITE MEN 73%

---

* Reflective Democracy Campaign, "Tipping the Scales: Challengers Take On the Old Boys' Club of Elected Prosecutors," October 2019.

White control of elected prosecutor positions has not changed
In 2015, prosecutors were 95% white. In 2019, they are still 95% white.

The gender (im)balance of elected prosecutors is changing
While nearly 75% of prosecutors are white men, women have increased at a rate of 34% since 2015, from 18% to 24% of prosecutors.

Change is possible - when there is competition
Prosecutors run unopposed 80% of the time, but in competitive races, the old boys' club starts to give way. White male over-representation is rampant, but not unsolvable.

When women of all races and men of color run for prosecutor in competitive elections, they're more likely to win than white men
In competitive 2018 elections, white men were 69% of candidates, but only 59% of winners. Women and people of color were 31% of candidates and 41% of winners.

Despite overall low numbers, women of color are making notable gains
There are nearly 50% more women of color prosecutors today as in 2015.

From *Charged: The New Movement to Transform American Prosecution and End Mass Incarceration**

Emily Bazelon

2019

In her first decade on the Supreme Court, Justice Sonia Soto-mayor became its fiercest voice for people . . . who are suspected of or charged with crimes. She proved herself, again and again, to be a tireless protector of our basic rights. In one unforget-table dissenting opinion in 2016, *Utah v. Strieff,* she described just how much those rights are at risk of being snuffed out, first for people whom police and prosecutors view with distrust, and then for the rest of us.

Utah v. Strieff involved an illegal police stop. In December 2006, the Salt Lake City police got an anonymous tip that a

* Emily Bazelon, From *Charged: The New Movement to Transform American Prosecu-tion and End Mass Incarceration* (New York: Random House, 2019).

house was being used for drug sales. An officer watched the house for a few hours and saw more people going in and out than he thought was typical. One of those people was a man named Edward Strieff. The officer stopped Strieff on his way out of the house (without seeing him go in or knowing how long he was inside), ran his license, and discovered he had an outstanding warrant for a minor traffic violation. The officer arrested Strieff, searched him, and found a baggie of methamphetamine.

The prosecution conceded that seeing Strieff come out of the house wasn't a sufficient basis for stopping him. But the trial court ruled that the drug evidence could be admitted against him anyway, saying the officer made a "good-faith mistake." The Supreme Court agreed, by a vote of five to three. The officer's discovery of the warrant for the traffic violation, Justice Clarence Thomas said, made up for the problem with the stop. Dissenting, Sotomayor wrote of the majority's decision:

"It says that your body is subject to invasion while courts excuse the violation of your rights. It implies that you are not a citizen of a democracy but the subject of a carceral state, just waiting to be cataloged. We must not pretend that the countless people who are routinely targeted by police are 'isolated.' They are the canaries in the coalmine whose deaths, civil and literal, warn us that no one can breathe in this atmosphere."

Sotomayor grew up in a housing project in the Bronx. In her first job out of law school, she worked as a prosecutor in the Manhattan D.A.'s office. She took the position, she told a packed auditorium at Yale Law School in the spring of 2017, because Robert Morgenthau, the legendary district attorney of Manhattan, said he could offer her "the opportunity to do more good for more people than anyone else."

Sotomayor spent five years in Morgenthau's office. At Yale, she said two things that were in tension with each other about the experience: she loved the job, and yet over time, being a prosecutor taught her that the criminal justice system "accomplishes nothing we think of as its purpose," Sotomayor told her audience. "We think we're keeping people safe from criminals. We're just making worse criminals."

We think we're keeping people safe. We're just making worse criminals. Sotomayor summed up how the criminal justice system continues to operate in most of the country. The bipartisan reform movement is about tearing down that kind of system. What comes next has to make the law of more value to the people it touches directly. Witnesses and victims often come from the same neighborhoods as the perpetrators and sometimes *are the same people.* They have to trust police and prosecutors in order to help them solve crimes. The system we should rebuild is one in which justice and mercy reinforce each other, in which success is measured by fortifying communities, not by putting people away in demand of an eye for an eye. Keeping people safe means making fewer criminals, and fairness is essential to that equation.

We can make incremental progress if we stop doing the stupid stuff, like weighing people down with court dates and convictions for smoking weed or playing dice or jumping a turnstile. (If it's a good idea to arrest poor people for not paying their subway fare, why don't we do the same thing to middle-class and wealthy drivers who blow through E-ZPass toll stations?) We won't get where the country needs to go, though, until we rethink the harder cases, too. Guns are dangerous, and when young people feel the need to carry them in neighborhoods like Brownsville, it's a warning sign: something is wrong. But that something is a lot more complicated than casting out the "evildoers" who carry pistols. Getting guns off the streets makes for a good slogan for city leaders, a seemingly unassailable political goal in the context of gun control. It's harder to help people than to lock them up. It's also almost always, in the end, far more pragmatic and worthwhile.

The movement to elect a new kind of prosecutor is the most promising means of reform I see on the political landscape. That doesn't make it a panacea. In her forthcoming book *Prisoners of Politics*, Rachel Barkow argues that serious criminal justice reform means minimizing the role of politics and elections in crime policy, not playing the political game differently. She fears the reform movement could fizzle, especially if crime rises. I think and hope otherwise, . . . but it's a risk worth acknowledging.

Another challenge for the movement is figuring out how demanding to be. In reporting on D.A.s from Eric Gonzalez to Kim Ogg to Kim Foxx to Larry Krasner, I've mapped the variations from evolution to revolution. It's a mistake, I think, for reformers to impose a purity test. It's the job of activists, however, to have high aspirations and to be impatient.

The movement for prosecutorial reform can't just install new D.A.s and count on them to do the job differently. Some activists talk about co-governing. They mean taking part in policy discussions and also watching in court and tracking data for the outcomes they care about. When D.A.s' offices operate as a black box, cloaking the exercise of discretion, they weaken the social compact. Revelations of wrongful convictions and concealed evidence are so unsettling because they show the government wielding its raw power in ways we usually cannot see. Prosecutors have to commit themselves to performance measures like reducing incarceration, racial disparity, the rate of reoffending, and findings of misconduct. They have to commit to increasing community satisfaction with local justice— and then show how they score.

The criminal justice system is ungainly and massive, and re-routing it is like turning an ocean liner. It's a behemoth, at once mighty and monstrous. There is much steam built up to keep it going along its current course, and many levers to pull to steer it in a different direction. Somewhere along the way, the balance of power between the prosecution, the defense, and the judiciary shifted. We have to readjust it. The stakes are so high— the well-being of so many communities and the trajectory of so many lives. Public safety depends on our collective faith in fairness and our view of the law as legitimate.

As a journalist, I've never felt a greater sense of urgency about exposing the roots of a problem and shining a light on the people working to solve it. I feel a great sense of possibility. We have to fix the broken parts of America's criminal justice system. And we the people have the power to do it, with our votes.

Reimagining Prosecution: A Growing Progressive Movement*

Angela J. Davis

2019

In *Berger v. United States*, the Supreme Court noted that the prosecutor's "interest . . . in a criminal prosecution is not that it shall win a case, but that justice shall be done." Nonetheless, most prosecutors have focused on seeking convictions in criminal cases. This perspective has greatly contributed to the phenomenon of mass incarceration and its many unjust collateral consequences. In recent years, some elected prosecutors have sought to change this narrative by using their power and discretion with the goals of not only enforcing the law, but also reducing mass incarceration, eliminating racial disparities, and seeking justice for all, including the accused. This small

* Angela J. Davis, "Reimagining Prosecution: A Growing Progressive Movement," *UCLA Criminal Justice Law Review* 3, no. 1 (2019): 2–27.

but growing movement of so-called "progressive" prosecutors has achieved varying levels of success.

Some of these prosecutors report modest improvements, but many have faced serious challenges from within and outside of their offices. In this article, I explore this new vision of prosecution, including its successes and challenges. Can progressive prosecutors make significant progress toward the goal of eliminating mass incarceration and unwarranted racial disparities? What are the factors that impact their ability to effect change and how can those factors be managed? Prosecutors are the most powerful officials in the criminal justice system. Thus, their discretionary decisions—especially their charging and plea-bargaining decisions—play a very significant role in contributing to mass incarceration and unwarranted racial disparities.

The charging and plea-bargaining decisions are entirely controlled by prosecutors. Just as a prosecutor may decide to "pile on" unmeritorious charges, he may decide to forgo charges altogether even if there is evidence to support a conviction. A prosecutor may offer a plea bargain but is not required to do so. He may decide to give one individual a break while prosecuting another similarly situated individual arrested for the same offense. Likewise, prosecutors may offer a better deal to one individual than to another who is similarly situated. This vast discretion in the charging and plea-bargaining process often results in unwarranted racial disparities.

Many prosecutors aggressively pursue charges in as many cases as possible, seek high cash bail, and advocate for lengthy prison sentences. But a prosecutor instead could use her power and discretion to institute policies and practices that would reduce the incarceration rate and unwarranted racial disparities. Such policies and practices would be in accord with the

Supreme Court's edict in *Berger* that prosecutors should seek justice, not convictions. In recent years, a growing number of elected prosecutors have chosen this path, attempting to balance the pursuit of public safety with the reduction of the prison and jail population.

THE ELECTION OF PROGRESSIVE PROSECUTORS

Most criminal cases—around 90 percent—are prosecuted on the state and local level, and most state prosecutors are elected officials. Although the electoral process is meant to serve as the mechanism of accountability for prosecutors, it has been largely ineffective for a variety of reasons. First, there is very little transparency in the prosecutorial function. Prosecutors' most important and consequential duties, charging and plea bargaining, are performed behind closed doors. It is impossible to hold prosecutors accountable without knowing how they carry out these important functions. Second, most people pay very little attention to prosecutor races. Finally, most prosecutors run unopposed and serve for decades.

We live in a democracy where we attest to hold accountable those to whom we grant power, yet the most powerful officials in the criminal justice system are rarely held accountable because of these flaws in the electoral process. Recent years have seen modest progress in improving the effectiveness of prosecutor elections. Organizations like Color of Change and the ACLU have mounted campaigns to educate the public about the importance of district attorney races.

Also, ironically, some of the police killings of unarmed black men in recent years served to educate the public about the power of prosecutors and their central role in the criminal process. The fact that very few prosecutors charged the police officers involved in these killings resulted in community members confronting prosecutors and demanding accountability. Consequently, these community members learned about the prosecutorial function in other contexts and began to pay attention to prosecutor elections.

As the prosecutor education campaigns evolved, several individuals began to run against incumbent prosecutors, offering a radically different vision of what it means to be a prosecutor. These challengers promised not only to pursue public safety but to use their power and discretion to reduce the prison and jail population and make the system fairer for all involved, including the accused. Some challenged incumbents who declined to prosecute police officers involved in the killings of unarmed black men and boys, campaigning in part on this issue. All promised to implement a progressive prosecutorial agenda in pursuit of criminal justice reform, including and especially alternatives to incarceration in appropriate cases.

DEFINING THE PROGRESSIVE PROSECUTOR

Progressive prosecutors are committed to reducing mass incarceration and racial disparities in the criminal justice system. There are several ways prosecutors can achieve these goals. Opposing cash bail can reduce the jail population. Forgoing charges in certain categories of cases and implementing diversion programs may reduce the incarceration rate. Diversion programs that do not require guilty pleas (and hence convictions) make it easier for participants to find employment and housing. Likewise, diversion programs that do not require the payment of fees and fines or impose other difficult conditions are more likely to reduce the number of people in prisons and jails. Prosecutors who commit never to charge juveniles as adults, even when the law permits them to do so, keep juveniles out of the criminal justice system and help to reduce the disproportionate number of black and brown youths tried in adult court. Prosecutors who refuse to seek the death penalty take an important step toward ending the well-documented racial disparities in the implementation of the death penalty. However, not every District Attorney will be able to successfully implement every goal. Many factors play a role, including the political climate of the jurisdiction, the prior experience of the District Attorney, and even the race and gender of the District Attorney.

POLITICS

In theory, progressive prosecutors duly elected by their constituents may argue that they were given a mandate to implement reform. After all, they ran on a progressive platform and won a majority of the votes. In practice, the political climate of their jurisdictions has an impact on their ability to effect change. For example, powerful groups like the FOP and the bail bond industry may confront and attack progressive prosecutors. The experiences of Larry Krasner in Philadelphia and Kim Foxx in Chicago provide cautionary examples. Krasner faces constant attacks by law enforcement organizations. Foxx had the support of the Chicago police commissioner but does not have backing from all the police chiefs in the surrounding suburbs in her county. Aramis Ayala's attempt to stop implementing the death penalty in her district demonstrates the extent of the potential power of political foes. A District Attorney attempting to implement criminal justice reform in Columbus, Mississippi, cannot run on the same platform as a District Attorney in Philadelphia, Pennsylvania, because Mississippi is much more conservative and the electorate would likely not be as receptive to radical changes. Yet when Scott Colom defeated incumbent Forrest Allgood in northeast Mississippi, advocates for criminal justice reform in Mississippi recognized the significance of his victory. Colom's proposed reforms included diversion for drug addicts, more rehabilitative services, and alternatives to incarceration in appropriate cases. These proposals may not sound very progressive in Philadelphia, Pennsylvania, but in Columbus, Mississippi, they represented a new vision for the District Attorney's office. Colom's predecessor, Allgood, had pushed for harsh sentences, and the Mississippi Supreme Court found that he had engaged in egregious misconduct. This highlighted the significance of Colom's promised reforms. Colom has followed through on his promises and is currently working with Tucker Carrington, the head of the Innocence Project at the University of Mississippi School of Law, to establish a conviction review unit.

CONCLUSION

District Attorneys committed to reforming the criminal justice system should plan carefully to confront the many internal and external challenges they will inevitably face. These challenges will vary by jurisdiction, experience, and background, and thus so will the strategies for addressing them. No single approach can achieve success in all jurisdictions, nor can every reform be implemented in every jurisdiction. For all these reasons, there should not be a litmus test or list of requirements for progressive prosecutors. Any attempt to reduce the incarceration rate and unwarranted racial disparities in the criminal justice system should be supported. An "all or nothing" approach will achieve nothing. In a country plagued by mass incarceration, racial inequities, and other injustices, the goal should be a fair and just criminal justice system with a much lower incarceration rate. Although radical change is desirable, it may not always be possible. Progress toward this goal should be the hallmark of the progressive prosecutor.

Memorandum on New Policies*

Larry Krasner

2018

NEW POLICIES ANNOUNCED FEBRUARY 15, 2018

These policies are an effort to end mass incarceration and bring balance back to sentencing. All policies are presumptive, not mandatory requirements. Where extraordinary circumstances suggest that an exception is appropriate, specific supervisory approval must be obtained. Wherever the term "supervisory approval" is used, it means that:

1. An Assistant District Attorney must obtain approval of the unit's supervisor, and
2. The supervisor must then obtain approval from the District Attorney, or in his absence, the approval of First Assistant Carolyn Temin or Robert Listenbee.

---

* Larry Krasner, Memorandum on New Policies to the Philadelphia District Attorney's Office, March 2018.

3. Bona fide verbal approvals and disapprovals are sufficient and must be noted in the case file, including the date of approval and identity of the requesting Assistant District Attorney and the supervisor who obtained approval or disapproval from the District Attorney.

DECLINE CERTAIN CHARGES

1. Do not charge possession of marijuana (cannabis) regardless of weight.
2. Do not charge any of the offenses relating to paraphernalia or buying from a person (BFP) where the drug involved is marijuana.
3. Do not charge prostitution cases against sex workers where a person who has been arrested has two, one, or no prostitution convictions. Withdraw all pending cases in these categories that would be declined for charging under this policy.
4. Individuals who have three or more prostitution convictions will be charged with prostitution and immediately referred to DAWN Court.

CHARGE LOWER GRADATIONS FOR CERTAIN OFFENSES

Rationale: summary gradation greatly reduces pre-trial incarceration rates as no bail is required and the shorter time required for hearings expedites Municipal Court and Common Pleas dockets.

1. Charge and dispose of retail theft cases as summary offenses unless the value of the item(s) stolen in a

particular case exceeds $500 or where the defendant has a very long history of theft and retail theft convictions.

2. You must seek supervisory approval to charge and dispose of retail theft cases at misdemeanor or felony levels.

3. Remember that a summary conviction permits a sentence of ninety days incarceration, fines of up to $250, and full restitution. These penalties are sufficient to hold a retail thief accountable.

4. In all cases, seek full restitution.

DIVERT MORE

All attorneys are directed to approach diversion and re-entry with greater flexibility and an eye toward achieving accountability and justice while avoiding convictions where appropriate. For example:

1. An otherwise law-abiding, responsible gun owner who is arrested because he does not have a permit to carry a firearm may apply for individualized consideration for diversion.

2. An otherwise law-abiding, first DUI (driving under the influence) defendant who has no driver's license (regardless of whether or not that defendant's immigration status interferes with obtaining a license under Pennsylvania law) may apply for individualized consideration for diversion with a requirement of efforts to overcome license impediments where possible as an aspect of any diversionary program.

3. A defendant charged with marijuana (cannabis) delivery

or PWID (Possession with the Intent to Deliver) may apply for diversion.

This is not a comprehensive list.

INCREASE PARTICIPATION IN RE-ENTRY PROGRAMS

In general, some effective re-entry programs have failed to attract more candidates due to rewards and incentives of the program that are minor compared with the major effort required of re-entering Philadelphians. Effective re-entry programs prevent crime and should apply to more re-entering Philadelphians. ADAs and staff involved in re-entry are directed to discuss and formulate suggestions to improve this situation by May 1, 2018.

PLEA OFFERS

Note: This policy does not apply to Homicides, Violent Crimes, Sexual Assault Crimes, Felon in Possession of a Weapon (6105), and Economic Crimes with a loss of $50,000 or more or cases involving attacks on the integrity of the judicial process (e.g., false reports to police, perjury, obstruction of the administration of justice, witness intimidation, etc.). All of these cases require supervisor approval as stated above.

1. Make plea offers below the bottom end of the mitigated range of the PA Sentencing Guidelines for most crimes.
2. Where an individual ADA believes an offer below the bottom end of the mitigated range is too low due to specific factors, that ADA must seek supervisory approval of a higher offer.

3. Where the applicable sentencing guidelines range is between zero and twenty-four months, ADAs should seek more house arrest, probationary, and alternative sentences in appropriate cases.

SENTENCING

At Sentencing, State on the Record the Benefits and Costs of the Sentence You Are Recommending

The United States has the highest rate of incarceration in the world. It has increased 500 percent over a few decades. Pennsylvania and Philadelphia have been incarcerating at an even higher rate than comparable U.S. states and cities for decades—a 700 percent increase over the same few decades in Pennsylvania; and Philadelphia in recent years has been the most incarcerated of the ten largest cities. Yet Pennsylvania and Philadelphia are not safer as a result, due to wasting resources in corrections rather than investing in other measures that reduce crime. Pennsylvania's and Philadelphia's over-incarceration have bankrupted investment in policing, public education, medical treatment of addiction, job training, and economic development—which prevent crime more effectively than money invested in corrections. Over-incarceration also tears the fabric of defendants' familial and work relationships that tend to rehabilitate defendants who are open to rehabilitation and thereby prevent crime. As a result, a return to lower rates of incarceration for those defendants who do not require lengthy sentences is necessary in order to shift resources to crime prevention. Ultimately, the highest goal of sentencing must be to seek justice for society as a whole (the Commonwealth includes victims, witnesses, defendants, and those not

directly involved in an individual case) while effectively preventing crimes in the future via methods that work. Each case,
each defendant, and each sentence is unique and requires your
careful consideration.

At sentencing, ADAs must state on the record their reasoning for requesting a particular sentence, and must state the
unique benefits and costs of the sentence (e.g., consider where
applicable the safety benefits, impact on victims, interruption
of defendants' connections to family, employment, needed
public benefits, and actual financial cost of incarceration). In
each case, place the financial cost of incarceration on the record as part of your explanation of the sentence recommended.

In talking about the financial cost to the taxpayer, use the
following, arguably low, but much-repeated cost of: $42,000
per year to incarcerate one person ($3,500 per month or $115
per day).

Facts You Should Know and Consider in Making Your Recommendation

1. The actual cost (including pension and other benefits
   to correctional employees, health care for incarcerated
   individuals, etc.) arguably is close to $60,000 now to in-
   carcerate one person for a year in Philadelphia County
   prison system. ($5,000 per month at $164 per day.)
2. As of March 1, 2018, Philadelphia County incarcerates
   approximately six thousand people at a total annual
   cost of around $360 million per year.
3. The cost of one year of unnecessary incarceration (at
   $42,000–$60,000) is in the range of the cost of one year's
   salary for a beginning teacher, police officer, firefighter,

social worker, Assistant District Attorney, or addiction counselor. You may use these comparisons on the record.

4. The average family's total income in Philadelphia in 2017 was approximately $41,000—which paid their housing, food, utilities, transportation, clothing, educational expense, and taxes.

Examples of How This Information Can Be Used at Sentencing

1. If you are seeking a sentence of three years incarceration, state on the record that the cost to the taxpayer will be $126,000 (3 x $42,000) if not more and explain why you believe that cost is justified.

2. In a very serious matter, where, for example, twenty-five years incarceration are sought and is appropriate, state on the record that the cost to the taxpayer is $1,050,000 (25 x $42,000) if not more and explain why you believe that cost is justified.

3. When recommending a sentence of probation, compare the cost of incarceration to the cost of probation. Emphasize the positive rehabilitative factors of a probationary sentence such as permitting the defendant to continue working and paying taxes, permitting the continuation of family life, education, and community inclusion.

Request Shorter Probation Tails (i.e., Consecutive Period of Probation) or No Probation Tail After a Sentence of Incarceration

Criminological studies show that most violations of probation occur within the first twelve months. Assuming that a defendant is violation free for twelve months, any remaining probation is simply excess baggage requiring unnecessary expenditure of funds for supervision. In addition, County Probation is overwhelmed with more than forty-four thousand supervisees, which makes supervising people who are more likely to commit serious crimes more difficult. There is no reason to assume a probationary tail must be two years or more in every single case. Carefully evaluate what, if any, probationary tail is appropriate upon completion of a sentence of incarceration.

Request Shorter Probationary Sentences Where No Sentence of Incarceration Is Sought

Criminological studies confirm that longer probationary periods often result in more failures than shorter ones where those studies have controlled for offense and criminal record. In addition, county probation is overwhelmed with more than forty-four thousand supervisees, which makes supervising people who are more likely to commit serious crimes more difficult.

Request No More Than a Six-Month VOP [Violation of Parole] Sentence for a Technical Violation Without Supervisory Approval

In many technical violation cases, no additional incarceration should be sought and no revocation is necessary. However, where the technical violation(s) calls for a more serious consequence, do not seek more than six to twelve months' incarceration unless you have approval from the District Attorney via your supervisor.

Supervisory Request No More Than a Two-Year VOP Sentence for a Direct Violation Without Approval

Every direct violation presents the opportunity for two sentencings (one on the old matter and one on the new matter) that take into account the fact of the defendant's commission of a new crime while under supervision. Obviously, commission of a new crime while under supervision is a factor tending to increase the sentence on the new matter. Therefore, ordinarily it is not necessary to seek a sentence of longer than two to four years for a direct VOP. However, where special factors arise, you may seek approval from the District Attorney via your supervisor to seek a lengthier direct VOP sentence.

Beyond Reform: Four Virtues of a Transformational Prosecutor*

*Taylor Pendergrass
and Somil Trivedi*

2021

The fourth and final virtue of a transformational prosecutor is a demonstrated commitment to shrinking the criminal legal system, including the role of the prosecutor itself. This is closely related to championing legislative change, in that shrinking the system as a whole will almost certainly involve pushing for legislative change that reduces prosecutors' power. However, this virtue is more expansive and potentially the most trans-formational, because it also contemplates prosecutors taking immediate and severely self-limiting acts like cutting their

---

* Taylor Pendergrass and Somil Trivedi, "Beyond Reform: Four Virtues of a Trans-formational Prosecutor," *Stanford Journal of Civil Rights and Civil Liberties* 16, no. 3 (2021): 435–455.

own headcounts and budgets, in order to seek—and potentially even transfer resources to—harm reduction solutions outside the criminal justice system. In light of the national conversation around police divestment in the wake of George Floyd's murder in Minneapolis, this virtue becomes even more timely and necessary.

In other words, a transformational prosecutor can and must shrink the entire system with every act they take. By the same token, a prosecutor—even a "reform-minded" one who espouses decarceral values and takes certain steps in that direction—cannot be considered transformational if they express those values and take those steps via the criminal system as it exists today, because that system is far too large, intrusive, punitive, and racist.

Crime of all types has decreased dramatically over the last quarter century, yet mass incarceration continues virtually unabated. Despite modest decreases since the mid-2000s, the arrest rate nationwide for nonserious offenses (e.g., drug abuse violations) is still higher than it was in 1980. State and federal legislators, often bowing to pro-carceral prosecutor lobbying, have passed more and more—and ever more punitive—criminal laws, sentencing enhancements, and investigatory tools.

This means that criminal dockets are still overflowing and prosecutors' caseloads—to say nothing of public defenders'—are still overwhelming, even though more and more of those cases are unnecessary for public safety. This in turn has created the conveyor-belt system of criminal justice we currently practice in America, in which the goal is to process as many people as possible as quickly as possible without much if any consideration for innocence, fairness, or actual harm reduction.

Hence, a second-wave, transformational prosecutor cannot

be satisfied by merely regulating the process or addressing individual policy tools like pretrial detention or mandatory minimums; that approach is in itself a mandatory minimum. Instead, a truly transformative prosecutor must shrink the system that created this state of affairs in the first place.

WHY SHRINKING THE CRIMINAL LEGAL SYSTEM IS TRANSFORMATIONAL

First, "shrinking the criminal legal system" may not be an easy concept for average individuals to understand. Indeed, the terms "criminal legal system" and "criminal justice system" are already misnomers; those who work in the field know that our country has thousands of individual systems across counties, cities, and the federal government. However, most Americans understand the concept of shrinking, and particularly shrinking government. Hence, without having to dig into the weeds of what it would take to shrink this particular part of government, one can imagine cross-ideological support for the notion in general.

And, of course, decarceration—including a numeric pledge—and other quantifiable metrics, like reducing charges, reducing jail intakes, eliminating wealth-based detention, slashing headcount, slashing budget, increasing community-based diversions, and the like, are all measurable indicators of a shrinking system.

While there are myriad avenues a prosecutor could take to shrink the system, we offer a few suggestions:

Simply saying it out loud. Even among the current wave of reform-minded prosecutors, we have not seen an example of this virtue being expressed on a consistent basis. Indeed, many who claim to be progressive are actively seeking to expand the system, asking us to trust them to operate it better. We will not. Others ask us to accept a tit-for-tat trade of mass incarceration for an expanded surveillance state. We will not. A transformational prosecutor must recognize that they are likely the most powerful player in their criminal justice system and must deploy that bully pulpit accordingly, forcing adjacent players like police, sheriffs, corrections officials, and judges to scramble and catch up.

Reinvest in the community. The most concrete way prosecutors can shrink the criminal system is by starving it of funding and giving those freed-up dollars to public defenders and eventually to non-criminal systems. For example, rather than using prosecutors to charge those with mental health, substance abuse, or housing challenges—often just to divert them back out, but under pain of state supervision and potential jail time—a transformational prosecutor will build up those non-criminal systems from the start and refuse to charge those individuals at all.

Establish a presumption against prosecution. Declining to prosecute certain categories of crimes is a hallmark of the current crop of reform prosecutors, and it has been game changing. However, a transformational prosecutor will go further and establish a rebuttable presumption against all prosecutions, looking first to the non-carceral, community-based harm reduction solutions mentioned above. Hence, rather than categorically refusing to prosecute a small number of crimes, transformational prosecutors will not refuse any prosecutions outright, but will be forced to formally justify and overcome this presumption in each one. While transformational, this proposition is not radical or unsupported; it is a logical outgrowth of the Framers' intent to make deprivation of liberty an extraordinary and extraordinarily difficult thing to do. We now have data showing that, in the vast majority of cases, incarceration is also an extraordinarily counterproductive and harmful thing to do. So prosecutors should make it the last resort, and establish a policy that makes that commitment real.

Second, shrinking the system is certainly generalizable and scalable. No matter the size or makeup of the jurisdiction, its criminal legal system can *always* get smaller, less punitive, and less racist. Smaller geographies may not have preexisting noncriminal support systems to fill in the gaps, but the savings from shrinking the criminal system could provide the seed capital.

Third and most importantly, shrinking the system is the most bold and far-reaching virtue a transformational prosecutor can exhibit, and one likely to remain essential in the third, fourth, and fifth waves of prosecutor reform. It is, indeed, the transformation itself. It is indisputable that the criminal legal system is far too large and fundamentally broken to justify a prosecutor's attempt to fix it by addition. What and how much prosecution is left after transformational shrinking can vary based on jurisdiction and local considerations—but shrinking is unquestionably necessary.

Can Prosecutors End Mass Incarceration?*

Rachel E. Barkow

2021

In her excellent book *Charged: The New Movement to Transform American Prosecution and End Mass Incarceration*, Emily Bazelon uses the story of two individuals to showcase the enormous power prosecutors have in a criminal case. The use of these narratives makes the book both a gripping read and a valuable primer for understanding how important local prosecutors are to the way punishment operates in America. Showing the authority prosecutors have over most aspects of punishment in America is the book's central descriptive contribution. But the book has a normative agenda as well. Bazelon argues that those seeking to dismantle mass incarceration should recognize that the power of prosecutors can be an effective lever of reform. She argues that by electing prosecutors concerned about mass incarceration, we can start to shift

* Rachel E. Barkow, "Can Prosecutors End Mass Incarceration?," *Michigan Law Review* 119, no. 6 (2021): 1365–1397.

course away from tough-on-crime rhetoric that in reality does a poor job keeping people safe and move toward policies that actually work. I agree wholeheartedly with Bazelon's descriptive claim that prosecutors are critical actors—probably the most important actor, if we had to choose just one—in administering criminal justice policy in America. I also agree that we would do well as voters to select prosecutors who understand what really works to fight crime and therefore know that mass incarceration is not the answer. Electing prosecutors committed to decarceration is an improvement over the status quo, and it should be a vital part of any reform agenda.

Bazelon notes at the end of *Charged* that a "challenge for the movement is figuring out how demanding to be" of self-identified progressive prosecutors, and she cautions against "a purity test." But she does insist on some benchmarks "like reducing incarceration, racial disparity, the rate of reoffending, and findings of misconduct." I agree with Bazelon that we cannot expect these prosecutors to uniformly pursue positions we would like, and her checklist of benchmarks is a good one. I would like to add some specific additional metrics to her list because I do not think this movement offers much in the way of positive and lasting change unless these prosecutors use their positions of leadership to pursue institutional changes. If progressive prosecutors want to transform criminal justice in America and if they only have so much political capital to spend before they risk losing their positions or facing too much pushback by other officials or lawyers in their own office, they need to choose the issues that will matter most.

One critical move is advocating for limits on the prosecutorial powers that legislators and courts have given them. That is obviously a lot to ask of someone: it is hard for anyone to relinquish power they already have, particularly if they think they will exercise it wisely. But that is what is required for fundamental change and for the election of more progressive prosecutors to be transformative instead of incremental. Just as it is insufficient to hire better police officers or train them more effectively in order to address systemic problems with violence and racial bias in policing, it is similarly not enough to elect better prosecutors to address systemic problems with prosecution. We need structural changes to do more than chip away at the edges of mass incarceration.

For starters, just as it is important to move police away from jobs better suited to other professionals, it is likewise critical to limit the reach of prosecutors. At a basic level, that means preventing prosecutors' offices from further expanding. Even some of the most progressive prosecutors seem to have lost sight of the fact that, while they might use extra personnel in the service of their progressive aims, their successors will simply have more bodies to bring more cases. John Pfaff has explained that one of the drivers of mass incarceration has been the simple fact that we have more prosecutors to bring cases. Thus keeping offices in check or downsizing them should be a key goal.

We also need to remove prosecutors from areas where they do not belong and where they have a conflict of interest that makes them ill-suited to a task. Prosecutors should make decisions about charging and enforcement; they should not be involved in decisions about forensics, corrections, clemency, or parole. While some progressive prosecutors might be more inclined to support decisions that favor defendants, most "[p]rosecutors will inevitably view these issues through a prism of what would be good for them and their cases and will not be able to assess objectively other interests that conflict with their own." For far too long we have seen prosecutors resist requests for reductions in sentences because their office brought those cases in the first place or support junk science because it helps them win cases. But they should not be involved in any of these decisions except to support the reformers working in those spaces.

We should thus see any prosecutor who claims to be progressive make clear they support second looks of sentences and presumptive release policies—and recognize that prosecutors themselves should not be vetoes for any of those decisions. At a minimum, they should not oppose parole and clemency requests because those decisions are based on what someone has done since their sentencing—facts prosecutors know nothing about. Prosecutors should also recognize that they are not qualified to set forensics policy and leave that to scientists. And to the extent prosecutors are involved in corrections, it should be to call out poor conditions and the absence of programming in prisons and jails because improving the way people are treated while they are incarcerated is critical for public safety and reentry outcomes.

In terms of the decisions that do fall within prosecutors' responsibilities, prosecutors will need to do more than just exercise their discretion with more wisdom than their predecessors. That kind of reform only lasts while the prosecutor is in office (and to the extent the prosecutor can get the line attorneys in the office on board). Instead, these prosecutors should use the authority of their office to push for needed institutional changes that limit the excessive powers of prosecutors. That means seeking changes in the law itself—both in case law and legislation.

Consider, for example, the policy of open discovery where defense lawyers have access to the prosecutor's files before deciding whether to plead guilty. In *Charged*, Bazelon discusses the factors that lead to convictions of innocent people, and one of them is the failure of prosecutors to turn over exculpatory evidence. "Chillingly, prosecutors may be more likely to withhold evidence when proof of guilt is uncertain," Bazelon observes. "If you think the suspect did it but you don't quite have the goods to convict, you may be tempted to put a thumb on the scale." A key guard against this is to have prosecutors open their files to defense lawyers. Bazelon notes that Texas passed a law mandating prosecutors to share their case files in the wake of a high-profile case of a prosecutor convicting an innocent man after failing to turn over exculpatory evidence. There are exceptions to protect confidential information and sensitive information, but otherwise, prosecutors have to turn over their files. The result has been extraordinary. Texas has had more exonerations than any other state, and with no evidence of witness intimidation or obstruction—problems prosecutors in other states fighting such laws have claimed would result from sharing their files. North Carolina has a similar open-file law, and their prosecutors now report it works well. Most prosecutors in other states have resisted similar reforms, however, because they think it makes it harder for them to win their cases. Some of the newly elected progressive prosecutors have adopted open files as an office policy, but not all of them have. Even more critically, however, prosecutors must vigorously support this as a legislative mandate. That would bind other prosecutors throughout the state and be harder to overturn. Brooklyn district attorney Eric Gonzalez, to his credit, supported state legislation that would mandate the kind of open file access his office was already providing. But many other progressive prosecutors have been silent on this issue. And even Gonzalez (along with other district attorneys) ended up opposing the reforms that were actually enacted because they went further than he would have liked. But for prosecutors to be real change agents, they need to be leading the charge for legislation like this.

One can see the same issue play out with cash bail. Cash bail gives prosecutors leverage because people detained pretrial are more likely to plead guilty. In Bazelon's words, "[j]ails serve as plea mills." She says, "Over the last two decades, all of the growth in the jail population has consisted of people detained pretrial." While this might make a prosecutor's job easier, cash bail is completely unnecessary for public safety. In fact, it harms public safety because pretrial detention is more likely to cause crime than prevent it. It also isn't necessary to get people to appear in court because other measures, like electronic reminders, work well. And the brunt of pretrial detention's harms fall disproportionately on people of color. Bazelon notes that ending cash bail should therefore "be the kind of commonsense measure just about everyone can agree on." Certainly, it should be something that anyone claiming to be a progressive prosecutor should agree on, because it harms public safety, costs a fortune, and causes so much human suffering. As with open-file discovery, we are seeing some of the prosecutors elected on decarceral platforms changing their office policies to limit the use of cash bail. Yet many of the so-called progressive prosecutors have yet to actively lobby for legislation to end cash bail in their jurisdictions. It is not enough to change office policies if you are not also seeking to make changes permanent and broadly applicable. Otherwise, those shifts are only as strong as the next election.

The same holds true for sentencing policy. It is not enough to pledge not to seek long sentences or file charges that bring mandatory minimums. Prosecutors must advocate to change the laws on the books as well, as the group of Virginia prosecutors recently did when they urged their legislature to abolish mandatory minimums. Doing so is consistent with prosecutors' mandate to further public safety and pursue justice. Mandatory minimum sentences are ineffective as deterrents and racially disparate in their application. Excessive sentences likewise fail to deter and at a certain point become criminogenic because of how difficult they make reentry. Bazelon quotes a report from the National Academy of Science in 2014 concluding that "the incremental deterrent effect of increases in lengthy prison sentences is modest at best." And as sentences get longer, it gets that much harder for people to reenter society. As Bazelon concludes, "we're long past the point of diminishing returns." Despite these facts, prosecutors all too often support mandatory minimums and long statutory sentence lengths because of the leverage it gives them to obtain guilty pleas and cooperation. If prosecutors care about better policies instead of what makes their jobs easier, sentencing reform should be at the top of their list of legislative reforms. They should be vocal advocates for shortening statutory sentences.

Advocating for legislative change is particularly critical when it comes to sentencing because most prosecutors have a limited toolkit when it comes to altering sentences already imposed. Mass incarceration is driven by two factors: the number of cases coming into the system (admissions) and the length of sentences. Prosecutors have discretion to change the rate of admissions, and for cases going forward, they can also influence sentences based on the charges they bring and the sentences they request (or accept in pleas). But for the people already serving their sentences, there is often little these prosecutors can do. Additionally, for many people seeking relief from an existing sentence—either on habeas or because of unconstitutional conditions in the prison—the relevant prosecutor dealing with the claim is the state attorney general. Even if a local progressive prosecutor would agree with the release, the state attorney general may not. Thus, the progressive-prosecutor movement needs to go beyond local elections and consider these statewide officeholders as critically important as well, because they are often crucial voices when sentences are being considered. Progressive prosecutors need to be calling attention to these other actors—judges, legislators, and attorneys general—and urging them to reform existing sentences.

Progressive prosecutors should also support caps on their own use of prisons. Because prisons are paid for by the state, they are a free resource for local prosecutors to use. Sound correctional policy would require prosecutors to internalize those costs so they do not overuse prisons, either by giving them financial bonuses for using them less or charging them for using them too much. Prosecutors should support these limits on the use of prison resources and support legislative efforts to downsize populations in prisons and jails.

A true progressive prosecutor will also support the constitutional rights of defendants.

That means more than not violating them. It also means taking positions in litigation that support those rights, even if it may mean losing a particular case. It is important to pay attention to how prosecutors are handling appeals and whether they are requiring people to waive their right to an appeal as part of their plea agreements. Bazelon notes that while more than a million people are convicted of felonies each year, there are only seventy thousand appeals. That is because a condition of many pleas is for defendants to waive their right to file an appeal. Indeed, some prosecutors go even further and require additional waivers. Federal prosecutors in California, for example, have required individuals to waive claims of compassionate release, even though the conditions that prompt such requests are by definition not known at the time of sentencing. As Justice Breyer noted in criticizing this practice, the government does this because "rather than risk a court decision it disagrees with, the Government can rely on its disproportionate power in negotiating the terms of the plea agreement to foreclose in advance any compassionate release motion it think[s] is unmeritorious." This makes prosecutors' jobs easier and gives them power to decide the merits of a case. But it is an end run around the judiciary's role, because it is up to judges to decide these motions, just as judges are to decide the legal issues on appeal that prosecutors get people to waive in these agreements. If progressive prosecutors care about dismantling mass incarceration and protecting constitutional rights, these waivers must no longer be sought.

When appeals are brought, prosecutors claiming the mantle of "progressive" need to be willing to concede error and make sure constitutional rights are being protected. That has yet to be a central part of this movement, but until it is, real progress on mass incarceration will stall because these rights are critical checks on overreach. Without Eighth Amendment checks on excessive punishment, robust enforcement against excessive fines and fees, and real limits on police overreach, we will not see big shifts in punishment in America. While it is up to judges to police these critical constitutional rights, prosecutors can play a key supporting role by taking litigating positions that protect those rights. Prosecutors should also be calling for an end to absolute immunity for their decisions and an end to qualified immunity for policing decisions because both of these doctrines impede the protection of constitutional rights.

Prosecutors also need to support other institutions that are using data and evidence to set criminal justice policies based on best practices instead of responding to political tides. This kind of insulation is important because if criminal justice policy depends on the current whims of the electorate, mass incarceration is here to stay. None of the reforms we have seen through the political process thus far have produced more than modest changes and they have been largely limited to drug and property crime. If reformers want to make a significant inroad into mass incarceration, they must address crimes involving violence because individuals convicted of those crimes make up roughly half of the state-prison population. Having a body more removed from the tabloid story of the day allows policies to be grounded in evidence of what works best to address crime, including violent crime. But those bodies need support from political actors, and especially from prosecutors. Prosecutors should support well-designed commissions charged with evaluating sentencing policies, prison conditions, limits on police use of force, prosecutorial misconduct, collateral consequences, and a variety of other criminal justice issues to support policies that actually work to reduce crime.

It is critical to get institutional changes such as these because simply announcing that an office will exercise its discretion differently is change without staying power should prosecutors lose their reelection bids. One can see an example of this at the federal level. Although hardly a revolutionary criminal justice reformer, Attorney General Eric Holder was committed to making changes at the Department of Justice to make the administration of criminal justice more equitable and less severe. The president for whom he worked, Barack Obama, wrote a law review article documenting his commitment to criminal justice reform. But the Obama-era effort was almost entirely rooted in policy changes in how discretion was exercised, so when Donald Trump took over and Jeff Sessions became the attorney general, all the policies immediately shifted.

For example, Attorney General Holder changed DOJ charging policy so prosecutors would not bring as many cases that would be subject to mandatory minimum sentences. But the Department did not support legislative changes that would have allowed judges to depart from mandatory minimums in all cases. The Department, in other words, opted to change its own discretionary policies but refused to tie its hands—and consequently, the hands of subsequent administrations—by supporting legislative changes. The result, predictably, was that DOJ prosecutors inconsistently followed the Holder charging memo, and when the Trump Administration took over, the discretionary charging policy was eliminated. Prosecutors were instructed to charge the most serious readily provable offense, including those with mandatory minimums. If the Obama Department of Justice had successfully lobbied for mandatory minimums to be repealed instead of fighting proposed legislation along those lines, the world would look much different even after the election. The Department did not make that push, however, because it did not want to relinquish its own powers, and without mandatory minimums to threaten, prosecutors lose much of their leverage in cases. Instead, the Administration wanted to keep discretion to decide when and whether to charge those mandatory minimums and the result is that none of its discretionary changes lasted.

Real change requires a shift in law—case law and legislation. And prosecutors can help make that happen. They are key litigators in court, and they are leading lobbyists on criminal law issues. People listen to them because they trust their commitment to public safety. Progressive prosecutors should thus use their capital to bring about as many institutional shifts as they can. Institutional changes are more lasting and extend beyond a single district. They help elected prosecutors get greater compliance from line attorneys within their offices and create a solid foundation that future progressive prosecutors can expand. So if the prosecutors Bazelon praises want to leave a lasting legacy, they will realize the key is to tie their own hands—because doing so will tie the hands of future prosecutors who will not exercise that discretion in the same way. Then this movement will truly live up to its promise.

Abolitionist Principles and Campaign Strategies for Prosecutor Organizing*

*Community Justice Exchange,
CourtWatch MA, Families for
Justice as Healing, Project NIA,
and Survived and Punished NY*

2019

In September 2019, several abolitionist organizations—Community Justice Exchange, CourtWatch MA, Families for Justice as Healing, Project NIA, and Survived and Punished NY—published "Abolitionist Principles and Campaign Strategies for Prosecutor Organizing," which outlines abolitionist principles, as well as strategies and tactics, for organizing campaigns targeted at prosecutors and prosecuting offices.

---

* Community Justice Exchange, CourtWatch MA, Families for Justice as Healing, Project NIA, and Survived and Punished NY, "Abolitionist Principles and Campaign Strategies for Prosecutor Organizing," 2019. Updated January 22, 2020.

The original document was inspired by conversations coming out of a national conference about "prosecutor accountability" hosted by Color of Change in June 2019. The conference included many organizations and actors that championed the election of so-called "progressive prosecutors" as a core decarceration strategy. At the conference, it became clear that an abolitionist framework for engaging with prosecutors was necessary in order to foster alignment and inter-movement accountability for groups and individuals committed to abolition as a political vision and a practical strategy for organizing. As the document clearly outlines, we believe that while significant movement energy and resources are devoted to supporting the election and work of prosecutors, it is important to clarify that no matter their personal politics, relying on the actions of prosecutors and, in particular, investing additional resources, work, and personnel in prosecuting offices is not an abolitionist strategy.

Since the document was published in 2019, the national, and many local, political landscapes across the United States have shifted. We have experienced an ongoing global pandemic, heightened organized abandonment and austerity from all levels of government, an unprecedented uprising of millions of people in protest of racist police violence, and the rise of right-wing fascism and repression. Prosecutors elected on the mantle of reform have become targets for the right, leading to the successful recall of District Attorney Chesa Boudin in San Francisco, CA,[1] the removals of head prosecutors in Florida and Texas,[2] as well as other targeted attacks including efforts by state legislatures to strip prosecutors' offices of power.[3] The reaction from some on the left has been an increase in uncritical support for "progressive prosecutors," even though while in office, these prosecutors have failed to produce promised decarceral results at scale and have consistently further increased their offices' resources, power, as well as their legitimacy among some liberal and leftist constituencies who otherwise might be opposed to the role of the prosecutor.[4] Being critical of these prosecutors, for some, has come to signify aligning with the right. For this reason, among others, the principles and assertions articulated in this document remain ever relevant. It is possible, we argue, to refuse fascism and right-wing authoritarianism without platforming and relying on the actors whose systemic role and purpose is to prosecute, incarcerate, and punish.

In the midst of these shifting political environments, since their release, the principles have also inspired organizing on the ground, as well as production of further analysis and resources. For example, leading up to the 2021 Manhattan District Attorney election, candidate questionnaires from mainstream criminal legal organizations included questions about whether the prosecutors would reduce their budgets and staff.[5] Additionally, a campaign that successfully led to the dismissal of all charges against a criminalized survivor, Tracy McCarter, in December 2022, was publicly messaged as a campaign for her freedom, for the freedom of all criminalized survivors, and for the abolition of prosecutors and the entire prison industrial complex.[6] Several authors of the original document have also gone on to build on the principles and create further analysis and resources for organizers, lawyers, and community members. This includes a law review article in the *Stanford Journal of Civil Rights and Civil Liberties*;[7] a web-based resource hub specifically for organizers looking for tools and analysis for organizing to make prosecutors, courts, policing, and prisons obsolete;[8] as well as specific voter education materials that directly reference the principles.[9]

While more and more people have begun to entertain the idea that police and prison abolition is necessary for a liberatory future, prosecutors and the courts continue to have a stranglehold on people's hearts and minds. This document remains a guiding tool for organizers and activists committed to prison industrial complex abolition.

As prison abolitionists, we are fighting for a world where the response to social problems does not include prisons, policing, prosecution, or any form of surveillance, supervision, or incarceration. These systems of punishment rely on, reinforce, and perpetuate structures of oppression: white supremacy, patriarchy, capitalism, xenophobia, ableism, and heterosexism. We aim to abolish these systems, not reform them. As abolitionists, we see a future without prosecutors and prosecution. Simply put, that is our orientation to prosecutor organizing. We focus on structural and systemic changes that lessen the power, size, and scope of the prosecuting office, and on running campaigns that build the size and strength of abolitionist movements. In most jurisdictions, prosecutors are elected officials tasked with distributing punishment within an unequal and violent society. Just like electing any elected official, electing a new prosecutor, even as part of a larger strategy, is never the end goal because it does not disrupt the existence of the prosecuting office or end the violence of criminalization. We believe that organizations engaged in prosecutor-focused electoral politics must be committed to base-building and be accountable to the communities most impacted by prosecution and mass criminalization.

As abolitionists, our job does not end with the election of any prosecutor, no matter what they claim to represent. Therefore, we reject the tendency toward cults of personality. We focus on what policies a prosecuting office enacts and supports others in enacting, what decisions a prosecuting office makes to release people from the grips of mass criminalization, and how a prosecuting office relates to, impedes, or advances our movements' demands. Our organizing focuses on how a prosecuting office's policies and practices result in decriminalization, decarceration, and shrinking the resources and power of the office of the prosecutor. Elected prosecutors are not co-strugglers, but targets we can push on the path to eliminating prosecution altogether.

WHAT DO WE BELIEVE? ABOLITIONIST PRINCIPLES FOR PROSECUTOR ORGANIZING

1. Prosecutors are law enforcement: they send people to prison and jail, parole and probation. A commitment to abolition includes the abolition of prosecutors, surveillance, and policing. This means that we seek the abolition of the role of prosecutor within the criminal punishment system.
2. Prosecution is a systemic and structural component of the criminal punishment system. Discussions of "good," "bad," "progressive," or "regressive" prosecutors keep the focus on individuals and are a distraction that impedes the need for structural and systemic change.
3. Abolition is opposed to prosecution. A commitment to abolition requires that we think outside the criminal punishment system for what accountability and healing from harm could look like. This means we condemn the prosecution of anyone, including police officers, people

in positions of power accused of financially-motivated crimes ("white collar crimes"), exploitative landlords, people accused of sexual or interpersonal harm, and so on.

4. Prosecutors are not social workers, therapists, housing advocates, or any other service-oriented role. They cannot and should not provide services to people who are in need. This is inherently in conflict with their pledge to serve and maintain the criminal punishment system. The best thing prosecutors can do for people who need services is get out of the way. Prosecuting offices should not receive more resources to provide social services or survivor/victim support, nor bolster other forms of confinement, stripping of rights, or institutions that use threat of punishment to force treatment or coerce services (such as drug courts and other forms of diversion court, mental health jailing).

   Resource shifting from carceral prosecution to carceral social services is not de-resourcing. Social services become another tool of the punishment system whether housed in or mandated by the prosecuting office. Giving more resources to death-making institutions is not abolitionist. It only cements and increases power and also cloaks the system in legitimacy. Instead, prosecutors should advocate for resources to be distributed to community organizations that already provide services and for policies that redistribute resources.

5. Prosecuting offices cannot be "co-governed" with/by community organizations. Given the inherent power imbalance, there is no shared power relationship between elected prosecutors and community organizations. Instead, community organizations are constituency or-

ganizations and can and should demand change from these elected officials within that relationship. This means using the tools of community accountability including phone calls, constituent meetings, protests, and the same demands we make of every and any elected official.

6. Prosecuting offices must be stripped of power and resources. Even as they restructure their offices and review prosecutions handled by their predecessor(s), prosecutors should not seek additional resources but work to redistribute resources internally to shrink the scale of current and future prosecutions as well as redress histories of aggressive prosecutions.

Should Good People Be Prosecutors?*

Paul Butler

2009

When I stopped being a prosecutor I told my friends it was because I didn't go to law school to put poor people in prison. My friends weren't surprised that I quit; they had been shocked that I became a prosecutor in the first place. For a progressive like me—a person who believed in redemption and second chances and robust civil liberties—the work presented obvious pitfalls. "Locking people up" was practically on the job description. Eric Holder, the first African American U.S. Attorney in D.C., and now President Obama's choice for attorney general, asked prospective prosecutors during interviews, "How would you feel about sending so many black men to jail?" Anyone who had a big problem with that presumably was not hired. I began the work, however, as a liberal critic of American criminal justice—the avenging Undercover Brother who would change

---

* Paul Butler, "Should Good People Be Prosecutors?," *Let's Get Free: A Hip-Hop Theory of Justice* (New York: The New Press, 2009).

the system from the inside. What happened instead was that I collaborated with the system's injustice.

Thinking about the business of prosecuting crimes brings questions about the utility and morality of American criminal justice into sharp relief. If there are too many people in prison, how should we feel about the men and women who put them there?

My conclusion is that prosecutors are more part of the problem than the solution. The adversarial nature of the justice system, the culture of the prosecutor's office, and the politics of crime pose insurmountable obstacles for prosecutors who are concerned with economic and racial justice. The day-to-day work of the prosecutor is geared toward punishing people whose lives are already messed up. This does not mean that criminals should be allowed to victimize others; some of the people in prison really belong there, for the protection of society. It suggests, however, that piling on is the main work of prosecutors. It is well intentioned, perhaps even necessary, but piling on nonetheless. Adding up the costs of a lifetime of deprivation and then presenting the bill to the person who suffered it seems an odd job for a humanitarian.

Also, prosecutors spend much of their time making arguments in favor of police power. They ask judges to adopt pinched interpretations of the Constitution and individual rights. When progressives bemoan the Supreme Court's approval of racial profiling, pretextual stops, widespread drug testing, camera surveillance, and police lying to suspects, they have prosecutors to thank. One of your primary functions as a prosecutor is to make the judge and jury believe the police. When the cops say that Kwame consented to the search of his backpack, and Kwame says he didn't consent, your job is to prove that Kwame is lying.

It is true that some prosecutors attempt to mitigate the harshness of the system, either openly or through the covert or subversive measures that I will discuss later in this part. Their principal work, however, is applying the criminal law, not ameliorating its negative effects. Becoming a prosecutor to help resolve unfairness in the criminal justice system is like enlisting in the army because you are opposed to the current war. It's like working as an oil refiner because you want to help the environment. Yes, you get to choose the toxic chemicals. True, the boss might allow you to leave one or two pristine bays untouched. Maybe, if you do really good work as a low-level polluter, they might make you the head polluter. But rather than calling yourself an "environmentalist," you should think of yourself as a polluter with a conscience.

I hope that the analysis in this part will be useful for any advocate for social change who ponders where she can do the most good. What is the role that our moral and political beliefs should play when we choose our work? When does compromise cross the line and become complicity? When does one do more harm than good by working within an unjust system?

Prosecutors have a lot of power.

I agree with that description absolutely; it's just that ultimately I would limit it to one prosecutor in particular. The head of a prosecution office is the most unregulated actor in the entire legal system. Basically, there are no rules. There's no law, for example, that says that simply because the prosecutor knows someone is guilty of a crime, that suspect must be charged. The lead prosecutor—the district attorney or the United States attorney—can make whatever decision he wants about whether to prosecute, and no judge or politician can overturn it.

The prosecutor often has more control than the judge over

the outcome of a case. Sentencing guidelines and mandatory minimum sentences have reduced the discretion that judges used to have to fit the punishment to the crime. The prosecutor can circumvent required sentences simply by charging a different crime, or leaving out some of the evidence. This is perfectly legal.

Federal law, for example, requires a minimum five-year sentence if someone uses a gun while engaged in drug trafficking, even if the gun is not brandished or discharged. The judge who refuses to impose this sentence would almost certainly be reversed on appeal. Let's say, however, that a prosecutor doesn't want the same defendant to receive the whole five years, perhaps because she is trying to entice the defendant to snitch in another case. She can simply charge the drug case, leaving out the evidence about the firearm. No one—not the judge, not the governor, not even the president of the United States—can require the head prosecutor to add the gun charge.

Line prosecutors "share" this power in the sense that they make the initial decisions about charging, plea bargains, and sentencing. As a baby prosecutor, I sometimes felt unworthy of the delegation of this much responsibility. Here I was, a kid only a few years out of law school, and cops and defense attorneys with much more experience had to suck up to me to get what they wanted. I loved it.

"Papering" was one of my favorite parts of the job. After the police arrested someone, they would bring their reports to the basement of the courthouse, where we prosecutors sat in cubicles. The police would line up to talk to us, and we would make the preliminary decisions about whether or not to bring charges. We considered factors like whether the defendant had a record, if the case had "jury appeal," whether there were victims who seemed like they would be cooperative, if the statements of the police officers seemed believable, and whether there would be problems getting all of the evidence admitted in court.

I soon realized, however, that my own power was limited. Whatever a line prosecutor decided, his or her recommendation had to be approved by a supervisor. If the case was high profile or the crime grave, the review went all the way up the chain of command.

In the state system, where 90 percent of criminal cases are brought, the head prosecutor is a politician who in most cases was elected pursuant to the dysfunctional politics of criminal justice in which people get votes by promising to put more people in cages.

The line prosecutor has to answer to the boss, who has to answer to those politics. This limits the effectiveness of wannabe progressive prosecutors who claim that they would be more sensitive than hard-core "law and order" types. These liberal prosecutors say they would exercise their discretion to be merciful and even to not charge when that was appropriate.

The reality is that the discretion of worker bees is tightly controlled. There are certain kinds of cases that come up all the time, and for those cases there are already rules in place. A classic case of this type is that of a first-time drug offender. Virtually every prosecuting office has a procedure for dealing with those cases, and the line attorney is expected to follow the program. In my experience, most people who work at prosecutors' offices—and especially those who reach the rank of supervisor—do not view mass incarceration and expanding police power as serious problems. To the contrary, they mistakenly believe that "tough" criminal justice makes us safer. Most will not be amenable to decisions in individual cases that are made with an eye toward locking up fewer people or limiting police power. Ultimately, the prosecutor with a social justice agenda would have to proceed more subversively than overtly.

While my experience is that line prosecutors don't have a lot of "free" discretion, there is another important limit on their power: they are stuck with the cases that the police bring. It's not as though a progressive prosecutor can say, "I don't want to try cases that are the result of selective law enforcement in poor neighborhoods" or "I want to opt out of cases that arise from racial profiling." That would be like a lawyer saying, "I want to work for a firm that pays big bucks but I don't want to represent rich people." If you are a typical prosecutor, you will spend most of your time locking up poor people. For better or worse, that's what most prosecutors do.

Is it possible to make a real difference from inside? If mere "reform" is required, working within the system might accomplish that change. If, on the other hand, a more substantial transformation is necessary, it becomes more evident that the change must come from without. Those who work inside can tinker with the punishment regime, but they probably cannot overhaul it.

To be a prosecutor . . . is to be an active participant in a system that defines too many activities as crimes, enforces its laws selectively, and incarcerates far too many of its citizens. If the punishment response had a substantial benefit to public safety, complicity might be warranted. It does not. The punishment regime creates a level of suffering—for prisoners, their families, and their communities—that should be intolerable in a civil society. An empathetic imagination of that pain—the degradation of our fellow human beings—helps us weigh the moral cost of complicity.

Part III

Public Defenders

We each became public defenders for different reasons, though our experiences share common threads. Premal grew up in Appalachia as a child of immigrant parents. She was drawn to public defender work because it takes on intersecting social injustices—and allowed her to question the often-hidden institutional choices that sustain them. James's parents were civil rights workers in the Student Nonviolent Coordinating Committee. He became a public defender because he believed that fighting mass incarceration was his generation's civil rights struggle. Maria came to public defense during law school, when as a summer clerk she worked on a death penalty case in New Orleans and was shocked by capital punishment's inhumanity.

Though we loved our work, we acknowledge the inherent tension in our choice: in order to challenge the criminal system, we became part of it. The readings that follow get to the heart of this tension, asking whether and how public defenders can resist mass incarceration—and whether and how they risk entrenching it.

Before 1963, poor people charged with crimes were not guaranteed to have lawyers standing beside them, helping them navigate the web of the criminal system. The Supreme Court's decision in *Gideon v. Wainwright* changed that. It pronounced that, in our adversarial system, due process requires effective counsel.[1] Today, approximately 80 percent of people charged with crimes are indigent. For each of them, their court-appointed lawyer is the only person in the courtroom who is there on their behalf and is ethically committed to them, their rights, and their needs.

The late Charles J. Ogletree Jr. knew what it meant to stand next to—and fight for—someone accused of a crime. Abbe Smith, too, understands the urgency of the role. In the articles we have excerpted, each of them provides a helpful entry point to understanding public defense and its complex function: resisting the system in which it exists. In "An Essay on the New Public Defender for the Twenty-First Century," Ogletree begins by pointing out something every public defender knows all too well: We aren't popular. As he explains,

> the public appears to dislike lawyers of all kinds, but it reserves a special contempt for those who represent indigent clients charged with crimes. After all, public defenders are called upon every day to represent indigents who are accused

of murder, rape, kidnapping, robbery, theft, drug usage and distribution, assault, and other conduct that threatens persons and property alike. Many believe that people accused of such crimes do not deserve to have any counsel at all, much less competent, well-trained counsel.

Ogletree argues that the public is wrong to be so hostile and makes the case for public defenders. Writing in 1995, as the prison system was hauling in more Black people than ever, Ogletree was among the first legal scholars to emphasize how public defenders advance racial justice. He writes, "Public defenders are the only representation to which many of the poor, who are disproportionately members of communities of color, will have access."

In "Defending Those People," Abbe Smith offers a more personal reflection on why she became a public defender. Smith says she is "drawn to any underdog—the little guy, not the big one; David, not Goliath; the Cubs, not the Yankees." Though she has no regrets about her chosen career, Smith is candid about the hard times: "The thing about siding with the underdog is you don't always win—in fact, mostly you don't—and it can be devastating when the government puts a human being under your care in a steel cage or kills them."

When lawyers like Ogletree and Smith have sufficient resources, they can make a profound difference. Every day across America, public defenders keep people out of jail and prison, educate judges and juries about the law and their clients' lives, push for better plea offers and reduced sentences, investigate and interrogate the government's allegations, find experts and evidence to support their clients in court, and expose police and prosecutorial misconduct. They act as a support system in what may be the worst time in a person's life.

There can be no question about public defense's urgent, intrinsic value: Extricating people from the criminal system, and mitigating the harm they experience, is critically important. And the idea that each person charged in the system could have a lawyer by their side, fighting for them, is exciting to many. But despite the Supreme Court's resounding proclamation, *Gideon*'s mandate has never been fulfilled.

For starters, despite the court's ruling, *Gideon* did not result in a robust, widespread public defense system. The decision offered no roadmap or structure to create public defender services that were properly funded or organized. Instead, it left jurisdictions to their own devices. Ultimately, counties, towns, and cities across the U.S. exhibited little to no political will to protect the lives, rights, and futures of those accused of crimes. To this day, public defense remains overburdened and under-resourced throughout the country.[2] In "Want to Reduce Mass Incarceration? Fund Public Defenders," Noah Berlatsky documents this systemic underfunding and argues that it must change if we are going to truly address mass incarceration.

Many in and around the public defense community cast this societal refusal to live up to *Gideon*'s mandate as a contributing factor to mass incarceration. But we offer two readings arguing that the mandate itself is part of the problem. The first comes from a law review article by Paul D. Butler, "Poor People Lose: *Gideon* and the Critique of Rights." Butler points out that since *Gideon* was decided, the prison population has exploded, and that this growth has been on the backs of poor people and Black people especially. While Butler doesn't overtly blame *Gideon* for these trends, he makes clear that the opinion plays a role in validating these changes. How so? By providing the promise of a lawyer in every criminal case, *Gideon* "invests the criminal justice system with a veneer of impartiality and respectability that it does not deserve."

In the second reading, "The End of Public Defenders," Matthew Caldwell draws on his own experience in public defense, describing why he came to feel that he had been "sold a bill of goods." He signed up for the job because he wanted to change the legal system. But when he became a public defender, he realized that he was only helping to defend a fantasy of courts as places that dispense justice. When public defenders counsel their clients to plead guilty, he argues, they imbue a fraudulent system with constitutional legitimacy. After all, if criminal defendants are represented by "embattled heroes sincerely wearing the badge of public defender," Caldwell says, "then perhaps the system doesn't seem so devious after all."

When read in connection with Berlatsky's essay documenting the underfunding of public defenders, Butler's and Caldwell's essays pose challenging questions. Should we give public defenders more money? Or would such an effort undermine the long-term goal of shrinking the criminal system?

In the next piece, "Why Public Defenders Matter More Than Ever in a Time of Reform," John F. Pfaff responds to Butler's concern that *Gideon* covers up a rotten system. In Pfaff's view, Butler's critique was correct when it was offered in 2013 but has since been overtaken by events. In particular, Pfaff points to the rise of the progressive prosecutor movement and its reformist candidates, who promise to make the criminal system smaller and less punitive. This movement gives public defenders a new role, says Pfaff: "They're in the best position to ensure that progressive-sounding prosecutors fulfill their campaign promises." Because public defenders are the only entity present at every court hearing, discovery conference, and plea-bargain meeting, Pfaff argues, there is no one better positioned to assess prosecutors and hold them accountable.

The late Jeff Adachi, a former chief public defender in San Francisco, shared Pfaff's view that public defenders merit a prominent role in today's criminal justice reform efforts. Writing as the Black Lives Matter movement gained prominence after the killings of Trayvon Martin and Michael Brown, Adachi sought to identify concrete ways for public defenders to advance racial justice. Noting that defenders are "already in the trenches," Adachi argued that they should maximize their unique position to do things like insist on diverse juries, confront biased judges and prosecutors, and challenge racial disparities in bail practices.

In the next reading, Alexis Hoag-Fordjour explores the attorney-client relationship. She argues that giving Black defendants the option of selecting a Black attorney could transform how they experience the system. "Black lawyers often have the experiential knowledge of what it is like to move through the world with the social meaning attached to Blackness and thus firsthand knowledge of the corresponding treatment and dangers," Hoag-Fordjour writes. As a result, she concludes, they can often better empathize with Black clients, are more likely to recognize their humanity, and will typically build more trusting relationships.

We end with two pieces that offer a path forward. The first is an excerpt from a voter guide created by a group of public defenders, analyzing the candidates for Manhattan district attorney in 2021. This excerpt highlights the value of public defenders' insights into the criminal system, including the role of prosecutors. By sharing the knowledge they've gained from helping their clients navigate the system's harms, public defenders can invite more people to learn about and challenge mass incarceration.

The final excerpt highlights a model of community organizing that is deeply tied to public defense: participatory defense. Participatory defense aims to support people charged with crimes, their families, and their communities. Defendants and their loved ones educate one another about the system: what to expect in court, how to address the judge during bail hearings, and how best to present information to the court. The participatory defense movement turns the traditional attorney-client model on its head by empowering communities to provide not only support, but also knowledge and advice. As a result, the public defender gains a partner in their courtroom advocacy.

More fundamentally, this model breaks down barriers between lawyers and the communities around them. In his talk "1,862 Fewer Years in Prison" and in his interview with Premal Dharia, Raj Jayadev reflects on the role participatory defense might play in the fight against mass incarceration: "We make the family an essential and effective part of the defense team, so they [can] change the outcome of cases and transform the landscape of power in the court system." Jayadev is a community organizer, and his larger goal is to help communities develop the capacity, from the ground up, to end the harms they experience through the criminal system. Changes this ambitious, he says, aren't going to come from "one clever litigator; they won't come from a Supreme Court case. The changes we want to create are going to require a larger force."

Gideon v. Wainwright*

Justice Hugo L. Black
1963

Reason and reflection require us to recognize that in our adversary system of criminal justice, any person haled into court, who is too poor to hire a lawyer, cannot be assured a fair trial unless counsel is provided for him. This seems to us to be an obvious truth. Governments, both state and federal, quite properly spend vast sums of money to establish machinery to try defendants accused of crime. Lawyers to prosecute are everywhere deemed essential to protect the public's interest in an orderly society. Similarly, there are few defendants charged with crime, few indeed, who fail to hire the best lawyers they can get to prepare and present their defenses. That the government hires lawyers to prosecute and defendants who have the money hire lawyers to defend are the strongest indications of the widespread belief that lawyers in criminal courts are necessities, not luxuries. The right of one charged with crime to counsel may not be deemed fundamental and essential to fair trials in some countries, but it is in ours. From the very beginning,

---

* *Gideon v. Wainwright*, 372 U.S. 335 (1963).

our state and national constitutions and laws have laid great emphasis on procedural and substantive safeguards designed to assure fair trials before impartial tribunals in which every defendant stands equal before the law. This noble ideal cannot be realized if the poor man charged with crime has to face his accusers without a lawyer to assist him. A defendant's need for a lawyer is nowhere better stated than in the moving words of Mr. Justice Sutherland in *Powell v. Alabama*:

> The right to be heard would be, in many cases, of little avail if it did not comprehend the right to be heard by counsel. Even the intelligent and educated layman has small and sometimes no skill in the science of law. If charged with crime, he is incapable, generally, of determining for himself whether the indictment is good or bad. He is unfamiliar with the rules of evidence. Left without the aid of counsel he may be put on trial without a proper charge, and convicted upon incompetent evidence, or evidence irrelevant to the issue or otherwise inadmissible. He lacks both the skill and knowledge adequately to prepare his defense, even though he have a perfect one [sic]. He requires the guiding hand of counsel at every step in the proceedings against him. Without it, though he be not guilty, he faces the danger of conviction because he does not know how to establish his innocence.

An Essay on the New Public Defender for the Twenty-First Century*

Charles J. Ogletree Jr.

1995

The role of serving as a public defender is, by its nature, a difficult one. Public criticism of the legal profession in general is quite widespread, resulting in ongoing calls within the profession to focus on changing its negative image. The public appears to dislike lawyers of all kinds, but it reserves a special contempt for those who represent indigent clients charged with crimes. After all, public defenders are called upon every day to represent indigents who are accused of murder, rape, kidnapping, robbery, theft, drug usage and distribution, assault, and other conduct that threatens persons and property alike. Many believe that people accused of such crimes do not deserve to

* Charles J. Ogletree Jr., "An Essay on the New Public Defender for the 21st Century," *Law and Contemporary Problems* 58, no. 1 (1995): 812–85.

have any counsel at all, much less competent, well-trained counsel.

Nevertheless, our adversarial system of law necessitates that we provide adequate assistance of counsel to anyone accused of a crime who cannot afford his or her own representation. An indigent—even one accused of committing heinous crimes—still has the right to the presumption of innocence and to a fair trial in which he can proffer a defense to the charges leveled against him. Without access to counsel, an innocent individual may be convicted of a crime merely because she happens to be poor. Providing competent counsel is the best means of ensuring the proper operation of the constitutional safeguards designed to protect the innocent and the less culpable from unfair punishment, including death. As Justice Black so eloquently recognized in *Gideon v. Wainwright*:

> Our state and national constitutions and laws have laid great emphasis on procedural and substantive safeguards designed to assure fair trials before impartial tribunals in which every defendant stands equal before the law. This noble idea cannot be realized if the poor man charged with crime has to face his accusers without a lawyer to assist him.

Without an assurance of adequate assistance of counsel for the indigent, the law draws a line between rich and poor, ensuring a fair trial to those on one side of the line and denying a fair trial to those on the other.

Moreover, failure to provide adequate assistance of counsel to accused indigents draws a line not only between rich and poor, but also between white and black. For the first time in our nation's history, the number of people who are incarcerated in jails and prisons surpasses one million. Recent reports indicate that unprecedented numbers of African-Americans, particularly young males, are involved in the criminal justice system. When discussing the inadequacies of the current system of providing counsel for the accused poor, one cannot ignore the correlation between race and poverty. If the criminal justice system deprives the poor generally of the right to a fair trial, that burden will fall disproportionately on communities of color because of the greater incidence of poverty in these communities and, hence, their greater reliance on public defender services.

The debate about public defender services also cannot ignore the fact that the same communities that suffer disproportionately from inadequate provision of legal services to the poor are already subject to peculiar disabilities in the criminal justice system. The most recent wave of criminal justice reforms has included the enactment of laws that appear to be aimed at members of certain races, leading to even higher levels of incarceration of African-American males. One of the most disturbing examples of race-based criminal law reform is the enactment of differing penalties for cocaine convictions based solely on the form in which the cocaine is possessed or distributed.

In *Minnesota v. Russell*, five African-American males challenged a state criminal prosecution for possession of crack cocaine. The defendants alleged that African-Americans, who constitute 96 percent of those charged with possession of crack cocaine, and white Americans, who constitute nearly 80 percent of those charged with possession of powder cocaine, were treated differently in the imposition of penalties for what is essentially the same crime, that is, possession or distribution of cocaine. Under Minnesota law at the time, the sentence for a conviction of possessing five grams of powder cocaine would likely result in probation. Alternatively, the sentence for a conviction of possessing five grams of crack cocaine would ordinarily result in a penalty of ten years' imprisonment. Moreover, the data presented at trial by the defendants indicated that an offender convicted of selling a given amount of crack cocaine would receive the same sentence as would an offender convicted of selling one hundred times that amount of powder cocaine. The Minnesota Supreme Court concluded that the statute failed the rational basis test drawn from the equal protection clause of the state constitution, which in some respects is more stringent than the federal test.

The federal courts have also noted the racial disparity in sentencing for cocaine possession and distribution caused by the dubious distinction drawn between crack and powder cocaine in the federal statutes. For example, Judge Louis Oberdorfer of the District Court for the District of Columbia held in *United States v. Walls* that the statutory mandatory minimum sentences for crack cocaine possession in some circumstances constituted cruel and unusual punishment in violation of the Eighth Amendment. Federal District Court Judge Clyde Cahill has also commented on the severe impact the disparity between crack and powder cocaine sentencing has had on the African-American community:

> While Congress may have had well-intentioned concerns, the Court is equally aware that this one provision, the crack statute, has been directly responsible for incarcerating nearly an entire generation of young black American men for very long periods, usually during the most productive time of their lives. Inasmuch as crack and powder cocaine are really the same drug . . . it appears likely that race rather than conduct was the determining factor.

Moreover, racial disparity in the federal system is not limited to sentencing for the possession and distribution of crack and powder cocaine; Douglas McDonald and Kenneth E. Carson have documented racial disparity in the application of the Federal Sentencing Guidelines generally.

In spite of the overwhelming evidence of dramatic increases in the arrest, prosecution, and conviction of African-American males, little attention has been given to the impact that improved public defender services would have on these numbers. Public defenders are the only representation to which many of the poor, who are disproportionately members of communities of color, will have access. If public defender services are inadequate, the accused poor will likely be deprived of constitutional procedural protections. Failure to ensure the adequacy of public defender programs produces a disproportionate impact not only on the poor, but also on members of communities of color, a result that is unacceptable in a society committed, as ours is by the Fourteenth Amendment, to equal treatment under the law.

Defending Those People*

Abbe Smith

2012

I am drawn to people in trouble. Maybe this is because I had a little sister who was often in trouble. My sister had "problems" as a young child. Once, in kindergarten, she was finger painting. When it was time to clean up and move to the next activity, the teacher said, "Okay, class. Time to put everything away." My sister ignored her. The teacher approached my sister and, calling her by name, directed her to put the paints away. My sister kept painting. When the teacher repeated her request, my sister picked up her paint-covered hands and wiped them on the teacher's dress.

I grew up intervening on my sister's behalf, fighting her battles—at home, school, and in the neighborhood. Sometimes I literally fought for her. There was a red-haired boy named Alan who, in second grade, called my sister a name. I gave him

* Abbe Smith, "Defending Those People," *Ohio State Journal of Criminal Law* 10, no. 1 (2012): 277–302.

a bloody lip, which got me sent to the principal's office. This was my first and only visit to the principal. It was worth it.

I don't think I've punched anyone since. I tend to fight my battles in court. From that point on, it wasn't a great leap to others in trouble. I mean "trouble" broadly, not just the kind my sister got in, or the kind that lands people in the criminal justice system. I feel a natural sympathy for people in difficulty or distress. It doesn't matter who they are. The fact that they are in trouble is what makes me want to defend them.

This is ironic since patience is generally not my strong suit—I can be brusque and dismissive. I am not known for my attention span—I tend to lose interest quickly (except when it's me who's talking; then I'm riveted). I have many more flaws: I can be a smart aleck, sarcasm is second nature, I don't suffer fools gladly. If I am any guide, you don't need to be the nicest person on Earth to want to help people in trouble.

I am probably nicer to people in trouble than I am to ordinary people—even more so if I don't know them. No one should take from this kindness to strangers any great meaning, biblical or otherwise. I might be nicer to strangers only in comparison to people I know. I laugh when a friend or family member takes a pratfall. I can barely stop laughing long enough to help them up.

I seem to broadcast a certain receptiveness to trouble. I am regularly accosted and confided in by people with problems: on the street, in the subway, and at the grocery store. This is multiplied many times in the courthouse. It never fails: the anxious person with a summons, subpoena, or son in jail manages to find me. I don't know why this is.

Ordinarily, I am not terribly interested in "needy" people. I don't have the stamina to weed through layers of need. But with people in criminal trouble there is a built-in narrative that draws me in—something happened and something else will happen to resolve it one way or another. It doesn't need to be a serious or high profile crime for there to be a good story: a gripping tale of comedy, tragedy, *theater*.

A student and I recently represented a man I'll call Lester Johnson, who was accused of shoplifting a pair of electric clippers from a CVS pharmacy. Even though the crime was captured on videotape, Mr. Johnson refused a plea for probation and insisted on going to trial. He was forty-nine years old. He had been in trouble in his youth, but not for years. He did a stupid, impetuous thing, but thought the store should have let him go when they recovered the clippers. He understood the system well enough to know that sometimes even clear-cut cases fall apart: witnesses don't show up, evidence is lost. He wanted a trial or a dismissal.

It turned out the trial date fell on Mr. Johnson's birthday.

When the government declared it was ready to go to trial—the store security guard was present, videotape in hand—Mr. Johnson said he was ready, too. It was unclear to me whether this was a matter of principle—the government should have to prove its case—or Mr. Johnson had backed himself into a corner by maintaining he wanted a trial.

I talked with him to try to understand exactly what his objectives were. We didn't have much time. We also didn't have much privacy—as often happens we talked in the hall just outside the courtroom. The judge had given the case a brief recess and would soon call us back.

Although the plea deal was off the table, Mr. Johnson still had the option of pleading guilty rather than going to trial. The judge who would hear the trial or plea was someone I'd appeared before many times. He was fair-minded. If Mr. Johnson pled guilty and expressed genuine regret at sentencing, I

believed he would be sentenced to no more than a year of probation. But pointless, time-consuming litigation would surely
test the judge's goodwill. I explained this to Mr. Johnson. I
made clear that we were prepared to go to trial if that's what he
wanted, but he should fully understand that a trial here would
be more like a "slow guilty plea." If Mr. Johnson's objective was
to avoid jail, he should plead guilty. If his objective was to have
his "day in court," no matter the consequences, he should go
to trial. I acknowledged that he might still receive probation
if convicted at trial. He remained adamant. We went back and
forth, but, in the end, I told him it was his decision and we
would go to trial.

I went to check on a case in another courtroom. By the
time I returned, things had changed drastically. A busload
of middle-school children had suddenly descended upon the
courtroom where the shoplifting trial would occur. There must
have been forty kids on some sort of field trip.

I grabbed Mr. Johnson and threw all that client-centered
counseling to the wind. "Forget trial," I said. "There's no way
the judge won't make an example of you in front of all those
children. He'll use you to teach them not to shoplift. He'll talk
about how we all suffer when people steal: shops have to hire
security, consumers have to pay higher prices, we are all under
constant surveillance. But if you plead guilty—if you 'man up'
and throw yourself on the mercy of the court—the judge will
be magnanimous. He will show those kids that judges have a
heart when an accused takes responsibility for his actions and
is contrite."

I didn't give him much of a choice; he went with the plea.
Mr. Johnson was so good during the plea and sentencing—he
was honest and forthcoming, made no excuses, said he was
ashamed of himself, and swore this would never happen

again—the judge gave him only six months nonreporting probation. When it was over, he threw his arms around me. He was delighted with the outcome. He said he couldn't thank me enough for saving his fiftieth birthday.

Most of those accused and convicted of crime are poor. Disproportionate numbers are nonwhite. There are now more black people currently under the control of the criminal justice system than were enslaved in 1850. I suppose this is why "nobody really cares" about the quality of criminal justice in the United States, or the fact that we currently lock up more people than any other nation on Earth in the "history of the free world." Who gives a damn about a bunch of poor, black people in prison?

I do. And so does every public defender in America—or at least they should. I often tell students I became a criminal lawyer because I read the book *To Kill a Mockingbird* (and saw the movie version) too many times as an impressionable child. For me, there is no more compelling figure than Atticus Finch, the archetypal criminal lawyer defending a wrongly accused poor black man. That Gregory Peck played Finch in the movie only contributes to his iconic stature.

Criminal defenders are, by and large, poverty lawyers. You can't spend any amount of time in criminal court and not see that it is a poor people's court. You can't step foot in a jail or prison and not notice they are full of poor people.

We are not very good at talking about poverty in this country. We don't seem to want to acknowledge its existence. But we must talk about poverty and advocate for those who bear the brunt of it. In his final column for *The New York Times*, Bob Herbert decried the lack of concern about poverty and called the growing divide between rich and poor "scandalous." This is not hyperbole: in 2009, the richest 5 percent of Americans claimed nearly 64 percent of the nation's wealth, while the bottom 80 percent held less than 13 percent.

I have never known poverty in any immediate sense. My own life could not be more different from that of most of my clients. I grew up with all kinds of advantages: no opportunities were beyond my reach. I am drawn to the poor because no one should be destitute and hungry, lacking decent housing, neighborhoods, schools, and medical care in the wealthiest nation on earth. I feel implicated by the inequality and unfairness of this.

The Reverend Martin Luther King Jr. could have been my kind of defender: "I choose to identify with the underprivileged. I choose to identify with the poor. I choose to give my life for the hungry. I choose to give my life for those who have been left out . . ."

Eugene Debs could have been my kind of defender too:

[Y]ears ago, I recognized my kinship with all living things, and I made up my mind that I was not one bit better than the meanest on earth . . . [W]hile there is a lower class, I am in it, while there is a criminal element I am of it, and while there is a soul in prison, I am not free.

But I confess that I am also drawn to any underdog—the little guy, not the big one; David, not Goliath; the Cubs, not the Yankees. I often tell students that growing up a Chicago Cubs fan probably helped pave my life path.

The underdog is not necessarily poor or black. [For example, two of my clients] are white and were some version of middle-class before their incarceration. But if they are ever released, neither will have an easy time of it. Neither came from money, is college educated, or a skilled worker. [One of my clients, named] Delores, worked as a nurse's aide before her arrest and conviction. As a convicted murderer, it's doubtful she'd find employment as any sort of caretaker. [Another client named] Ronnie was a struggling high school student. He has never held a job outside the prison walls.

Moreover, some criminal justice underdogs were once top dogs. That's the terrifying thing about a criminal prosecution: the once mighty can suddenly be brought low. Although I have represented very few non-indigent clients, the fear, anxiety, and vulnerability that accompany a criminal accusation transcend class.

There's also something fun about fighting for the underdog in criminal court: the stakes are high, the battle hard-fought, the outcome uncertain. The lines are also refreshingly clear. Defenders fight for underdogs against the enormous power of the State. It's the Good Fight.

What's more, we have to be that much better—tougher, smarter, more creative, more resourceful—in order to level the playing field. As one writer puts it: "It's always a stacked deck for the state and often the defense attorney's very best work is simply not good enough to overcome the power and the might." This can be frightening, but it is also exciting. Sometimes you can literally beat the government. There's nothing more thrilling than this, nothing more intoxicating. The wins help keep you going.

But the thing about siding with the underdog is you don't always win—in fact, mostly you don't—and it can be devastating when the government puts a human being under your care in a steel cage or kills them. Each defender has to figure out a reason to continue the fight.

Want to Reduce Mass Incarceration? Fund Public Defenders*

Noah Berlatsky
2018

How can we reduce mass incarceration? Policy advocates in the past have argued we should decriminalize some drugs, or end mandatory minimum sentences. Today, many activists argue we need to elect more progressive district attorneys and prosecutors.

But one group that could have a major effect on prison populations is often ignored: public defenders.

Public defenders aren't senators or presidents; they don't get a lot of time in the media spotlight. As a result, it can be easy to forget them when thinking about criminal justice policy. But while mass incarceration is a national problem, it is fueled by local decisions and actions. The nitty gritty, small-scale effec-

* Noah Berlatsky, "Want to Reduce Mass Incarceration? Fund Public Defenders," *Medium*, September 11, 2018.

tive administration of justice for individuals can add up over time and be just as effective as sweeping policy changes.

Public defenders may be neglected, but researchers and policymakers have begun to show the connection between prosecutors and the prison boom. Individual prosecutors have great discretion in how they charge crimes, and in what prison sentences they ask for. John Pfaff, a professor of law at Fordham University, has analyzed filings in state courts which show that prison populations ballooned over the 1990s and 2000s largely because of prosecutorial decisions.

Pfaff's data set started in 1994, and showed that at that time, one of every three arrests was charged as a felony case. By 2008, which is when the data set ends, the number had doubled to two out of three arrests charged as felonies.

In response to this information, progressives have been pushing to elect reform-minded prosecutors who are committed to reducing unnecessary felony charges and reducing prison populations. Kim Ogg in Houston, for example, has decided not to prosecute many marijuana cases. Larry Krasner in Philadelphia has ordered his prosecutors to offer plea deals that start at the lower end of sentencing guidelines, rather than pushing for the longest possible prison time.

John Pfaff told me that he believes reforming prosecutors such as Krasner and Ogg can have a long term effect. However, he points out a couple of caveats.

First, he says, reform prosecutors are generally only elected in places with progressive voters—which generally means urban counties. Rural areas are much less likely to elect such prosecutors. "Decarceration since 2010 hasn't really been the United States decarcerating, it hasn't even really been the story of certain states decarcerating," Pfaff says. "It's been the story of urban counties in a lot of states decarcerating. While smaller counties actually are sending more people to prison than in 2010."

The other limitation of electing progressive DAs, Pfaff says, is that especially in large urban offices, DAs may have limited control over policy. A progressive DA can order people not to set bail for marijuana offenses, for example. But subordinates may push back, or drag their feet in implementing the policy. Kim Ogg recognized this problem, and fired thirty-seven veteran prosecutors as soon as she took office, because she felt that progressive change required a new management team. However, even with a large-scale upper management changeover, it takes time to shift priorities that have been entrenched for decades. Prosecutors have long worked to put people behind bars for as long as possible. Changing that will take time.

In theory, public defenders are supposed to provide a counterweight to prosecutors. Public defenders work to make sure that indigent defendants have advocates who work to reduce their sentences, or to find evidence suggesting they shouldn't be sentenced at all.

Unfortunately, public defender offices are in a state of crisis. State governments have slashed budgets for public defenders, leaving thousands of defendants without adequate representation. In 2017, the ACLU sued Missouri's public defender system, in which PDs find themselves with three times as many cases as they can handle. The Southern Poverty Law Center is suing Louisiana in a similar case on the grounds that the ill-funded system fails to provide adequate defense for the indigent.

In an article in the *Georgetown Journal of Legal Ethics*, Colleen Cullen writes that "public defense offices across the country are in crisis and the primary reason is the lack of adequate funding." Cullen also points out that public defender offices often lack investigative staff, which means that public defenders do investigative work themselves, further reducing the amount of time they can spend in court or on legal work.

When defendants don't get adequate representation, they receive longer sentences. Even before trial, without adequate defense the accused may be hit with high bail, which means they end up sitting in jail before they've even been convicted of crime; five hundred thousand pre-trial detainees spend time in jail every year. In contrast, Cullen told me, during her own time in the well-funded Georgetown legal clinic, not a single one of her clients was sentenced. "Just looking at my own personal anecdotal experience, the more time and effort you're able to put into your case, the better outcomes you'll see for your clients."

Cullen recommends that states need to hire more public defenders. But John Pfaff and others have pointed out that there is also a potential national solution. Congress has the power to allocate national funds for public defenders, if it chooses to do so.

Currently, Pfaff told me, national spending on indigent defense is somewhere around $4.5 billion. Congress could double that by spending $9 billion a year—a fraction of the roughly $200 billion spent on criminal justice each year.

A national grant for public defense would face some logistical barriers. Some states might try to cut their own funds for defense when they receive the grants. Some states have no central office set up, so distributing funds could be difficult.

However, there are advantages to the national funding solution over the attempt to simply hire more defenders. Putting in place reform prosecutors requires winning numerous elections and then engaging in a long bureaucratic fight. Money for public defenders just requires putting it on the national Democratic agenda, and then waiting until a Democratic Congress is in place. The overall cost is relatively low, and Democrats have been more and more open on the national level to criminal justice reform.

Adequately funded public defender offices could reduce sentences across the country, and start to roll back some of the worst excesses of mass incarceration. Just as important, Pfaff says, public defenders with adequate resources could hold prosecutors accountable when they say they want to reduce sentencing. If a reform prosecutor says she wants to stop prosecuting cannabis cases, public defenders are in a position to report on whether such a policy actually goes into effect.

At the moment, public defenders can't even provide adequate defense for their clients. But if their offices were actually funded and fully staffed, they could start serving as a check on prosecutors in the political arena as well as in the courts.

Those charged with keeping people out of prison year after year, day after day, are public defenders. If we want to reduce mass incarceration, we should make sure they have the resources to do their jobs.

Poor People Lose: *Gideon* and the Critique of Rights*

Paul D. Butler
2013

Gideon v. Wainwright is widely regarded as a milestone in American criminal justice.

When it was decided in 1963, it was seen as a major step forward in assuring fairness to poor people and racial minorities. Yet, fifty years later, low-income and African-American people in the criminal justice system are considerably worse off. It would be preferable to be a poor black charged with a crime in 1962 than now, if one's objective is to avoid prison or serve as little time as possible.

The "critique of rights," as articulated by critical legal theorists, posits that "nothing whatever follows from a court's adoption of some legal rule" and that "winning a legal victory can actually impede further progressive change." My thesis

* Paul D. Butler, "Poor People Lose: *Gideon* and the Critique of Rights," *The Yale Law Journal* 122, no. 8 (June 2013): 2176–2204.

is that *Gideon* demonstrates the critique of rights. Arguably, *Gideon* has not improved the situation of accused persons, and may even have worsened their plight.

The reason that prisons are filled with poor people, and that rich people rarely go to prison, is not because the rich have better lawyers than the poor. It is because prison is for the poor, and not the rich. In criminal cases poor people lose most of the time, not because indigent defense is inadequately funded, although it is, and not because defense attorneys for poor people are ineffective, although some are. Poor people lose, most of the time, because in American criminal justice, poor people are losers. Prison is designed for them. This is the real crisis of indigent defense. *Gideon* obscures this reality, and in this sense stands in the way of the political mobilization that will be required to transform criminal justice.

Gideon is not responsible for the exponential increase in incarceration or the vast rise in racial disparities in criminal justice. As I explain later, however, *Gideon* bears some responsibility for legitimating these developments and defusing political resistance to them. It invests the criminal justice system with a veneer of impartiality and respectability that it does not deserve. *Gideon* created the false consciousness that criminal justice would get better. It actually got worse. Even full enforcement of *Gideon* would not significantly improve the wretchedness of American criminal justice.

Approximately two decades after *Gideon*, two trends began in criminal justice, the effects of which were to overwhelm any benefits that *Gideon* provided to low-income accused persons. First, the United States experienced the most pronounced increase in incarceration in the history of the world. Second, there was a corresponding exponential increase in racial disparities in incarceration.

This dramatic expansion of incarceration was accomplished on the backs of poor people. The Bureau of Justice Statistics reports that the "generally accepted indigency rate" for state felony cases near the time when *Gideon* was decided was 43 percent. Today approximately 80 percent of people charged with crime are poor.

Other data further illustrate the correlation between poverty and incarceration. In 1997, more than half of state prisoners earned less than $1,000 in the month before their arrest. This would result in an annual income of less than $12,000, well below the $25,654 median per capita income in 1997. The same year, 35 percent of state inmates were unemployed in the month before their arrest, compared to the national unemployment rate of 4.9 percent.

Approximately 70 percent of state prisoners have not graduated from high school. Only 13 percent of incarcerated adults have any post-high school education, compared with almost 50 percent of the non-incarcerated population.

College graduation, on the other hand, serves to insulate Americans from incarceration. Only 0.1 percent of bachelor's degree holders are incarcerated, compared to 6.3 percent of high school dropouts. Put another way, high school dropouts are sixty-three times more likely to be locked up than college graduates.

The post-*Gideon* expansion of the prison population was also accomplished on the backs of black people. There have always been racial disparities in American criminal justice, but from the 1920s through the 1970s they were "only" about two-to-one. Now the black/white incarceration disparity is seven-to-one. There are more African Americans under correctional supervision than there were slaves in 1850. As Michelle Alexander states, "If mass incarceration is considered as a system of social control—specifically, racial control—then the system is a fantastic success."

In summary, poor people and blacks have never fared as well as the nonpoor and the nonblack in American criminal justice. Since the 1970s, however, the disparities have gotten much worse. Something happened that dramatically increased incarceration and dramatically raised the percentage of the incarcerated who are poor and black. What happened is usually attributed to two main causes: the war on drugs and the law-and-order or so-called tough-on-crime policies of American leaders since the Nixon Administration.

What if every person accused of a crime had an excellent lawyer? Proponents of *Gideon* suggest it would be an important step in making criminal justice more equitable. For example, David Cole writes that the "story of the enforcement of the right to counsel suggests that our failure to make good on *Gideon*'s promise is no mere mistake. Rather, it is the single most important mechanism by which the courts and society ensure a double standard in constitutional rights protection in the criminal law."

In reality, full enforcement of *Gideon* probably would not significantly impact the "double standard." If mass incarceration and racial disparities were caused by poor defense attorneys, it would make sense to think of *Gideon* as the appropriate solution. But defenders are not the cause.

Gideon was decided during the 1960s, a period during which, according to Mark Tushnet, the Supreme Court took a "brief, perhaps aberrational, and sometimes overstated role . . . in advancing progressive goals." Perhaps that was why it seemed, at the time, like a victory for the poor and minorities. *Gideon* was one of those classic Warren Court opinions that provided hope not just about criminal justice, but about economic and racial justice as well.

That hope is long gone. If *Gideon* was supposed to make the criminal justice system fairer for poor people and minorities, it has been a spectacular failure. The National Right to Counsel Committee, a panel that was created in 2004 to conduct a comprehensive survey of the state of indigent defense, reported:

> The right to counsel is now accepted as a fundamental precept of American justice. . . . Yet, today, in criminal and juvenile proceedings in state courts, sometimes counsel is not provided at all, and it often is supplied in ways that make a mockery of the great promise of the *Gideon* decision and the Supreme Court's soaring rhetoric.

Nancy Leong notes that *Gideon* has been "widely and accurately hailed as a milestone in protecting the rights of individual defendants." This assertion is correct, as far as it goes. *Gideon* did protect the "rights" of defendants; it turns out, however, that protecting defendants' rights is quite different from protecting defendants. Fifty years after *Gideon*, poor people have both the right to counsel and the most massive level of incarceration in the world. As stated earlier in this essay, since *Gideon*, rates of incarceration (which, in the United States, applies mainly to the poor) and racial disparities have multiplied. The right to have a lawyer, at trial or even during the plea bargaining stage, has little impact on either of those central problems.

What poor people, and black people, need from criminal justice is to be stopped less, arrested less, prosecuted less, incarcerated less. Considering other needs that poor people have—food and shelter—Mark Tushnet has stated, "[D]emanding that those needs be satisfied—whether or not satisfying them can today persuasively be characterized as enforcing a right—strikes me as more likely to succeed than claiming that existing rights to food and shelter must be enforced."

Gideon diverts attention from economic and racial critiques of the criminal justice system. In addition to its diversion function, *Gideon* also provides a legitimation of the status quo. The poor—especially the poor and black—are incarcerated at exponentially greater levels now than when *Gideon* was decided. If more poor people are represented by lawyers because of *Gideon*, arguably their trials or plea bargains are fairer than before *Gideon*, when they did not have lawyers. Thus, the poor have simultaneously received a fairer process and more punishment. *Gideon* makes it more work—and thus more difficult—to make economic and racial critiques of criminal justice. This is not to say people cannot and do not make those claims, but rather that *Gideon* makes their arguments less persuasive. It creates a formal equality between the rich and the poor because now they both have lawyers. The vast overrepresentation of the poor in America's prisons appears more like a narrative about personal responsibility than an indictment of criminal justice. In the words of one commentator, "Procedural fairness not only produces faith in the outcome of individual trials; it reinforces faith in the legal system as a whole."

The End of Public Defenders*

Matthew Caldwell
2022

A little more than fifteen years ago, I began my career as a public defender. Propelled by outrage, I was encouraged to see my work as a crucial check on law enforcement—and I did. A few years in, working in Miami and then various offices in New York City, I began to question the role of public defenders. Are we a check or a collaborator? I wanted to be part of an equalizing force, and yet it felt that much of my job came down to assisting the court, however unwillingly, in extracting guilty pleas from my clients and thereby burying misconduct on the part of the police, the prosecution, and the court. Many of my colleagues were noticing the same thing. Was our perspective unreasonably cynical? We saw the creation of the public defender system as an inspired moment in our nation's history, when human rights and decency won out.

For years, I lived in this schism: Where what I was seeing

---

* Matthew Caldwell, "The End of Public Defenders," *Inquest*, February 25, 2022.

and what I was told I should be seeing didn't line up. Was I hallucinating that parts of my job were aligned with the interests of law enforcement? About a year ago, I read a new history of the public defender that said to me, *What you're seeing is real.* The creation of the public defender was not a victory of human rights, I came to learn. Instead, it was a formative step in the expansion of our system of mass arrest, guilty pleas, and incarceration. I had been sold a bill of goods, it turned out, as far as my role in our criminal legal system goes, but I had also found a new well of outrage to draw upon—and with it, a path forward.

As Sara Mayeux recounts in her excellent *Free Justice: A History of the Public Defender in Twentieth-Century America*, what we call our public defender system wasn't created by Progressive Era lawyers, or by socialists, or by a man named Gideon holding the line against injustice. Rather, as Mayeux tells the story, it was the result of many years of behind-the-curtain work by white, wealthy attorneys. The solution that public defenders offered, in their view, was a path through which the legal establishment could avoid overhauling the criminal "justice" system by simply providing lawyers to everyone caught in it.

Voices of the poor, and anyone who was not an elite attorney, were excluded from any meaningful input in the design of the public defender system. By the middle of the twentieth century, the Cold War was all-consuming for these attorneys, and a motivating interest for their concept of the public defender became positioning "democratic justice" over communism. In this context, defense counsel in a purely adversarial legal system was "elevated into an essential element of what made trials not only fair, but also democratic," Mayeux writes. In other words, the real problem was not actual racial and economic injustice, but the appearance of procedural injustice. It wasn't that there were too many unlawful arrests, but that we had too few lawyers ready to process them all.

Cases like that of the Scottsboro Boys and *Betts v. Brady* laid bare an emerging catastrophe: the police and professional prosecutors, who were still finding their footing in this nascent system of punishment, saw their role as making arrests and securing convictions. The legal establishment, however, saw the problem as a lack of adequate counsel. The solution was not to reform the police, prosecutors, or the courts, if that even occurred to them. Their solution was to give everyone lawyers, allowing the great and ruinous gears of our fledgling criminal "justice" system to grind on—and with that, to destroy entire communities. The public defender system, in other words, wasn't created to defend the public, nor was it designed to deliver justice. It was built to handle the traffic. The Supreme Court essentially ratified the work of these elite, establishment attorneys in 1963 in the landmark *Gideon v. Wainwright*.

That case was decided long before it got to Washington. As Mayeux notes, one justice who played a role in its outcome later remarked that "no lawyer could have lost that case." *Gideon*, though widely touted as a triumph for David, was entirely Goliath's victory in that it finally scrubbed *the public* out of the public defender. Mass incarceration exists and grows not in spite of but by way of our public defense system.

We continue to use the term *public defender* because we want it to be true, even though the conception of the institutional defender was essential in the development of the criminal legal system. By and large, we maintain a concept of our American criminal courtroom as an acceptable venue for productive engagement of adequately matched adversaries. The title *public defender* helps to obscure the overriding purpose of our courts: to remind workers and the poor that they are not in control and, should they forget, that there is a fate worse than poverty waiting for them. Slapping *that* term onto *this* system erroneously suggests that some kind of popular uprising is possible within its structure—and that's the point. We want the fantasy. This idea of a corps of lawyers acting as a bulwark against injustice lends an air of legitimacy to the enterprise of police barreling through poor communities, often with excessive force and other demeaning tactics, to arrest millions of people who are then processed through the legal system by prosecutors and judges.

With this legitimacy comes structural support. Many of our clients are arrested in overpoliced, under-resourced neighborhoods and plead guilty to simply end the case and its intractable disruption to their life; many more do so to avoid the risk of extreme punishment after trial. By participating in this process, public defenders imbue the ensuing convictions with a kind of constitutional integrity, rendering them all but impervious to attack on appeal. The same protection is granted to any police action that gave rise to the arrest. Almost every illegal stop and instance of misconduct by the police is excused by a guilty plea, a process that depends on the presence of a lawyer. If, in the public imagination, those lawyers are embattled heroes sincerely wearing the badge of public defender, however, then perhaps the process doesn't seem so devious after all.

The integral role of public defenders within our system of mass incarceration lives alongside our active support of reform. Many, in fact, take the job for the purpose of being a part of changing the criminal legal system. I know I did. And all of us do play a crucial role in the individual lives of our clients once they are trafficked into the criminal legal system by the police. One of the things that's most confounding about being a public defender is our bifurcated awareness: that the work is critical and useful on an individual scale, even as it directly supports a violent system of racist control of the poor. It is impossible to do the former without the latter, overwhelmingly so considering that so much of our work ends in standing next to a client as they plead guilty.

Public defenders, myself included, march in protest against injustice in the criminal legal system, as we are right to do. But we mustn't also blind ourselves to how our daily work contributes to the expansion of the system we are protesting. This is true even for those of us who practice our craft at the highest levels. The legitimacy of the system depends on a warehouse of quick-witted defense attorneys whom police and judges can point to when asked whether their actions were, or are, constitutional. Without us, there wouldn't be mass arrests and inhumane conditions of confinement. The system might just grind to a halt.

In New York City, for example, public defender offices quietly compete against each other in a bidding process to represent all the people whom the police are expected to arrest in a given year. An office may contract to represent forty thousand people in the coming year, and that office is expected to meet that forty thousand number to remain competitive in subsequent contract negotiations. On the one hand we decry unnecessary arrests, but on the other we need to make our numbers in order to get paid. How can we conduct ourselves that way and still claim that the endless flood of arrests is something that is happening to us and we are powerless to stop it? When are we going to stop merely protesting the inadequacy of police reform and take greater responsibility in forcing the hand of police, prosecutors, and the courts?

Every day that this status quo persists, we show that we are not antagonists of the system. We *are* the system.

Why Public Defenders Matter More Than Ever in a Time of Reform*

John F. Pfaff

2018

In 1963, the Supreme Court handed down *Gideon v. Wainwright*, which held that the government had to provide a lawyer to any poor defendant facing prison time. While often trumpeted as one of the Court's greatest modern decisions, it has also been embroiled in controversy from the beginning. Like all Supreme Court opinions that impose new obligations on state governments, *Gideon* was an unfunded mandate—and, given the political unpopularity of criminal defendants, the states have aggressively gone out of their way to make sure that this constitutional obligation stays unfunded.

Critics of the American criminal justice system have often

* John F. Pfaff, "Why Public Defenders Matter More Than Ever in a Time of Reform," *The Appeal*, April 18, 2018.

pointed to *Gideon*'s failure as a major cause of mass incarceration, and of mass punishment more broadly. And they have proposed myriad ways, including increasing defender funding, to try to fix or repair or improve how we provide legal services to the poor. I count myself among those who have done so, having argued that funding indigent defense nationwide is one of the few steps the federal government could take that would really make a difference (although this is obviously not something that *this* administration would do).

To many, realizing *Gideon*'s vision of effective counsel for all is seen as one of the, if not *the*, most important steps toward real criminal justice reform that we can take. Indeed, one of the more high-profile reform groups is Gideon's Promise, a nonprofit that partners with public defender offices around the country to implement best practices in public defense and has been the subject of a documentary aired on HBO.

There is no doubt that the work public defenders do is vitally important, and there is no doubt that they are underfunded—both in absolute terms, and compared to far better-funded prosecutor offices. Improved funding for indigent defense should be an important part of criminal justice reform.

But what if an emphasis on *Gideon* raises serious problems at a more fundamental level? What if pouring money into indigent defense really wouldn't make the sort of difference for which many hope? What if *Gideon* distracts us from what really matters—or, worse, what if focusing on *Gideon* makes more impactful reforms *harder*?

Georgetown University law professor Paul Butler made just this argument a few years ago in a provocatively titled *Yale Law Journal* piece, "Poor People Lose: *Gideon* and the Critique of Rights" (a not-at-all-stuffy-law-review essay everyone should read). Butler raised several powerful points, but here I want to focus on just one of them: that mass incarceration and mass punishment are not really the product of procedural break-downs in individual cases—which is the implicit assumption of *Gideon*-focused reforms—but rather the result of systemic and systematic decisions about who to arrest, to charge, to send to prison.

I think Butler's critique is spot-on. And, even just a few years ago, it was a powerful argument against directing too much attention and resources toward *Gideon*. But the politics of criminal justice have changed sharply over the past few years, and so too has, perhaps, the role that *Gideon* can play in bringing about real change.

For Butler and others, the jumping-off point of *Gideon*'s limitation is something that often gets overlooked in all the discussions of wrongful convictions, *Brady* violations,[1] false confessions, bad forensics, and conviction integrity units: most—perhaps almost all—who are arrested, charged, convicted, and sentenced are guilty of a crime. Our criminal laws are sprawling, open-ended codes that punish people for wide swaths of behavior. More often than not, defense work is about triage, about minimizing the harms that come from an almost-guaranteed—and legally sound—conviction.

The core problem with *Gideon*-focused reform is that mass incarceration is driven by decisions made by police and prosecutors about *who* to arrest and *who* to charge, not procedural issues about *how* the arrest is made or *how* the trial or plea bargain is conducted. The criminal justice system is a blunt tool, and not everyone who violates the terms of a criminal statute should be arrested, charged, convicted, sentenced.

In fact, Butler suggests that focusing on *Gideon* might make reforms *harder*, by effectively white-washing the substantive injustices of our criminal justice system, such as disparities in which groups (such as low-income Black men) face higher risks of arrests, charges, and convictions, for the same conduct.

So while evidence suggests that competent indigent defense makes a difference—what few studies we have suggest that those with better lawyers are less likely to be convicted or serve less prison time—the traditional role of public defenders is individualistic and reactive: They handle the specific cases that the police arrest and the prosecutors charge.

In other words, while improving the often-frightening procedural failings of the criminal process is important work, real reform lies far more in changing the systemic choices made by police and prosecutors. The decisions about where to deploy police, what sort of arrest policies to have, what sort of cases prosecutors get charged vs. dismissed—these are the decisions that really drive mass punishment.

This is why, Butler suggests, focusing on *Gideon* risks making reform harder. If everyone has a decent lawyer, then we might be less troubled by *why* some people are more likely to need that lawyer in the first place.

Yet, suddenly, perhaps public defenders are in a position to make these changes. Perhaps today, *Gideon* can serve a new substantive function.

Over the past few years, at least in more urban counties, voters have started to push prosecutors to adopt less harsh and more progressive policies. The changes they demand are systemic, not individualistic: to no longer ask for cash bail in entire categories of cases, to stop prosecuting entire types of offenses (such as marijuana and low-level theft), and so on. Prosecutors are facing political pressure to shift from "tough on crime" to something far more like "smart on crime," and they are increasingly making promises along those lines.

But promises are just words, and sometimes it seems like prosecutors running for election or re-election are quickly learning a set of reformist buzzwords they can trot out to voters—but then struggle to implement in practice. Many observers were deeply disappointed with former Brooklyn District Attorney Ken Thompson's broken promises on declining to prosecute low-level marijuana cases. Thompson died of cancer in the fall of 2016 and court monitors report that under Brooklyn's current DA, Eric Gonzalez, they still see marijuana possession cases whenever they're in court. Manhattan DA Cy Vance, meanwhile, continues to promise to stop charging people with jumping turnstiles, yet seems to keep doing so.

The potential disconnect between promise and practice has become sufficiently concerning that at least in New York City, a group of nonprofits, including a coalition of public defenders, recently created Court Watch NYC, which sends observers to courts across the city to make sure that DAs are living up to their reformist promises.

The role of public defenders is thus clear: They're in the best position to ensure that progressive-sounding prosecutors fulfill their campaign promises. Unlike court watchers, they are present at every step of the process—not just public hearings, some of which might be held in the middle of the night—but the behind-closed-doors plea bargaining processes that resolve about 95 percent of all cases. They see the charges that prosecutors threaten and then withdraw, the factors that seem to shape prosecutors' decisions about when they drop charges and when they move forward, and so on.

Real reform requires real data, but prosecutor offices are notoriously stingy with their numbers. About 80 percent of all defendants nationwide qualify for indigent representation, which means that while defender offices do not handle every case, they handle most, and a data-rich annual report from a public defender's office would inevitably provide a detailed picture of what the prosecutor's office is up to as well.

As voters, or at least urban voters, increasingly demand a new form of criminal justice, there is increasingly a role for public defenders to ensure that *substantive, systemic* change happens. All of this, however, takes time—and money. If public defender offices cannot fulfill their basic ethical—and constitutional—obligations to represent their clients, they certainly can't start generating data or court-watching reports.

In fact, the role of public defender offices could expand even more. When criticized for being excessively harsh, prosecutors often like to say that they are only doing what the legislature has instructed them to do. It's a doubly disingenuous claim, not just because "prosecutorial discretion" means that prosecutors are not *required* to be as harsh as the legislature permits, only that they can be—but because many of those tough laws come about from aggressive lobbying by statewide district attorney associations.

Historically, public defenders have played primarily procedural roles—profoundly important, constitutional roles to be sure, and ones that should be far better funded than they are, even if you ignore all the arguments I've made here. But mass incarceration and mass punishment are not really the products of procedural failings at the trial stage. They are far more the result of discretionary choices by police and prosecutors, as well as judges and legislators. Yet in this reformist moment, as voters demand smarter policies from still-opaque prosecutor offices, and as legislators seem more open to less-punitive approaches to social problems, public defenders are well positioned to play a critical role—which makes the role of *Gideon* all the more important.

Ten Things Public Defenders Can Do to Stand Up for Racial Justice*

Jeff Adachi
2015

The wheels of justice may turn slowly, but they still flatten countless Americans trapped beneath their weight.

We'll look back at this moment in history as a tipping point: When entire communities scarred from police brutality and weary from racial profiling looked upon the broken bodies of unarmed citizens and said "enough is enough." When the Black Lives Matter movement harnessed the frustration wrought by mass incarceration and delivered it directly to Main Street.

Next stop: the courtroom. And there is nobody in the system more qualified to confront bias and demand change than public defenders.

---

* Jeff Adachi, "Ten Things Public Defenders Can Do to Stand Up for Racial Justice," *Medium*, September 28, 2015.

There are more than twenty-five thousand public defenders and thousands more legal aid attorneys across the country who fight like hell for the rights of their clients. Most of these clients are black and brown. All are poor.

The color of our clients matters because the U.S. criminal justice system has a race problem. Uncontroverted studies show African Americans are more likely to be stopped, detained, imprisoned, and convicted than their white counterparts. Many roads led to this morass of racial disparity: biased policing, prosecutorial overcharging, and explicit and implicit bias by judges who set bail and sentence persons convicted of crimes.

It is public defender clients who bear the brunt of racial discrimination. The fact is, we are already in the trenches. So let's brush up on our fighting techniques. Here are ten things that public defenders can do to litigate racial justice issues in court:

1. Talk About Race with Prospective Jurors

   In cases where the race of the accused is an issue, or there are other issues such as cross-racial identification, public defenders must screen jurors who may hold biases that affect their decision-making. This includes discussing implicit bias, the unconscious cognitive processes that cause us to rely on stereotypes in our judgments. The U.S. Supreme Court has held that lawyers have a constitutional right to question jurors on racial prejudices when a "reasonable probability" exists that such views would affect their ability to be fair.

2. Insist on Diverse Juries

   While we are often reminded that we are entitled to a jury of our peers, the reality can be quite different. In San Francisco, we recently convened a panel of ninety prospective jurors for the trial of our black client. There wasn't a single African American in the bunch. A study by Duke University found juries formed from all-white jury pools convicted black defendants 16 percent more often than white defendants. Public defenders should make note when there are no minorities on a jury and even consider filing to jury challenge when the panel is not representative of the client's community.

3. Report Prosecutors Who Use Their Peremptory Challenges to Strike Black Jurors Without Just Cause

The High Court ruled in the landmark *Batson v. Kentucky* that prosecutors cannot use their jury challenges to strike a person due to race. Unfortunately, the practice remains rampant according to recent studies. Public defenders need to make *Batson* challenges whenever prosecutors exercise their challenges in a discriminatory manner. Prosecutors who violate their oath of fairness can also be reported to the state bar for discipline.

4. Report and Challenge Biased Judges

Most states have ethical codes that prohibit judges from discriminating based on race. Yet studies have shown that judges are as susceptible to the same explicit and implicit biases that plague all of us. Statutes often allow parties to challenge a judge who has expressed racial biases, and public defenders should raise these challenges when grounds exist. Judges who express bias should also be reported to judicial discipline bodies.

5. Insist on Bail Hearings and Raise Racial Disparities in Pre-trial Incarceration

Studies have shown that minorities are more likely than whites to be held in jail while awaiting trial. Many jurisdictions disproportionately confine people of color by setting unreasonably high bails. Public defenders can and should demand bail hearings, even after bail is set, to challenge the amount and raise the issue of disproportionate confinement. We recently began doing this in San Francisco, and experienced a 30 percent success rate in winning freedom for our clients or reducing their bail.

6. Sponsor a Court Watch Program

Why has police brutality received so much more attention than injustice in the courtroom? Because what happens in court is largely hidden from the public's view. Many Americans are surprised to discover they have a right to watch what happens inside the halls of justice. San Francisco's Court Watch program encourages community members and youth to attend court hearings. The group confers with public defenders to learn more about the system and its treatment of minorities, so they may become watchdogs of fairness in the courtroom.

7. Identify Unfair Charging Patterns by Prosecutors

Public defenders should review their cases to determine if the prosecution is charging individuals of one race differently than another. Recently, I had a case where a young African American man with no prior record was charged with felony gun possession while a white man accused of the same crime under similar circumstances was charged as a misdemeanor. Raising this glaring inequity resulted in a favorable outcome for my client. In another local case, the federal public defender made a motion for discriminatory prosecution following drug stings in which all thirty-seven people arrested were African American. One of the officers involved in the arrests was caught on video directing his team to arrest an African-American rather than a non-African-American alleged drug dealer.

8. Collect Statistics

Unless you can show the data, you're just acting on a hunch. Public defenders can play a vital role by collecting statistics on illegal stops and searches, racial profiling and other forms of police or governmental misconduct. San Francisco recently passed legislation requiring the police department to keep statistics on race and gender in all of its traffic stops, detentions, arrests, and searches. San Francisco's Reentry Council also commissioned a report quantifying unequal treatment from arrest to sentencing.

9. Form a Racial Justice Committee

Harness your collective power by organizing to propose solutions to eradicating racism in the system. Our office formed a racial justice committee in 2013, and the committee was successful in implementing a nine-point plan for reform, which included body cameras, collection of race statistics, and other initiatives. Our attorneys also banded together with public defenders from other counties to create the Bay Area-wide Public Defenders for Racial Justice, which provides valuable training. Draw from the collective brain trust in your office and work with other agents, such as the ACLU, Black Lives Matter, and local legislators, to implement needed system reforms.

10. Let Your Clients Know You Care

As public defenders, we often become jaded to the system treating people differently based on their race. It may seem like a hopelessly entrenched problem. But

we need to talk with our clients about these realities so
they will be empowered to stand up for justice in their
own case—whether that means going to trial, or simply understanding their public defender "gets it" and is
sensitive to the struggle going on in this country.

Public defenders can support the Black Lives Matter movement by litigating against racial injustice wherever we find it.
We must also educate community members on the vital role
that public defenders play as watchdogs of the constitution and
protectors of civil rights. It is our obligation to ensure the system is accountable to the public it serves. We must work collectively and collaboratively to improve outcomes for our clients
and their families and strategically fight for the eradication of
racism in the criminal justice system.

Black on Black Representation*

Alexis Hoag-Fordjour

2021

Black people are overrepresented in the criminal legal system, the majority of whom are indigent and qualify for public defenders or appointed counsel. Given the lack of racial diversity in the legal profession, the system overwhelmingly appoints white lawyers to represent indigent Black clients. For instance, over 70 percent of assistant federal public defenders are white, with white men making up the largest subgroup at 40.5 percent; among Criminal Justice Act attorneys who federal courts appoint to represent indigent defendants, approximately 80 percent are white.

As a solution, this article calls for the expansion of the Sixth Amendment right to counsel of choice for all indigent defendants. Extending choice to indigent defendants reinforces the principles underlying the Sixth Amendment right to counsel

---

* Alexis Hoag-Fordjour, "Black on Black Representation," *New York University Law Review* 96, no. 5 (November 2021): 1493–1548.

and can help strengthen the attorney-client relationship. Given the focus of this article, the expansion would also grant a defendant the autonomy to request counsel who shares their race and/or to select culturally competent counsel if they believed that lawyer could best represent them. Empowering indigent Black people to select, should they desire, Black and/or culturally competent public defenders also has the potential to help mitigate anti-Black racism in the criminal legal system.

Black lawyers often have the experiential knowledge of what it is like to move through the world with the social meaning attached to Blackness and thus firsthand knowledge of the corresponding treatment and dangers. I call this "embodied empathy." As a result, many Black public defenders have a greater ability to understand and empathize with the stressors and circumstances that resulted in the criminal charges their clients face, and to recognize the humanity in their clients. This embodied empathy enables many Black defenders to build rapport more readily with their clients and to establish trust, both of which can contribute to improved representation. Constitutionally effective representation depends upon a trusting attorney-client relationship. And as this article demonstrates, Black clients tend to form a more trusting relationship with Black counsel given the shared social meaning assigned to race in this country.

The overrepresentation of Black people in the criminal legal system reflects longstanding structural racism born from slavery and the racial hierarchy that resulted. It also stems from the strength of anti-Black bias that stereotypes Black people as dangerous and criminal. These stereotypes are direct descendants of slavery, which produced a racialized caste system. In her book, *Caste*, journalist Isabel Wilkerson explains: "What people look like, or, rather, the race they have been assigned

or are perceived to belong to, is the visible cue to their caste."
The public then relies on caste as an "historic flash card" to
determine "how [people] are to be treated, where they are expected to live, . . . [and] whether they may be shot by authorities
with impunity." Historian Khalil Muhammad calls it "racial
criminalization: the stigmatization of crime as '[B]lack'" while
simultaneously "masking . . . crime among whites as individual failure." Studies show that police stop and question Black
people at higher rates; prosecutors file more serious charges
when the suspect is Black and the victim is white; defense attorneys are more likely to recommend plea bargains for Black
clients that impose longer sentences than those they would
recommend for similarly situated white clients; and judges and
juries impermissibly consider race when determining whether
to convict and what sentence to impose.

What if the law empowered indigent defendants to choose
counsel who they believed could best represent them? Some
federal appellate courts have concluded that the right to counsel "would be without substance if it did not include the right to
a meaningful attorney-client relationship."

For many defendants, quality representation includes how
well counsel hears, believes, and understands them and
how well counsel tells their story. Whether counsel is competent and has the capacity to provide adequate representation—
factors trial courts consider when defendants request to substitute counsel—misses the mark. Further, the Court frames
these factors as a negative—the floor that counsel should not
fall below. Instead, a defendant may prioritize positive factors,
such as a lawyer with the ability to overcome the presumption
of dangerousness and criminality that society and the legal
system assign Black defendants. In fact, "[o]ur system of laws
generally presumes that the criminal defendant . . . knows

his own best interests and does not need them dictated by the State."

Black public defenders may be able to more readily see, hear, and understand their Black clients and, as importantly, Black clients tend to more readily see, hear, and understand their Black lawyers. At each turn in the system, a Black indigent defendant faces potentially hostile decisionmakers whose anti-Black bias may cloud judgment and detrimentally impact the defendant's case. Public defenders, like all of us, harbor anti-Black bias. Such bias can manifest in small or large ways, such as defense counsel mistaking another Black person in a courtroom for their client, or in negotiating a less favorable plea agreement on behalf of a Black client relative to an otherwise similarly situated white client. However, research shows that Black defenders harbor less anti-Black bias than do their non-Black counterparts. Moreover, Black defenders may be more likely to recognize racism and raise race-based challenges by virtue of their experience as Black people. In this way, Black defense counsel are particularly well-situated to challenge anti-Black racial bias whenever it arises in the client's case.

Two decades after [researchers] recognized that extending the right [to choose counsel] would likely improve the attorney-client relationship, their arguments led a small community in Texas to enable indigent defendants to select counsel of their choosing among a list of court-approved lawyers. The one-year pilot program, the first of its kind in the nation, appeared to work. Relative to non-choice defendants, client choice defendants were more likely to perceive that their lawyer treated them with respect. With regard to outcomes, although most cases involved the defendant pleading guilty, significantly more choice defendants pled to lesser charges, more choice defendants went to trial than non-choice, and choice defendants were more likely to receive a sentence of community service rather than incarceration.

These benefits to the outcomes of choice defendants' cases demonstrate that there may be something more at stake than merely exercising agency, which by itself is still a worthy priority. These benefits suggest that when a defendant is able to exercise choice, it fosters trust; and with trust comes an improved attorney-client relationship, which can offer multiple benefits, including better case outcomes.

Manhattan DA Race 2021: A Voter Guide*

Five Boro Defenders
2021

NOT AN ENDORSEMENT

As public defenders and students of abolition, we do not embrace any candidate for District Attorney. The role of the prosecutor, no matter how "progressive," will always be harmful to the communities we represent because of our fundamental belief that prosecutors do not deliver justice. Justice comes from accountability within the community. Prosecutors do not make us safe; safety arises when a community has its basic health, economic, housing, and educational needs met.

We witness daily the harm created by the racist and dangerously retributive policies of Manhattan District Attorney

---

* Five Boro Defenders, *Manhattan DA Race 2021: A Voter Guide* (self-published, 2021). Five Boro Defenders (5BD) describes itself as "an informal collective of public defenders, civil rights attorneys, and advocates fighting for the rights of indigent New Yorkers."

Cy Vance and his assistants in the name of the "People of New York"—policies which reinforce and contribute to the continuing harm of racist policing and mass incarceration. The role of the prosecutor in our legal system, no matter who they are, is a role that harms individuals and communities. With this in mind, we recognize that some candidates are likely to cause more harm than others. The aim of this guide is to inform voters and would-be endorsers as to where we, as practitioners, believe candidates fall on a harm-to-community scale as compared to one another and to Vance.

Vance is responsible for caging the most New Yorkers on Rikers Island out of any citywide District Attorney. He pursues low-level offenses and refuses to hold police accountable, and has not addressed deep corruption within his office. He has notoriously served the wealthy and special interests, declining to pursue cases against campaign donors such as Harvey Weinstein and the Trump family until it was politically expedient, all while relentlessly incarcerating and targeting Black and brown New Yorkers for prosecution. True transformative change will require a DA that addresses the devastating legacy Vance will leave behind.

WE WANT TO SHRINK THE POWER OF THE DA

The DA decides who to charge, what to charge, what kind of alternatives to incarceration to offer, and what length of sentence to seek. A position imbued with this much power and discretion is downright dangerous. While certainly a "progressive prosecutor" is a better alternative to a traditional law-and-order prosecutor, too often these self-styled "progressive" candidates want to maintain their discretion and power while simply reorganizing and redirecting it. We want to end it. No one politician should wield such extraordinary power. No one politician should control such a massive budget. Vance's 2019 budget was the largest of all six citywide offices, including the special narcotics prosecutor. Despite a decrease in crime, Vance has consistently increased the size of his largest-in-NYC staff, all while prosecuting the people of the third most populous borough.

We want to defund and shrink the power of the DA in service of our mission to abolish the DA, just as we fight to defund and abolish the police. We want to divest from the prison industrial complex and ensure that funding goes directly to support communities through community-led initiatives like violence interrupters, safe injection sites, community and youth centers, public health sites, mental health resources, child care, public schools, and after-school programs—in short, resources that will make communities safer and ensure that communities thrive, free of jail and prison walls.

GUIDE CREATION AND METHODOLOGY

This guide is not the opinion of 5BD as a whole, but of our working group, largely made up of practitioners in Manhattan criminal courts. Our evaluations are based on ninety-minute interviews with the candidates that took place in November 2020, public statements, and information they have provided on websites and social media, synthesized and filtered through our experiences witnessing the racist and dangerously retributive policies of DA Vance and his assistants. We recognize that candidates continue to introduce new policy papers and even change positions as the race continues. We did our best to encapsulate the information we had access to at the close of

2020 in our analysis and evaluations. After publication of this guide, we will continue to monitor changes or inconsistencies in platforms or positions and provide updates via our Twitter account.

This guide has a clear point of view: we are adversaries of the prosecutor and students of abolition who want to shrink the power of the prosecutor until it is abolished. Our questions were designed to understand and evaluate which candidate's policies would focus on shrinking their power, not redirecting it. We sought to understand which candidates understood the racism that pervades every aspect of policing and prosecution and who has a plan to address and eradicate that harm. We also evaluated the candidates' ability to follow through on their proposals, their understanding of the intricacies of criminal law, and the inner workings of the Manhattan DA's office. We wanted to know if candidates had a plan to "clean house" and whether they had a team ready to implement their policies.

We organized our interview questions into distinct issue areas and provided those general topics, but not the specific questions, to the candidates before the interviews. While candidates were allotted ninety minutes for the interview, every candidate was asked to restrict their answers to our specific questions and we often found ourselves without sufficient time to allow a candidate to expand at great length upon an issue of particular interest to their campaign. Additionally, for every issue area, we finished with "commitment" questions to which we asked candidates to only answer yes or no. After the interviews, we further refined the topics into the issue areas discussed below. We considered the candidates' commitment to anti-racism in every issue area. It should be noted that some topics span many issue areas—for example, gang policing and prosecutions. When considering responses on gang policing and prosecutions, we mostly scored those answers in our "policing the police" issue area but also considered some aspects of candidate answers in the "support for decarceral outcomes and sentencing" issue area.

OUR RUBRIC

Every member of the working group who took part in the evaluations participated in or watched every candidate interview and then worked in both small-group and large-group evaluations using a rubric we created together to rank each candidate's positions and policies. We first ranked Vance based on our experiences as practitioners to get a baseline. We then ranked each candidate, keeping in mind Vance's scores and our score for the other candidates. We assessed candidates' interview answers, public platforms, known history, and public comments in specific focus areas and applied the rubric to answers from each area. We then broke down each rubric into numeric values for easy assignment and placed the candidates on a comparative scale ranging from most potential harm to least potential harm.

OUR FOCUS AREAS

DEFUNDING THE DA AND PROSECUTORIAL
   ACCOUNTABILITY
COMBATTING SYSTEMIC RACISM
POLICING THE POLICE
ABOLISHING CASH BAIL AND PRETRIAL
   DETENTION

ENDING THE CRIMINALIZATION OF POVERTY,
   MENTAL ILLNESS, AND SUBSTANCE USE
SUPPORT FOR DECARCERAL OUTCOMES AND
   SENTENCING
COMMITMENT TO THE PRESUMPTION OF
   INNOCENCE
CORRECTING PAST HARMS

1,862 Fewer Years
in Prison*

Raj Jayadev
2015

These photos behind me are of people waiting in line back in my hometown of San José, California, getting ready to go into court. They're connected by one looming, anxiety-filled question, "Will I go to prison or jail? Will I be part of the over two million people incarcerated in this country?"

[Many of these] people [feel like they have to] face the justice system [alone. And] unsure of how to navigate those courts [and] separated from their families and communities, almost all take a plea deal, meaning they'll never see their day in a trial court.

But we have a response. We make the family an essential and effective part of the defense team, so they could change the

---

* Raj Jayadev, "1,862 Fewer Years in Prison," *PopTech*, October 23, 2015, 5:44 (video transcript, edited with author's permission).

outcome of cases and transform the landscape of power in the court system.

We call this model participatory defense. It works like this: people who are facing the justice system convene in a weekly meeting with other families who have loved ones that are facing the courts. Together they build a community out of what otherwise would have been an isolating, intimidating process. When they meet, they begin by writing the names of their loved ones on a whiteboard. Collectively, they go through every single name, identifying specific places where the family can have tangible impact on the outcome of the case. They identify tactics like creating biographical material, so that their loved one is understood by the courts as a person, not as just a case file. They review police reports and point out inconsistencies that prove innocence. They work with the public defender, who now has a new resource at their disposal, and who is as committed as they are in seeking justice for the client.

The results have been remarkable. We've seen charges dismissed and sentences significantly reduced. We've seen not-guilty verdicts. We've seen successful appeals by people who were initially wrongfully convicted.

We have one ceremony we do each time a loved one comes home. Up until then, they've been just a name that we've seen on the board or only understood through a mom's story. That person is given an eraser, and they walk over to the board, and they erase their name. And it means that the family has been made whole. For those other families who are just starting the journey, going through the most frightening times of their lives, it means that there is hope for them too if they engage and participate.

To show you how this works, I want to introduce you to Cornell. Cornell pled guilty to a low-level drug charge, but he was facing a five-year prison sentence. As a single father, his main concern was, what would happen with his two young girls if he got locked up? So we gave him a camera. We said, "take pictures of what it's like being a dad." He took pictures of making the girls breakfast, taking them to school, and driving them to volleyball practice. He made a photo essay that he gave to his public defender, who used it at the sentencing hearing.

The result? That five years of prison was transformed into a six-month outpatient drug program. That meant Cornell could be with his two young girls, and his daughters would have a father in their lives. And Cornell could get the treatment that he was seeking for himself and for the future of his family.

Cornell is not the only story like this. We have one metric that we use in participatory defense, which we call "time saved." It's a play on the term "time served," which is what the courts call terms of incarceration. We look at what the family was facing when they first came to us versus what they actually received. Cornell represents five years in time saved. When we reviewed all our cases, we totaled the numbers, and we had 1,862 years of time saved. Those are years with parents in their children's lives, of young people going to college instead of prison, of generational cycles of suffering that had been eliminated. All from the power, will, and intellect of families.

We're training communities all across the country now. And when you go back to your hometown, I would ask that you do this: if you see a line peeking out the courthouse doors in your city, know that those people are not necessarily just the fodder of mass incarceration on a conveyor belt to jail or prison. They are potentially the founding mothers and fathers of a new movement that may change the way justice is experienced and exercised in America forever.

Interview with Raj Jayadev, Conducted by Premal Dharia*

Summer 2023

Dharia: It is exciting to talk to you almost a decade after you gave this talk. Looking back on your work, can you say something about how the participatory defense model has changed the court process?

Jayadev: Here's an example. We created a form that public defenders can use with families who come to court. At a bail hearing, the public defender turns to the courtroom pews and says, "Hey, if you are here for a loved one, De-Bug[1] is in the back of the room, they're going to help you understand what's going on today. And they will explain how your presence here could have an impact on the bail decision."

Then people's families walk up to the De-Bug represen-

---

* Interview with Raj Jayadev, Conducted by Premal Dharia, Summer 2023.

tative, and fill out this little form explaining things like, "my son's lived here his whole life," or "my mom just started college, and she'll lose that if she stays locked up," or "my dad is the one that takes the kids to school." Those type of things. Then we give that sheet to the public defenders like a cheat sheet. Now the public defender can tell a judge about why incarceration is particularly harmful for this person. Their family can then stand up in court, the auntie and uncle are here. And they can say, "Judge, you have no reason anymore to keep this high bail or keep our loved one detained pretrial." And this process has had impact. We saw dramatic decreases of people being held on money bail or detained pretrial.

Dharia: Can you talk about how your work has grown since you gave that talk?

Jayadev: Since then, the core group of folks that built the practice have gone to other places across the country to train people in the practice. We now have over forty participatory defense hubs across the country who are all doing the same practice. They draw from the same values and principles that motivate our work in San Jose, but they fold it into the rhythm and culture of the places they go. We see that each has had the same type of impact—each new site has its own erasing-the-name ceremonies, each has moms that first came for their sons, who then become part of the leadership that are growing and sustaining participatory defense. That's the physics of this work. That's how participatory distinguishes itself from, say, going to a legal clinic and getting a lawyer to work on your case.

Dharia: Beyond individual cases, can you talk about your work from a community organizing standpoint?

Jayadev: At the base of it, we're organizers at De-Bug and so
we're interested in building ground-up transformative
power. That's why participatory defense feels so kindred to
other types of organizing outside of the courts; it has the
same ingredients. We're just applying community organizing principles onto a core process—the court system—that
has been insulated from community power.

One natural consequence of a community getting together and working on individual cases is they end up seeing where to apply collective pressure to the infrastructure
of the system. And some of those systemic changes can
only happen if collective power is applied. We believe these
changes won't come because of one clever litigator; they
won't come from a Supreme Court case. The changes we
want to create are going to require a larger force.

Part IV

Judges

Robert Saleem Holbrook, who spent over twenty years in prison and now leads the Abolitionist Law Center in Pittsburgh, has a clear view of judicial authority. "The thing with judges' power—it's like oxygen, right? You're not really conscious of oxygen until you're deprived of it," he told reporter Ian Ward in 2021, for an article we have included in this part. "And with judges, you're not conscious of their power until you're in their courtroom or you see them obstructing your interest through the judicial system."

Law professor Rachel Barkow agrees with Holbrook. In a recent speech to the Cato Institute, she explained how the Supreme Court sustains mass incarceration: "The justices may not have designed our world of mass incarceration, but they have made sure its foundation stays firmly in place."[1] Barkow's insight about the nine Supreme Court justices applies with equal force to the other 3,200 federal judges and the tens of thousands of state and local judges across the country. They have all played a role in sustaining mass incarceration. Here, we examine how they can help to unwind it.

Part IV's readings follow the flow of a court case in the criminal system, and we begin where most cases do: with the first contact between police and civilians. As Part I demonstrates, discriminatory and abusive police practices—including disproportionately stopping Black drivers and pedestrians—are one of the gateways to mass incarceration. Judges have long been complicit in such practices because they set the legal rules that permit them. For example, the U.S. Supreme Court has endorsed "stop and frisk," which disproportionately targets Black and brown people far beyond just arrests.[2] The Court further insulated abusive practices like racial profiling from legal challenge when, decades later, it upheld pretextual traffic stops.[3] Given the current composition of the Supreme Court, its trend of allowing the police maximum authority is likely to continue.

But while federal courts garner outsized attention in the national conversation, state courts have just as much power— or more—in the criminal system.[4] Even if federal courts are unwilling to protect individual rights, state courts can do so under their state laws and constitutions. Journalist Ally Jarmanning provides an example in "Mass. High Court Lowers Burden for Proving Racial Bias in Police Stops." Before 2020, Massachusetts required anyone who accused the police of racial profiling in a traffic stop to produce extensive statistical evidence in support of their claim. But in *Commonwealth v. Long*, the Massachusetts Supreme Judicial Court set a more flexible standard, allowing people to support a racial profiling claim with a range of evidence, including their own account of what happened.[5] If the government fails to rebut that evidence, the judge must suppress anything the police seized during the stop.

After arrest comes a court appearance in which a judge or magistrate decides whether to release the accused or lock them up until trial. At this point, a person is supposedly protected by foundational concepts in U.S. law: the presumption of innocence and its counterpart, the presumption of liberty. As the Supreme Court explained in *United States v. Salerno*, "In our society, liberty is the norm, and detention prior to trial or without trial is the carefully limited exception."[6]

Despite this mandate, American jails are crowded with people waiting for trial. We have more people in jail hoping for their day in court than most other countries have in their entire prison systems.[7] Most are there because they cannot afford to post money bail.[8] How does that happen? In most states, judges make decisions about bail and detention in just a few minutes, without carefully assessing the accused person's circumstances. Often, too, the accused do not even have a public defender standing next to them to explain their situation. Instead of treating money bail as the exception, many courts impose it as a matter of course. Indeed, for some judges, the question isn't *whether* to impose money bail but *how much*. When this happens, if you're poor, you're stuck.

The decision to lock someone up before trial can have devastating ripple effects. Research shows that people detained before trial are more likely to plead guilty, receive harsher prison sentences once they do, and be charged with a new crime in the future.[9] They are also more likely to lose their jobs, homes, and even custody of their children. Finally, they are more likely to suffer mental health issues and experience the lasting effects of trauma.

If that sounds unfair to you, you're not alone. Over the past decade, initiatives to transform the pretrial detention system have gained traction across the country. Journalists have documented the horrors of jails like Rikers Island in New York City. Ordinary people have donated to local bail funds and advocated for systemic change. Lawyers have filed lawsuits seeking reform, and state legislators have rewritten laws governing pretrial release. Some states—such as Illinois in 2023—have abolished cash bail entirely.[10]

In this part, we highlight two examples of bail reform at the state level. In 2019, New York passed a law prohibiting judges from setting money bail for people charged with certain types of misdemeanor and nonviolent offenses.[11] For charges where money bail is permitted, the law requires judges to consider whether it would impose an "undue hardship" on the accused. Despite this legislative change, however, judges kept setting money bail amounts that poor people could not pay.[12] In "Judge Frees Man from Rikers in Exceptional Decision Citing Bail and Jail Conditions," Sam Mellins recounts this history and highlights a judge, Wanda L. Licitra of the Bronx Criminal Court, who bucked the trend. In applying the bail reform statute's terms, Judge Licitra cites Mr. Ayala's five-day pretrial detention as evidence of "undue hardship" to justify releasing him from jail. Although her decision is not binding on other judges, we encourage them to follow her example.

Across the Hudson River, New Jersey has also transformed its bail laws—achieving, in the words of one commentator, "something increasingly rare in American politics: a big, transformative piece of legislation achieved through broad-based compromise."[13] In 2017, New Jersey essentially eliminated cash bail; three years later, the number of people locked up awaiting trial had declined by 40 percent.

Yet bail reform in New Jersey didn't come easily, and it isn't flawless. We describe what happened in the state through a conversation with two unlikely allies: former New Jersey prosecutor Elie Honig and ACLU attorney Alexander Shalom. New Jersey prosecutors, police officers, and the bail bond industry all opposed bail reform, Honig explains. Speaking to fellow prosecutors, Honig came to see why many of them were committed to the existing system. People who can't pay the money bail imposed by a judge feel pressured to plead guilty just to get out—and when they do, prosecutors can clear the case from their docket without bothering with a trial.

Reforms singularly focused on money bail can sometimes do more damage than good. For example, they can even entrench or expand non-money-related pretrial detention or create entirely new problems. [14] Shalom is quick to point out that from the ACLU's perspective, the new law has its defects. It relies on racially biased risk-assessment algorithms and doesn't mandate release in any cases, even ones involving minor charges. And yet, the reform has helped thousands of people remain in their homes and communities. In Shalom's view, "It is far from perfect. But you know what it's better than? The totally failed system that it replaced."[15]

We then turn to trials. As we discussed in Part II, trials are not commonplace because our system gives prosecutors so much leverage to force guilty pleas. But when they do occur, they put ordinary community members at the very center of the criminal system—as jurors.

Jurors have awesome power. They get to answer questions like: Is the government's main witness biased against the accused? Is the police officer telling the truth about what happened when they stopped the car or made the arrest? Is there an innocent explanation for what happened? At the end of the day, jurors have the greatest authority of all: to decide whether or not to convict.

Yet some potential jurors—including many who believe our legal system is unjust—seek to avoid being chosen for jury service. William Snowden argues that sitting on a jury is imperative—especially for those who doubt the system's fairness. As he explains, juries can check the government, limit prosecutorial overreach, and even save a life. But to do that, they must be racially and economically diverse and include people with a range of perspectives and life experiences. Just like voting at the ballot box on election day, he says, showing up to vote in the jury box "isn't someone else's duty, it's yours."

We then move to what is often considered the last stage of the court case: sentencing. When we think of sentencing, we normally think of that dramatic moment when a judge announces how many years a person will serve. But should that be the final word?

A number of legislatures have passed or are considering something called "second look" sentencing, which gives judges the power to determine whether a lengthy sentence imposed long ago remains appropriate. These reckonings are not easy. Consider that as of 2020, more than two hundred thousand people were serving life sentences, often for killing, seriously injuring, or sexually assaulting other people.[16] Some people serving long but less-than-life sentences have also been convicted of such crimes. There is no way to undo mass incarceration without addressing the long sentences imposed for serious acts of violence.

Washington, D.C., has led the "second look" movement, and we include *United States v. Halim Flowers*, an opinion highlighting the city's new approach to sentencing. Under D.C.'s Incarceration Reduction Amendment Act (IRAA), people who were younger than twenty-five years old at the time of the crime and have served at least fifteen years can ask a court to reconsider their sentence.[17] The driving force behind the law, which was passed in 2016 and later amended, was an evolving understanding of how brains develop. Recognizing that adolescents and young adults lack the reasoning skills and judgment of older adults, proponents said courts shouldn't impose extraordinarily long sentences on young people without giving them a subsequent chance to show how they've changed. In the story we share, sixteen-year-old Halim Flowers and another teenage friend went to someone's home and robbed the men inside. During the robbery, one of the men was killed. In 1997, at the height of the expanding carceral state, and before we really understood how long it takes for the adolescent brain to develop, the sentencing judge ordered Flowers to spend thirty years to life in prison.

More than two decades later, the new law required another judge to weigh the harm Flowers caused as a teenager against the harm his continued incarceration caused him and his community. While acknowledging the violence in Flowers's past, the judge considered who Flowers had become in the twenty-one years he had spent behind bars: "Mr. Flowers has transformed himself to a mature man, remorseful, and motivated and equipped to be a respectable, contributing member of our community." Since his release, Flowers's contributions to the community have been extraordinary. He's an author, poet, and visual artist whose work appears in galleries around the world.

Next, we feature an opinion that grapples with undoing racist sentencing practices. In 1997, a Connecticut trial judge sentenced Keith Belcher, a Black fourteen-year-old, to sixty years in prison on charges of kidnapping, sexual assault, robbery, and burglary. In doing so, the judge cited the now-debunked theory of teenage "superpredators," which claimed that America faced an unprecedented threat from a new generation of remorseless teenagers. Twenty-five years later, in *State of Connecticut v. Keith Belcher*, the state supreme court overturned the sentence. We include the opinion by Justice Raheem L. Mullins, who discussed the history of the superpredator theory and the racial bias that motivated it.

When activists organize to elect a diverse, thoughtful, and progressive-minded judiciary, they make it more likely that decisions like *Belcher* will be handed down. Ian Ward describes such efforts in his article "How Progressives Are Knocking Out Local Judges Across the Country." For instance, he reports on reform groups in Allegheny County, Pennsylvania, and in Philadelphia that either endorsed candidates for courts of common pleas or put forward their own slate of candidates. In both cases, the majority of these candidates won. Ward argues that "if judges cannot be arbiters of pure justice, they can at least be representatives of a new type of politics—one that is more attuned to the injustices of America's criminal justice system."

While Ward tells ordinary people how they can elect better judges, former federal judge Nancy Gertner has a different audience—those who already sit as judges themselves. In "Reimagining Judging," Gertner urges her colleagues to take action to reform the carceral system. She has a host of ideas for how judges can do that, including: 1) educating themselves on how trauma has influenced the lives of the criminal defendants who appear before them, 2) conducting case audits after any wrongful conviction to determine how and why the system failed, and 3) commissioning statistical reviews of judges' case files to check for racial bias. Finally, Judge Gertner asks her colleagues to speak out against laws that lead to unfair outcomes. There is a long history of judges dutifully applying such laws, privately bemoaning their impact, but saying nothing about them in their opinions. Gertner counsels a different course of action: When America's harsh criminal laws compel the wrong result, she says, a judge should write an opinion acknowledging the injustice. These opinions, Gertner argues, have the power to change criminal justice narratives, laws, and minds.

Mass. High Court Lowers Burden for Proving Racial Bias in Police Stops*

Ally Jarmanning

2020

The Supreme Judicial Court of Massachusetts (SJC) has lowered the burden for proving a police traffic stop was racially motivated, and acknowledged that the court's previous solution for ferreting out racial bias by police wasn't working.

In the far-reaching decision, the high court said people who are stopped by police and charged with a crime can now hold up aspects of the stop—from how long police followed them to how the officer handles the stop—to help make their case. The old standard required a statistical analysis to prove racial bias by an officer.

Without a workable remedy, "the right of drivers to be free

---

* Ally Jarmanning, "Mass. High Court Lowers Burden for Proving Racial Bias in Police Stops," WBUR News, September 17, 2020.

from racial profiling will remain illusory," Justice Frank Gaziano wrote in the opinion, issued Thursday.

"The discriminatory enforcement of traffic laws is not a minor annoyance to those who are racially profiled," he wrote.
"To the contrary, these discriminatory practices cause great
harm."

Only one person had successfully suppressed evidence in a
case because of racial bias in the twelve years since the previous
decision established the statistics-based standard. Defense attorneys say that's not for lack of trying.

The court blamed it on the lack of available police data, and
laid blame on the state legislature for not passing a law requiring it.

"We urge the legislature to require the collection and analysis of officer-specific data," Gaziano wrote. "This type of data
collection would help protect drivers from racially discriminatory traffic stops, and also would protect police officers who do
not engage in such discriminatory stops."

Legislative leaders are debating a compromise police reform bill. The Senate version of the bill would mandate all police departments to collect data about each traffic stop, while
the House bill says nothing about data.

Matthew Segal, legal director of the American Civil Liberties Union of Massachusetts, said the legislature, governor, and
police departments "forced the court's hand" by not fixing the
problem of not having publicly available police data.

"We have more than one branch of government in this
commonwealth, and it should not fall to the court to do everything," he said. "We need the other branches of government in
this state to step up and do their job."

The decision comes a week after a SJC-commissioned study
found that Black and Latino people were more likely to be

locked up for drugs and weapons offenses and get longer sentences than white people.

The SJC decision, which centered on the traffic stop of a Black man named Edward Long, was one of three released Thursday that addressed the police stops of Black teenagers and men.

In one, where a Black teen ran from Boston police and was charged with murder after a gun was found near him, the court ruled the stop was lawful. But they noted that police witnessing nervous and evasive behavior isn't enough to stop someone who is Black, because of a pattern of racial profiling by police.

"Just as an innocent African-American male might flee in order to avoid the danger or indignity of a police stop, the fear of such an encounter might lead an African-American male to be nervous or evasive in his dealings with police officers," wrote Gaziano, who also authored that opinion.

In the third decision, the court ruled that a Black man stopped by Framingham police and allegedly beaten by the officers can pursue a civil suit against the police for part of the encounter, even though a jury convicted him of some charges related to the stop.

Chauncey Wood, who authored a friend-of-the-court brief on behalf of the Massachusetts Association of Criminal Defense Lawyers, said the court has continued to show a willingness to find a practical solution to deal with racial injustice.

"I'm excited that the court is really wrestling with, on a fundamental level, how to address a profound problem in our society—like racism—in an effective, practical way," he said. "I think everybody on the court recognizes that the goal is an effective, practical solution to this problem that eliminates, as much as possible, racial profiling in traffic enforcement."

The Long decision centered on a traffic stop made by Boston police's gang unit in 2017. Long, who is Black, was driving his girlfriend's Mercedes that morning in Dorchester when the officers saw him drive by. Long was driving lawfully, but the officers ran the license plate and saw the car didn't have an inspection sticker.

They stopped Long and discovered he didn't have a driver's license, and had two default warrants for operating without a license and failure to identify himself. The officers arrested him and called for a tow truck to take the car. They found an unlicensed gun when they searched the vehicle in anticipation of the tow.

To prove the stop was racially biased, Long's court-appointed lawyer, John P. Warren, hired a statistician to analyze what are known as Field Interrogation Stops. Over a seven-year period, 80 percent of the drivers stopped by the two officers who arrested Long were Black.

In the decision Thursday, the SJC wrote that Long proved racial bias—even under the old standard. But they also acknowledged that current burden was too high.

Now, they wrote, judges should look at the circumstance of the stop. How long did the officer follow the car? Is this officer assigned to patrol, or another unit that doesn't typically make traffic stops? Did the officer keep questioning the driver even after they provided their license and registration? Do the police department policies allow unmarked vehicles to make routine traffic stops?

"The truth is that someone who looks like me—I'm white— has a different experience when they're driving as compared to someone who looks like Mr. Long, who's Black," Warren said.

But going into court to prove that was next to impossible.

"This [decision] is going to enable other defendants to

actually be able to raise these claims and challenge stops that are made on the basis of race," Warren said.

Suffolk County District Attorney Rachael Rollins, whose office prosecuted the two Boston cases and whose office argued against the appeal, said in a statement that the decisions reflect the legal system's "ability to evolve and adapt" its understanding of racial disparities through the entire legal system.

"With these decisions, the public is seeing that the appellate process is one avenue available to bring about changes within the system, as occurred here," she said. "I want to thank the SJC justices for their thoughtful consideration and progressive analysis of these important issues."

A Boston police spokesperson said the department needed time to review the ruling before commenting.

The late Chief Justice Ralph Gants, who died unexpectedly this week and has been credited with pursuing racial justice through the court, wrote a concurring opinion in the Long case. It's the unanimous view of the court, he wrote, that its prohibition against racial profiling must be given teeth.

Judge Frees Man from Rikers in Exceptional Decision Citing Bail and Jail Conditions*

Sam Mellins
2022

In a striking written decision issued last week, Bronx Criminal Court Judge Wanda Licitra ordered the release of a man who had been incarcerated on Rikers Island due to his inability to pay bail along with the violent and increasingly lethal conditions at the city's main jail.

The man, who is referred to in the decision only by his last name, Ayala, had been sent to Rikers because he was accused of violating an order of protection. That enabled a prior judge to set cash bail, and Ayala didn't have the $500 required to be released.

He was fifty-six years old, in "frail condition," and had no

---

* Sam Mellins, "Judge Frees Man from Rikers in Exceptional Decision Citing Bail and Jail Conditions," *The City*, September 21, 2022.

criminal record, though he had been arrested several times and had multiple open cases for offenses including drunk driving and assault.

Licitra's unusual written decision ordering the man's release was based in large part on the requirement in New York's sweeping 2019 bail reform law that judges take into account a defendant's financial circumstances and their "ability to post bail without posing undue hardship." Licitra, a former public defender, reasoned that the fact that Ayala was still at Rikers was evidence that the $500 bail constituted an "undue hardship."

The decision, which isn't binding on other judges, also cited the high levels of violence and death among people incarcerated at Rikers as reasons to release the defendant.

Licitra's choice to publish a written opinion for a bail hearing, rather than issuing a verbal decision, was a break from usual practice that could prompt other judges and lawyers to reassess how the 2019 reforms should be implemented, say court observers.

"If every judge applied this kind of careful parsing and reasoning, and gave fair application to the statute's terms, more people would be released from Rikers," said Jonathan Oberman, a criminal law professor at Cardozo School of Law.

If other judges were to embrace Licitra's logic, it would significantly change the way bail functions in New York. The vast majority of people in jail in New York state have not been convicted of a crime, but are awaiting trial and unable to post bail, like Ayala.

"I don't think when they changed the bail statute that they wanted a fifty-six-year-old guy with no record being held in jail on a criminal conduct misdemeanor," said Mark Bederow, a defense attorney who formerly worked as a prosecutor at the Manhattan District Attorney's office. "This is one of those cases that the advocates in favor of bail reform would check in their column as one where the D.A. was not being reasonable."

The office of Bronx District Attorney Darcel Clark, which is prosecuting Ayala and opposed his release, did not respond to a request for comment. Nor did the New York Police Department or New York's District Attorneys Association.

BETRAYED PROMISE

New York's 2019 overhaul of bail law was meant to fix a justice system that was commonly perceived as treating rich and poor people differently, as low-income New Yorkers were forced to await trial from jail while those with means could buy their freedom.

Its approach contrasted with that of New Jersey, which eliminated cash bail entirely in 2017 but granted judges power to order certain defendants held behind bars before trial if they presented public safety risks. New York, which has never allowed judges to consider "dangerousness," retained bail as a means to ensure people showed up at trial—but limited its use mostly to certain felonies in certain circumstances.

In an April 2019 statement praising the changes, state Senate Majority Leader Andrea Stewart-Cousins said that the new laws would "ensure that no New Yorker is incarcerated because of their inability to pay."

But that's not how the law has functioned in practice. While it has dramatically reduced New York's pretrial population by rendering most misdemeanors ineligible for bail, it did not cause the dollar amounts of cash bail to decrease, when judges do apply it.

Instead, judges have continued to set bail beyond many low-income defendants' ability to pay. When the Vera Institute of Justice examined arraignments in five upstate counties, it found defendants' ability to pay wasn't even discussed in more than 70 percent of cases in which bail was set, said Jullian Harris-Calvin, director of the organization's Greater Justice New York program.

In 2020, the first year that the bail reform law was in effect, only 39 percent of felony defendants who had bail set could pay within a week of being sent to jail—the same number as in 2019, the year before bail reform took effect, according to a report from the nonpartisan Center for Court Innovation. Fewer than half could pay within ninety days, a slight decline from 2019.

In some cases, defense lawyers have attempted to get their clients released by arguing that setting bail beyond a defendant's ability to pay violates the "undue hardship" provision of the law. But those arguments hadn't found much success until now; a public defender representing clients in the Bronx, who requested anonymity to prevent reprisals against their clients, said Licitra's decision is the first time they can recall a judge applying that logic.

"If you and your family clearly are not able to meet the bail requirements in terms of the amount, that's never really swayed the courts," the public defender said.

For decades, judges in New York have only been allowed to set bail as a means of ensuring defendants return to court to face trial. New York is the only state that does not allow judges to take into account whether they believe that defendants are a public safety risk. Instead, judges are mandated to use the "least restrictive" means of ensuring that defendants return to court for their scheduled appearances.

Simply failing to show up to court is rare in New York. In 2020, fewer than one in ten defendants missed any of the court dates in their cases, according to a report from the nonprofit New York City Criminal Justice Agency, though that rate was slightly higher for people accused of felonies.

Ayala had previously missed court dates in separate cases, such as a case stemming from a drunk driving charge in February 2022, before he was sent to jail on September 9. Other judges might have used those missed appearances as evidence that bail was required to ensure he would return to court. But Licitra noted that he had appeared at multiple court dates after those missed appearances, which she took as evidence he wasn't trying to escape the court.

"Not every instance in which a person misses their court date is evidence of 'running away' from the prosecution," Licitra wrote. This perspective, while not ubiquitous, is shared by some other judges in New York courts, the public defender said.

"A MORE RESTRICTIVE KIND OF CONTROL"

Licitra's ruling also applied the 2019 reform laws to the violent conditions at Rikers Island to justify releasing Ayala. Leaning on the law's mandate to use the "least restrictive" means to get someone to return to court, Licitra argued that "worse jail conditions are a more restrictive kind of control," noting that a man had died at Rikers on the very day that she issued the ruling in Ayala's case.

Licitra isn't the first judge to order someone released before their trial because of the conditions on Rikers Island. In December 2021, Supreme Court Judge April Newbauer ordered the release of a man incarcerated at Rikers on a felony burglary charge, ruling that the level of violence at Rikers justified releasing him and allowing him to wear an electronic monitor while awaiting trial. (Newbauer's decision was based on federal constitutional provisions prohibiting cruel and unusual punishment and establishing the right to due process, not the New York state law, which Licitra relied on.)

Whether the ruling will produce wider change is an open question. As a criminal court judge, Licitra only rules on misdemeanors and the initial stages of felony proceedings, and doesn't have any jurisdiction over other criminal court judges or the higher-ranking Supreme Court judges who hear felonies. Other judges can simply choose to ignore her ruling.

But others may be influenced by Licitra's reasoning, some defense attorneys hope. The Bronx public defender said they plan to use the decision to try to persuade other judges to take a "more head-on approach to the bail reform law."

"Just having something that we can rely on and point to is very big," they said. "She's giving us the tools."

New Jersey Bail Conversation*

Alexander Shalom and Elie Honig, Interviewed by James Forman Jr.

Monday, July 24, 2023

Forman: Why did each of you consider bail reform so urgent?

Shalom: When I interviewed for the job at the ACLU, they asked me, "What is the issue in the criminal justice space that most needs fixing? Where are people of color most directly harmed?" Now, I had been a public defender, so I was ready for this question. I described the total unfairness of the money bail system. I explained how my clients had been forced to plead guilty to crimes they didn't commit—or at least crimes they wouldn't have been convicted of—only because they wanted to get out of jail. I detailed how many of

---

* Former prosecutor Elie Honig and ACLU attorney Alexander Shalom both served on New Jersey's Joint Committee on Criminal Justice, tasked with evaluating and reforming the state's bail system. They reflect on their experiences in this conversation with James Forman Jr., which took place on July 24, 2023.

my clients were simply too poor to get out. The people interviewing me were smart lawyers, but they didn't know about
this horrible bail system, and they were appalled. They loved
my answer. So they said, "Great, tell us how to fix it."

I was like, "Wait, you asked me to describe a problem,
not fix it. I don't know how to fix it!" I would spend the next
few years at the ACLU trying to figure that out.

Forman: Elie, what about you? Why did bail matter to you so
much?

Honig: I had been a federal prosecutor for eight and a half
years. And when I came up over to the New Jersey system,
and saw the way that cash bail was being used, my first
thought was, "What the hell is going on?" It made no sense,
in two respects. One, you had absurd numbers of low-risk
poor people locked up just because they couldn't post low
cash bail amounts. The New Jersey Drug Policy Alliance
did a study that was very influential in the state—it showed
that 12 percent of our entire incarcerated population were
pretrial detainees held on bail of $2,500 or less.[1] You might
think prosecutors would want this, but my view is that we
have no need for low-risk people to waste their lives behind
prison unnecessarily.

On the other hand, cash bail was getting set even for high-
risk people, even for people charged with murders, regardless of the danger they posed. I remember we prosecuted a
hideous double murder case where the defendant had killed
two people, cut off their hands, cut off their heads, and buried the heads and the hands in a separate grave site from the
torsos.

I said to the prosecutor on the case, "Well, obviously
we'll get that guy locked up, and then we'll go from there."
And he says, "Well, there is no getting locked up." I said,

"What do you mean? This guy's obviously dangerous and he's a flight risk." And the prosecutor said "Yeah, but in New Jersey everyone gets cash bail, it's just a question of how much." Now, the amount would be very high in a case like this, but if you could afford it, you could get out.

This just made no sense.

Forman: Let's talk about the politics of change. How did you and others change the law?

Honig: Look, bail reform is an easy sell to the ACLU or public defender audience. In the judiciary, it's a medium easy sell. We were fortunate to have an influential and outstanding Chief Justice, Stuart Rabner, who really guided everyone through this.

But it's harder to walk into a room of cops and prosecutors and explain that we're going to change this system. I remember going from office to office around the state, and prosecutors would tell me, "We're going to be letting too many people out," and "This is going to become catch and release." We tried to explain why it wouldn't and we tried to defend the trade-offs: maybe it's worth it to let out more low-risk people if we get to detain more high-risk ones.

But underneath the stated concern was another concern, which didn't get talked about as much. I remember speaking to an auditorium full of prosecutors from all over the state. And they were looking at me like, "Here's this former Fed who is now in Trenton and he's giving orders."

I was taking questions from the crowd and one guy gets up and says, "Why is anyone going to plead guilty anymore?" And I'm wondering, what does this have to do with bail reform? People will plead guilty for all the reasons they pled guilty before bail reform. And then I realized,

he's talking about one of our secrets: how some prosecutors keep poor people in jail, knowing they can't afford to
post bond, to pressure them to take a plea. And I told him,
"Oh, I understand. You're going to miss the 'time served
plea.' That lovely plea that lets you clean your docket sheet.
A guy's coming up for his next pretrial conference. He's
been locked up for eight months on $3,000 bail. If he pleads
guilty today, he's getting time served and you get to clear it
off your docket."

And I actually did something I almost never do, which
is I got a little angry in front of the crowd. I said, "Listen, if
you're a prosecutor for that reason, because you just want
to rack up time served pleas, you need to rethink why you
have this job."

And it wasn't just prosecutors. Some public defenders
liked time served pleas, because it helped them clean their
dockets, too. And judges liked them, because judges in this
state get evaluated by their clearance rates. So there was resistance from lots of places.

Also, the cops were brutal. Not all of them, to be clear.
There were a lot of cops who took the time to understand
this. And some were absolutely for it, including the state
police. But there were also some chiefs of police and rank-
and-file cops who thought this was going to be madness,
who thought this was going to lead to *The Purge*.

The bigger, more systemic source of opposition came
from the bail bonds industry—a multibillion-dollar industry. They were smart enough to see that this was going to
wipe them out.

They got their hooks into a couple of legislators, liberal
Democrats, who said, "Well, I'm not so sure I'm on board

with this. This bail reform is going to lock up disproportionate numbers of minorities." And we said, "You know who's in prison now, right? So that's who is going to start getting out if we can get this passed."

By the way, the bail bonds industry was right to see the threat. This multibillion-dollar industry has essentially disappeared in New Jersey. I was walking through New Brunswick a few years ago and I came across a storefront that had an old sign hanging that said "bail bonds" and it was covered by a new one that said, "coming soon," and it was advertising a new craft brewery.

I took a picture and sent it to Alex and the Chief Justice and said, "This is progress."

Forman: The new bail law passed in 2017. Can you talk about how it works and how it is different from the old system?

Honig: In the old system, a person would get arrested and a judge would set some cash bail amount pending trial. That amount was supposed to be based only on the risk that the person would flee, and nothing else.

It was basically a mechanical process. The judge would say, here's your charges and your history, and here's the cash bail amount. If you could post the cash bail, you would walk out. Or if you only had 10 percent, you could give 10 percent—and sometimes even less—to a bail bondsman, and they would get you out. But if you were poor enough that you couldn't pay the 10 percent, then you sat in jail, you waited, and you were left to rot. A lot of times you sat in jail for longer than you would have served if you were convicted.

Under the new system, which kicked in on January 1, 2017, you get arrested and you are assigned a risk assessment score. You are scored on two scales, basically: whether you are a risk of flight and whether you are a danger to the community. The score is based on factors like, does the person have a record, have they failed to appear in court before, and things like that. It was designed by the Arnold Foundation.

To be clear, the score is just a starting point. Both the prosecutor and the defense still get to make arguments about whether the person should be released. So if the person has a low score—which says they aren't a flight risk or a danger—the prosecutor can still say, "Wait, Your Honor, here are reasons this person should be detained." Same for the defense. Even if the score is high they can argue that the person should be released on conditions.

Shalom: So what Elie says is right, but let me just add a little to it from my perspective. One of my concerns with risk assessment tools is that algorithmic justice often comes with tremendous bias against certain groups—especially poor people and people of color. So to be honest, I've never gotten fully comfortable with it. But what makes me support this approach is that all those same biases existed in the old system as well. Judges would say they were only assessing risk of flight, but they were obviously looking at factors that disproportionately harmed my clients—problematic factors like prior convictions or prior failures to appear. What you should know is that sometimes a person failed to appear, but they weren't trying to skip court. Instead they were poor and life is so much harder when you're poor and you struggle with transportation, child care, and housing insecurity.

Also importantly, the current system includes some significant due process protections. U.S. Supreme Court Chief

Justice William Rehnquist wrote that in this country, liberty is the norm and detention prior to trial is the carefully limited exception. In New Jersey that means the new bail law includes a presumption of release, a presumption that people get out pretrial because they haven't been convicted of a crime. The presumption of release is broad; it includes almost every crime except for murder. There's also a right to counsel in any detention hearing. If the state moves for detention, you can cross-examine witnesses and call your own witnesses. There's robust discovery, there's an expedited right to appeal.

Forman: Alex, can you talk about the law's impact? Are fewer people being locked up?

Shalom: Yes. Now, Covid complicates the data, but here's the overview. Before the law went into effect, we had about 9,000 people detained pretrial in New Jersey. Almost immediately, we were able to start reducing that number, and the number got to as low as 4,500. So in other words, a 50 percent reduction.

Since Covid, it has gone up. As was true in much of the country, crime rose in New Jersey during the pandemic, although violent crime didn't go up that much here. But the result was an increase in the number of people detained pretrial, to about seven thousand on any given day right now. So not as low as our lowest number, but still fewer than before the law was passed.

Also, crucially, again looking at the time outside of Covid, it is important to note that as we released more people, crime did not go up. And people kept coming to court for their court hearings. We instituted a text message reminder system, which really works. It's honestly made more of a difference than I thought it would. Of course we should be doing more to help people get to court more easily. We should have travel vouchers and child care. But it turns out just a simple text message helps. Because when you're poor, and life is so overwhelming, sometimes you just forget.

There's one more thing I have to say about violent crime. Bail reform isn't about eliminating risk. It's about reducing it. So when we did this, we knew something would go wrong, that somebody would commit a crime while they were released. But we all agreed that we'd try to figure out what went wrong, we'd try to fix things, but we wouldn't point fingers at the new system. If somebody committed a crime, before the press got all worked up, we'd remind reporters that this happened under the old money bail system too. Elie and the attorney general's office truly deserve a lot of credit for this, because there were folks on the law enforcement side who wanted to point fingers. But the prosecutors at the top resisted that, and after a few years, people were able to see that the system was working. It is far from perfect. But you know what it's better than? The totally failed system that it replaced.

Forman: My last question is about what advice you have for people in other states who might want to change their bail laws. Lots of places still have terrible systems—as bad or worse than the one New Jersey had previously. If somebody lives in a state like that and wants to make a difference—whether they are a legislator, an advocate, or an everyday citizen—what would you tell them?

Honig: It takes guts. It's not easy. This doesn't work if you aren't willing to put aside partisan views—whether you're a Democrat, conservative Republican, prosecutor, defense lawyer, you name it. If you're in your own lane and refusing to consider anything outside of your lane, it's not going to happen.

The other thing is, it's so much easier *not* to do this. It's so much easier to keep the status quo—because when you change the system, and anything goes wrong, people will look for someone to blame. So the question you have to ask yourself is, what am I in this job for? Am I here to protect my hide and move on to the next ineffectual project? Or am I here to make a difference? It might sound naïve, but that's the truth.

The other thing I would tell people is that if you can muster the political will, and the partnership to get it done, it works. Bail reform leads to fewer people in prison and it does not jeopardize public safety. In fact, it may even help public safety. So it takes a lot of guts, but it will yield actual tangible results.

Shalom: I have a few categories of advice. The first is, when you're thinking about what the reforms should look like, you have to be clear on what's driving you. I think you have to be driven by liberty. Bail reform has to be about freedom. These are people who have not been convicted of a crime. So whether you're talking about whether to detain somebody, or what sort of conditions of release to impose, we have to center liberty because these are innocent people.

The second thing is that not one of these reforms we talked about works without counsel. So if you are in a place that doesn't provide meaningful defense for poor people, start there. Because you can't have bail reform without a right to counsel.

Last, you have to be willing to compromise. It is okay to

say, "This is not the system I would draw up, but I still support this change." Why? Because in the next ten years, it's going to mean tens of thousands of people are going to be free. That matters to them, their families, and their communities. We can keep working toward the ideal of getting everyone free. But until we're there, let's just free more people.

How to Save a Life from the Jury Box*

William Snowden

2019

All right, Jimmy, the first thing you tell them is you can't be on the jury because your dog was hit by a truck and today's the funeral. Nah, Jimmy, just tell them you don't have the time. It's easier than that: wear a red "Make America Great Again" hat and you'll be out in no time.

Look to the person to the left of you; now, look to the person to the right. One of these people has tried to get out of jury duty, but when they do that, sometimes, what we get is this: "I looked around the courtroom, the judge was white, the prosecutor was white, the jury was white. Even though I was innocent, I knew I had no chance." These are the words of an exonerated death row prisoner. These words highlight a problem that we have in our country: our juries lack diversity. Not just diversity of

---

* William Snowden, "How to Save a Life from the Jury Box," New Leaders Council Spark! Talk, YouTube, August 30, 2019, 5:10 (video).

race, but diversity of thought, diversity of experience, diversity in every sense of the word. And this lack of diversity is leading to a lack of fairness.

My name is William Snowden, I'm the founder of the Juror Project. Our mission is to increase diversity of jury panels as well as improve people's perspective of jury duty. As progressives in this country, this is your call to action. I chose to be a public defender in Louisiana because it's one of the prison capitals of the world; simply put, they're locking up too many Black people, too many people of color, and the majority of these people are poor.

So I made it my responsibility to create the Juror Project and go out into the community and have conversations with folks about how the criminal justice system isn't always just, and how we can take power and bring criminal justice reform through the jury box by increasing diversity.

It's really a simple idea based in the roots of the benefits of diversity. We're all familiar with and know why we need a diverse boardroom, or why we need a diverse classroom. Well, for the sake of the fairness of our criminal justice system, we need diverse juries too, and here's why.

One of my first cases, I represented a man named Clarence. He was charged with possession of heroin. If he were to go to trial and lose, he'd be facing a life sentence in prison—not for possession with intent to distribute, not for actual distribution, but for being a heroin addict on his third strike. Clarence wanted help, and we all wanted to help him, but we all agreed that the help he deserved wasn't a life sentence in prison. But the law said otherwise.

With this new attorney general in office, the war on drugs is back, but we've seen this war before. We know that casualties of this war are going to be people of color and poor people. We all know that this war on drugs leads to generations of mass incarceration, generations of single-parent homes, and generations of wrongful convictions. Now, more than ever, we need more diversity in that deliberation room. We need folks representing with a diverse perspective, that the war on drugs is a failed policy. We need folks talking about how drug addiction is a health problem, not a crime problem.

And we know what happens when we don't have this diversity. For example, in Louisiana they studied more than three hundred trials over a ten-year period. When there were not more than two Black people on the jury, there were zero acquittals. But what happens when we increase the diversity? Well, in that same study, when there were three or more African Americans on the jury, the acquittal rate increased to 12 percent. When there were five or more African Americans on the jury, the acquittal rate increased to 19 percent. That's direct evidence and direct proof that with an increase in diversity, there's actually an increase in fairness. At the Juror Project, what we like to say is that's what our criminal justice system is about: a fairer system.

Although this research is based on diversity of race, we can imagine the impact when we increase diversity with more women, or with more young people, and, of course, with more progressives. But when you or Jimmy try to get out of jury duty, that's potentially one less person bringing diversity to the jury room. That's potentially one less perspective that could change the outcome of the case, and that's potentially one less vote that could save Clarence's life.

Jury duty isn't someone else's duty, it's yours, and I want you to be excited about this opportunity. The next time you get a jury summons I want you to use the hashtag "jury duty is my duty."

Right here, right now in this room, we not only have the power to change the criminal justice system, but we also have the power to save someone's life. I want you to be part of this process and change the narrative around jury duty, and I want you to start today. Thank you.

United States v.
Halim Flowers*

Judge Ronna Lee Beck
2019

Before the court is Mr. Flowers's motion for reduction of sentence under the Incarceration Reduction Amendment Act of 2016, his supplemental memorandum of law in support of the motion, the government's opposition, and Mr. Flowers's reply to the government's opposition. The court conducted an evidentiary hearing on March 15, 2019, and granted the instant motion. On March 21, 2019, the court resentenced Mr. Flowers. The court now issues its "opinion in writing stating the reasons for granting . . . the application" for relief under the Incarceration Reduction Amendment Act (the "IRAA").

This case arose out of the senseless shooting death of fifty-one-year-old Elvern Gregory Cooper during the commission of a burglary committed by sixteen-year-old Halim Flowers

---

* *United States v. Halim Flowers*, No. 1997 FEL 000631 (D.C. Superior Court, March 26, 2019).

and his juvenile codefendant, Momolu Stewart. Mr. Flowers was tried before Judge Harold Cushenberry in 1997. A jury found Mr. Flowers guilty of two counts of first-degree burglary while armed; first-degree felony murder while armed; second-degree murder; assault with intent to commit robbery while armed; two counts of possession of a firearm during a crime of violence or dangerous crime; and carrying a pistol without a license. Mr. Flowers ultimately was sentenced to an aggregate term of thirty years to life in prison.

On March 6, 2018, [the] defendant filed his motion for reduction of sentence pursuant to the IRAA after having served approximately twenty-one years in prison.

The IRAA allows people who were under the age of eighteen at the time of the offense to move the sentencing court for a reduction of sentence, provided the movant meets the criteria outlined in the statute.

One of the IRAA's goals is to comply with Supreme Court precedent that juveniles are "constitutionally different from adults for the purposes of sentencing." The Council intended that sentencing be age-appropriate and relied on four recent Supreme Court juvenile sentencing cases in its analysis. These cases together assert that because juveniles are inherently less culpable than adults, they are less deserving of the most severe punishments.

The Court in *Graham* noted that "developments in psychology and brain science continue to show fundamental differences between juvenile and adult minds. For example, parts of the brain involved in behavior control continue to mature through late adolescence." The Court reasoned that such findings, those of "transient rashness, proclivity for risk, and inability to assess consequences," reduced a juvenile's "moral culpability" and increased the "prospect that, as the years go by and neurological development occurs, his deficiencies will be reformed."

In passing the IRAA, the Council considered similar research on the development of the brain during adolescence. This research provides that the frontal lobes of the brain may not be fully developed until the midtwenties, meaning that adolescents possess impaired judgment and difficulty grasping consequences.

The Council understood the constitutional need for juvenile offenders to have the opportunity to receive lesser penalties as compared with adults. The Council did not intend to minimize the seriousness of crimes committed by juveniles: "While the severity of these crimes is not open to debate, the rationality of continuing to imprison an individual into old age for a crime they committed as a child, without any opportunity to review that decision, is subject to serious question in the District and across the country." To reduce a term of imprisonment pursuant to the IRAA, the court must find, after considering all eleven factors set forth in the statute, that "the defendant is not a danger to the safety of any person or the community and that the interests of justice warrant a sentence modification."

The factors the court is required to consider, and has considered in this case, are the following: (1) the defendant's age at the time of the offense; (2) the nature of the offense and the history and characteristics of the defendant; (3) whether the defendant has substantially complied with the rules of the institution to which he or she has been confined and whether the defendant has completed any educational, vocational, or other program, where available; (4) any report or recommendation received from the United States Attorney; (5) whether the defendant has demonstrated maturity, rehabilitation, and a fitness to reenter society sufficient to justify a sentence reduction; (6) any statement, provided orally or in writing, provided pursuant to § 23-1904 or 18 U.S.C. § 3771 by a victim of the offense for which the defendant is imprisoned, or by a family member of the victim if the victim is deceased; (7) any reports of physical, mental, or psychiatric examinations of the defendant conducted by licensed health-care professionals; (8) the defendant's family and community circumstances at the time of the offense, including any history of abuse, trauma, or involvement in the child welfare system; (9) the extent of the defendant's role in the offense and whether and to what extent an adult was involved in the offense; (10) the diminished culpability of juveniles as compared to that of adults, and the hallmark features of youth, including immaturity, impetuosity, and failure to appreciate risks and consequences, which counsel against sentencing them to a lifetime in prison; and (11) any other information the court deems relevant to its decision.

A. IRAA FACTORS

Ed. Note: The judge discusses each of the factors listed above and applies those factors to Mr. Flowers. By way of example, we include her analysis of one such factor below.

The Diminished Culpability of Juveniles as Compared to That of Adults, and the Hallmark Features of Youth, Including Immaturity, Impetuosity, and Failure to Appreciate Risks and Consequences, Which Counsel Against Sentencing Them to a Lifetime in Prison

The defense argues that felony murder participants who did not themselves kill or intend to kill possess diminished culpability as compared with principal offenders. "When compared to an adult murderer, a juvenile offender who did not kill or intend to kill has a twice diminished moral culpability."

Thus, the defense argues, Mr. Flowers is "less of a danger to society because he was not the principal actor in the death of Mr. Cooper." The government points out that "[a]lthough defendant was not the person who pulled the trigger, he participated in the events that led Stewart to fire the shots that ended Mr. Cooper's life." Before the killing took place, Mr. Flowers unsuccessfully attempted to rob Mr. Cooper at gunpoint, and then returned to the same apartment twice thereafter.

There is no question that Mr. Flowers's actions were deliberate and senseless. The government also submits that because Mr. Flowers's sentence complies with *Miller* [*Miller v. Alabama*, 567 U.S. 460 (2012)], his release should be left to the parole board. This argument ignores the purpose of the IRAA. At four months past his sixteenth birthday, Mr. Flowers's senseless burglary and murder were the product of impetuosity, immaturity, and a failure to appreciate risks and consequences. While he was arrested for weapons-related offenses prior to the instant offense, he was not a hardened criminal. In addition, it is noteworthy that Mr. Flowers was not the principal offender in Mr. Cooper's death.

B. A REDUCTION IN SENTENCE IS WARRANTED

The IRAA was a recognition that juveniles are constitutionally different from adults for purposes of sentencing. Mr. Flowers's young life, like the lives of so many people who are defendants in serious criminal cases, was filled with trauma. Mr. Flowers had stopped going to school and became involved in criminal activity. At about four months past his sixteenth birthday, five-foot-tall and one-hundred-pound Mr. Flowers was responsible for the senseless shooting death of fifty-one-year-old Elvern Gregory Cooper.

Mr. Flowers did not shoot the fatal shot and did not intend for Mr. Cooper or anyone else to be killed, but he set in motion the felony murder that resulted in Mr. Cooper's death. If the IRAA was designed for anyone, it was designed for people like Mr. Flowers. In summary, during his more than twenty-one years of incarceration, Mr. Flowers has transformed himself to a mature man, remorseful, and motivated and equipped to be a respectable, contributing member of our community. In the last fourteen years, Mr. Flowers remarkably has had no disciplinary infractions whatsoever. His participation in programs and work to better himself and to help others is truly impressive. He has a home that he owns to return to that has been maintained by his mother. He has considerable family and other support in the community and a detailed reentry plan and employment prospects.

Ed. Note: Based on the aforementioned factors and circumstances, the court found that Mr. Flowers is not a danger to any person or the community and the interests of justice would be served by reducing his sentence.

State of Connecticut v. Keith Belcher*

Justice Raheem L. Mullins

2022

The defendant, Keith Belcher, a juvenile offender, appeals from the trial court's denial of his motion to correct an illegal sentence. After his conviction, the defendant received a total effective sentence of sixty years of incarceration. He claims, inter alia, that the trial court improperly denied his motion to correct on the basis of the court's conclusion that the sentencing court did not impose the sentence in an illegal manner by relying on materially false information.

Our review of the record reveals that the defendant established that the sentencing court substantially relied on materially false information in imposing his sentence, specifically, on the court's view that the defendant was a "charter member" of a mythical group of teenage "superpredators." Therefore, we conclude that the trial court abused its discretion in denying the defendant's motion to correct. Accordingly, we reverse the

* *State of Connecticut v. Keith Belcher*, 268 A.3d Conn. 616 (2022).

judgment of the trial court, and the case is remanded with direction to grant the defendant's motion and for resentencing.

The following facts and procedural history are relevant to this appeal. "The defendant was fourteen years of age when, on December 24, 1993, he and a companion approached the victim in front of her apartment in Bridgeport. The victim was unloading groceries from her car when the defendant approached her from behind, pulled out a gun[,] and demanded that she give him her purse. When she informed the defendant that the purse was upstairs, he dragged her up to the apartment to retrieve it, all the time holding the gun on her." While in the apartment, the defendant sexually assaulted the victim twice, attempted to do so a third time, and pistol-whipped her.

Soon thereafter, based on the victim's identification of him from police photographs, the police arrested the defendant. Proceedings against him were initiated in the docket for juvenile matters of the Superior Court. Following a hearing, the court granted the state's motion to transfer the defendant's case to the regular criminal docket of the Superior Court.

We have emphasized that the protection against sentencing in an illegal manner "reflects the fundamental proposition that [t]he defendant has a legitimate interest in the character of the procedure [that] leads to the imposition of sentence even if he may have no right to object to a particular result of the sentencing process."

We also have acknowledged that "[a] sentencing judge has very broad discretion in imposing any sentence within the statutory limits and in exercising that discretion he may and should consider matters that would not be admissible at trial. Consistent with due process the trial court may consider responsible unsworn or out-of-court information relative to the circumstances of the crime and to the convicted person's life and circumstance. It is a fundamental sentencing principle that a sentencing judge may appropriately conduct an inquiry broad in scope, and largely unlimited either as to the kind of information he may consider or the source from which it may come. Finally, although a trial court's discretion is not completely unfettered, and information may be considered as a basis for a sentence only if it has some minimal indicium of reliability . . . [a]s long as the sentencing judge has a reasonable, persuasive basis for relying on the information which he uses to fashion his ultimate sentence, an appellate court should not interfere with his discretion."

We consider each of these factors in turn. First, a review of the superpredator theory and its history demonstrates that the theory constituted materially false and unreliable information. In the mid-1990s, Professor John DiIulio of Princeton University coined the term "superpredator."

DiIulio, whose work the sentencing court referenced specifically, warned that "the demographic bulge of the next [ten] years will unleash an army of young male predatory street criminals who will make even the leaders of the Bloods and Crips . . . look tame by comparison." DiIulio predicted that this coming wave of superpredators would include "elementary school youngsters who pack guns instead of lunches" and "have absolutely no respect for human life . . ."

He further warned: "On the horizon . . . are tens of thousands of severely morally impoverished juvenile superpredators. They are perfectly capable of committing the most heinous acts of physical violence for the most trivial reasons (for example, a perception of slight disrespect or the accident of being in their path). They fear neither the stigma of arrest nor the pain of imprisonment. They live by the meanest code of the meanest streets, a code that reinforces rather than restrains their violent, hair-trigger mentality. In prison or out, the things that super-predators get by their criminal behavior—sex, drugs, money—are their own immediate rewards. Nothing else matters to them. So for as long as their youthful energies hold out, they will do what comes 'naturally': murder, rape, rob, assault, burglarize, deal deadly drugs, and get high."

These dire predictions centered disproportionately on the demonization of Black male teens. In fact, contrary to DiIulio's assertion, even at the time that he coined the term in the mid-1990s, juvenile offense rates already had dropped significantly from their peak across demographic groups. The falsity of Di-Iulio's claim was demonstrated in a 2000 bulletin of the United States Department of Justice, which provided a data-driven assessment of juvenile crime patterns through the 1990s.

We conclude that the superpredator theory was baseless when it originally was espoused and has since been thoroughly debunked and universally rejected as a myth, and it therefore constituted false and unreliable information that a sentencing court ought not consider in crafting a sentence for a juvenile offender.

In the context of the sentencing of the defendant, a Black teenager, the court's reliance on the materially false super-predator myth is especially detrimental to the integrity of the sentencing procedure for two reasons. First, reliance on that myth invoked racial stereotypes, thus calling into question whether the defendant would have received as lengthy a sentence were he not Black. Second, the use of the superpredator myth supported treating the characteristics of youth as an aggravating, rather than a mitigating, factor. To fully appreciate how the use of this term was not simply a gloss but, rather, an inappropriate sentencing consideration, some historical and sociological context is needed.

The superpredator theory tapped into and amplified racial stereotypes that date back to the founding of our nation. Specifically relevant to the present case, the dehumanization of Black children pervades this country's history. In 1776, when Thomas Jefferson, a slave owner, declared "all men are created equal," in many of the colonies, Black adults and children were property and "were not legally considered human . . ."

As one legal scholar has observed, throughout the history of our country, our policies have reflected that only some children—white ones—have deserved societal protection. Notably, the protections and progressive social innovations afforded by these reforms were not provided to Black children, who were considered "'unsalvageable and undeserving'" of the "citizen-building ideals" that had prompted the changes. As a result, by 1850, rather than being sent to reform schools, "a disproportionate number of Black youths were jailed in cities with majority white populations." At the time that adolescence was being recognized as a distinct developmental stage for white children, many Black children remained enslaved and were viewed as subhuman.

The historical fiction that Black adolescents are not actually "children," meriting societal protection, stems from the dehumanization of Black Americans and is one of the roots of the disparate treatment of Black teens by the justice system.

Against this backdrop, the superpredator myth employed a particular tool of dehumanization—portraying Black people as animals. The news coverage in the mid-1990s, which depicted "young Black males, showing them [handcuffed] and shackled, held down by [the] police, or led into courtrooms wearing orange jumpsuits" left little doubt that the "packs" were Black teens.

The superpredator myth triggered and amplified the fears inspired by these dehumanizing racial stereotypes, thus perpet-

uating the systemic racial inequities that historically have pervaded our criminal justice system. Looming on the apocalyptic
horizon were tens of thousands of these fabricated, subhuman
superpredators, who would "do what comes 'naturally': murder,
rape, rob, assault, burglarize, deal deadly drugs, and get high."
And the consequences of the changes to juvenile justice fell disproportionately on Black teens.

The second reason the superpredator myth constituted particularly harmful materially false information for sentencing
purposes is because it turns upside down the constitutional
mandate of *Roper* [*Roper v. Simmons*, 543 U.S. 551 (2005)] and
its progeny. By labeling a juvenile as a superpredator, the very
characteristics of youth that should serve as mitigating factors
in sentencing—impulsivity, submission to peer pressure, de-
ficient judgment—are treated instead as aggravating factors
justifying harsher punishment.

In summary, by invoking the superpredator theory to sentence the young, Black male defendant in the present case, the
sentencing court, perhaps even without realizing it, relied on
materially false, racial stereotypes that perpetuate systemic
inequities—demanding harsher sentences—that date back
to the founding of our nation. In addition, contrary to *Roper*
and its progeny, in relying on the superpredator myth, the
sentencing court counted the characteristics of youth as an aggravating factor against the defendant. Although we do not
mean to suggest that the sentencing judge intended to perpetuate a race based stereotype, we cannot overlook the fact that
the superpredator myth is precisely the type of materially false
information that courts should not rely on in making sentencing decisions. Whether used wittingly or unwittingly, reliance
on such a baseless, illegitimate theory calls into question the
legitimacy of the sentencing procedure and the sentence.

Having concluded that the superpredator doctrine was materially false information, we next must determine whether the sentencing court *substantially relied* on the materially false and unreliable superpredator theory in arriving at the defendant's sentence.

The sentencing court described the superpredator group as "a group of radically impulsive, brutally remorseless youngsters who assault, rape, rob and burglarize." Echoing DiIulio's description of superpredators, the court stated to the defendant: "You have no fears, from your conduct, of the pains of imprisonment; nor do you suffer from the pangs of conscience." The court went further and called the defendant a "charter member" of that fictitious group. This was more than a mere gloss or broad statement. Consequently, we conclude that reliance on the false and pernicious superpredator theory in the present case so infected the sentencing that the sentence was imposed in an illegal manner.

It is axiomatic "that [t]he defendant has a legitimate interest in the character of the procedure which leads to the imposition of sentence . . ." We conclude that, because the superpredator theory constituted materially false, and, therefore, unreliable, evidence on which the sentencing court substantially relied, the trial court abused its discretion in denying the defendant's motion to correct an illegal sentence. The defendant's sentence was imposed in an illegal manner, in violation of his right to due process.

The trial court's decision is reversed and the case is remanded to that court with direction to grant the defendant's motion to correct an illegal sentence and for resentencing.

How Progressives Are Knocking Out Local Judges Across the Country*

Ian Ward

2021

On February 28, 1991, seventeen-year-old Robert Saleem Holbrook sat before a judge in a Philadelphia courtroom waiting to learn if he would spend the rest of his life behind bars.

Thirteen months earlier, on the night of his sixteenth birthday, Holbrook had served as a lookout for a drug deal gone wrong that ended in the murder of one of the participants. Despite never laying a hand on the victim, Holbrook was charged with first-degree murder, a capital offense in Pennsylvania. Facing the death sentence, he entered a plea deal for general murder, hoping that the judge overseeing his case would settle on a third-degree murder charge, which carried a penalty of

* Ian Ward, "How Progressives Are Knocking Out Local Judges Across the Country," *Politico*, September 3, 2021.

ten to twenty years in prison. Instead, claiming that his hands were tied by mandatory sentencing guidelines, the judge found Holbrook guilty of murder in the first degree. Under Pennsylvania law, the conviction carried a punishment of life in prison without the possibility of parole.

Thirty years later, Holbrook is, to use the lingo of the criminal justice system, "decarcerated," thanks to a 2012 decision by the United States Supreme Court that found that life sentences without the possibility of parole for minors violated the Eighth Amendment. Although Holbrook's days as an inmate are behind him, the lessons he learned while sitting in the courtroom as a seventeen-year-old criminal defendant are still very much with him.

One particular insight has stuck with him: the judges who preside over America's courtrooms are as much participants in contested political battles as they are executors of blind justice.

"What I saw in the courtroom, and what many other people like me saw—we don't see justice in courtrooms. We see politics being expressed in the courtroom," Holbrook said. "The judge in my courtroom—as a juvenile facing the death sentence for being a lookout to a drug-related homicide that I didn't see, or even have any idea that was going to happen—he was not pursuing justice. In my case, he was pursuing politics . . . It was politics that had me sitting in that courtroom facing the death sentence at the age of [sixteen]."

Now the executive director of Straight Ahead, the political action wing of the Abolitionist Law Center in [Pennsylvania], Holbrook has decided that if judges cannot be arbiters of pure justice, they can at least be representatives of a new type of politics—one that is more attuned to the injustices of America's criminal justice system. And Holbrook is not alone. In a handful of cities around the country, criminal justice reformers are organizing to get reform-minded judges elected to local benches, setting in motion a movement to "flip the bench" in favor of more progressive judges.

At a moment when politicians at the national level are cautiously backing away from more aggressive proposals to reform the nation's criminal justice system, the movement to flip the bench offers an alternative forward path for reform—albeit one that most challenges the left's conventional view of elected judges as instruments of tough-on-crime policies.

Holbrook and his fellow reformers face an uphill battle. In the vast majority of counties around the country, tough-on-crime messaging continues to dominate judicial races, and voters remain largely in the dark about the function and responsibilities of their local magistrates—let alone the role that progressive judges could play in a broader criminal justice reform agenda. On top of that, reformers are having to contend with the complexity of the different systems that states and local counties use to select judges, a dynamic that makes it difficult to scale grassroot movements up beyond the local level.

Yet despite these less-than-optimal political circumstances, the movement has shown some early signs of success. In early 2021, Holbrook's organization formed a coalition with four other criminal justice reform groups to endorse a slate of eight candidates running in the Democratic primary for spots on the court of common pleas in Allegheny County, the county in western Pennsylvania that includes Pittsburgh. In the May primary election, five of the coalition's candidates won. In neighboring Philadelphia, the criminal justice reform group Reclaim Philadelphia put forward its own slate of eight candidates for their county's court of common pleas, seven of whom won. Both counties lean heavily Democratic, and the reformist candidates are expected to prevail in the November general elections.

These recent results out of Pennsylvania bolstered a broader movement for judicial reform that has picked up momentum over the past three years. In 2018, activists in Harris County, Texas, successfully unseated fifty-nine Republican judges and replaced them with a slew of more reform-friendly candidates, including at least one self-proclaimed democratic socialist. Since then, activists in a growing number of counties around the country have repeated their success. In Clark County, Nevada, which includes Las Vegas, seven former public defenders won seats on local benches in 2020. Judicial candidates with similarly progressive credentials also secured seats in New Orleans and Cincinnati.

The judges come from different professional backgrounds—many previously worked as public defenders or as civil rights attorneys—and they have not rallied behind a unified platform or a clearly defined judicial philosophy. Yet they share a common goal: to use the discretion that is afforded to judges to remake America's justice system from the inside out. To Holbrook, their effort is symbolic as well as pragmatic.

"In America, the courtroom is the ultimate expression of law, because it is the courtroom that takes you into the carceral state and that leads you into the prison," Holbrook said. "It is an area that must be contested as hard as any other area."

Unless you've spent a significant amount of time in a trial courtroom, your understanding of judges' power likely remains little more than a vague set of impressions drawn from episodes of *Judge Judy* and *Law and Order*. But for those who have spent time in a courtroom—especially as a criminal defendant—that power is all too real.

"The thing with judges' power—it's like oxygen, right? You're not really conscious of oxygen until you're deprived of it," Holbrook said. "And with judges, you're not conscious of their power until you're in their courtroom or you see them obstructing your interest through the judicial system."

When it comes to many criminal proceedings, it is not an exaggeration to say that judges' decisions can be a matter of life and death. In some jurisdictions, state legislatures have adopted mandatory minimum sentencing guidelines and other provisions to constrain judges' discretion.

But in many cases, judges are afforded fairly broad discretion to apply a state's rules of criminal procedure, rules of evidence, and sentencing guidelines. In practice, that means that judges frequently have the power to decide whether a defendant is held on pretrial bail, what sort of plea bargain prosecutors can negotiate between defendants and victims, what the ultimate terms of a sentencing agreement look like, and how long a person must remain on parole or probation after serving his sentence.

In family and housing courts, judges can steer cases toward less punitive outcomes by opting against lengthy probation periods for minors convicted of nonviolent offenses, for example, or by granting more lenient stays in eviction disputes between tenants and landlords.

In part because of the wide array of judge's responsibilities, Americans have never agreed on the best way to select judges to the bench, and our collective indecision is reflected in the complex patchwork of state laws that govern judicial selection. Although public debates surrounding the optimal method of judicial selection tend to divide the approaches into two distinct categories—those that rely on popular election versus those that rely on some sort of appointment—the reality of judicial selection defies simple categorization.

In practice, most states deploy hybrid models that mix and match different selection methodologies, often depending on

270

Ian Ward

the type of court in question. In Kansas, for example, some judicial districts empower a commission to appoint judges to the district court—a system known as "merit selection"—while others use partisan elections, where candidates are required to list their party affiliation. Meanwhile, judges on the Kansas Court of Appeals are appointed by the governor, confirmed by the state senate, and then subject to face a yes-or-no retention election after one year—at which point they are allowed to serve a four-year term before facing another retention election. In the case of the state Supreme Court, Kansas uses a commission-based appointment without legislative confirmation, followed by retention elections.

By contrast, Alabama selects all state judges across all levels of the judiciary through partisan elections. Multiply this complexity across all fifty states, and the truly byzantine nature of judicial selection in America begins to come into focus.

Notwithstanding this complexity, nearly all state judges face some sort of electoral scrutiny. According to a 2015 study by the Brennan Center, roughly 87 percent of judges will face at least one election during their careers on the bench.

The nature of this scrutiny varies from race to race—some judges run in hotly contested partisan elections, while others merely face up-down retention votes—but historically, one dynamic has united most judicial elections: they favor hard-line, tough-on-crime candidates.

"Tough-on-crime messaging has been overwhelmingly the dominant message in judicial elections across the country," said Alicia Bannon, the managing director of the Democracy Program at the Brennan Center for Justice. "That's true both in terms of professional backgrounds, where it is very unusual, for example, to see judges come from public defender backgrounds or civil rights backgrounds, as well as in the kind of messaging you see in campaigns, where it's so much more common for judicial candidates to be targeted [for being] soft on crime and praised as tough on crime."

Elected judges' reputation for stringency has historically inspired a deep-seated skepticism of judicial elections among progressives, for whom the mere mention of an elected judge conjures up visions of Wild West hanging judges and Hollywood hard-liners. As a result, reformers have traditionally not contested these elections, assuming they would favor tough-on-crime candidates by default.

"Among people who were involved in criminal justice reform, decarceration, or even abolition, the prosecutor's office and the judicial elections were traditionally viewed as areas that we just weren't going to contest," Holbrook said.

However, that reflexive skepticism has begun to erode in the past three years, as criminal justice reformers have begun to grapple with the implications—and the limitations—of their movement's success. In particular, activists are learning from the early experiences of progressive prosecutors including Larry Krasner in Philadelphia, Chesa Boudin in San Francisco, Kim Foxx in Chicago, and Rachael Rollins in Boston, all of whom have assumed office since 2017. Now in power, many of these prosecutors are being met with fierce resistance from local judges, who object to either the substance or the method of their reforms. In Philadelphia, for example, local judges have repeatedly stymied Krasner's efforts to reform the city's parole and probation systems, arguing that Krasner's reforms prioritize the needs of criminals over those of victims and the public.

"We are seeing that when you elect someone like Krasner, then immediately the judiciary starts pushing back against him," said John Pfaff, a professor of law at Fordham University who studies the role of prosecutorial discretion in driving high prison populations. "Historically speaking, judges seem to be fairly deferential to prosecutors . . . but that in some way reflects the fact that those judges were former prosecutors for the same office that was still asking for bail, and therefore had a fair amount in common ideologically. When you change who the D.A. is, it's become clear that judges will resist."

Reform-minded prosecutors have run into resistance from the bench on a slew of other issues, as well. Local judges have also refused to sign off on more lenient plea deals and resentencing bargains that progressive prosecutors have negotiated, declined requests for retrials in cases of past prosecutorial misconduct, and even stood in the way of prosecutors' efforts to dismiss low-level nonviolent charges during the height of the Covid-19 pandemic.

The response to such forceful judicial pushback, reformers have realized, is not to fall back on conventional left-wing criticism of elected judges, or even to advocate for more judicial appointments. The more expedient approach is simple: begin seriously contesting judicial elections.

"We had the whole [movement] around progressive D.A.s that took off after Larry Krasner's campaign back in 2017, because there are more cities where people have realized, 'Hey, wait, we can do this,'" Holbrook said. "And when it comes to what can be done with district races across the country in places where you can elect the judge, I think it's also [the case], too. People are just saying, 'Wait, we can also have an effect on this—we should be involved in this.'"

Encouraged by their recent victories in Pennsylvania, Nevada, New Orleans, and Ohio, judicial reformers are hoping to translate these early wins into a broader movement to flip state and local benches around the country.

As a model for the future of the movement, they look to the

way that Krasner's victory in 2017 inspired reformers around the country to rally behind other progressive prosecutors—which is not surprising, given that many of the same activists who are organizing around judicial elections are the same ones who helped orchestrate Krasner's victory four years ago.

"I think we're at the beginning of a wave, just like 2017 was the beginning of the wave of progressive prosecutor reform," said Amanda McIllmurray, the political director of Reclaim Philadelphia. "I think this cycle is really the beginning of a progressive judicial reform."

But whether these early ripples of reform can grow into a full-blown wave will depend on how reformers navigate a complex matrix of political dynamics surrounding judicial elections.

For one, judicial elections tend to be what political scientists call "low-information, low-visibility" elections—in other words, voters tend to know next to nothing about the judicial candidates they're asked to vote for.

"I'm a law professor who takes voting for judges very, very seriously, and I struggle to learn anything about these judges beyond, at best, where they went to law school and what their job was before they became a judge," said Pfaff, who noted that even local outlets don't tend to publish detailed information on judicial candidates during busy election cycles. "Even if you want to be a high-information voter, you can't be, outside of sending emails to each individual judge to find out what they think."

Facing the dearth of public information about judicial candidates, organizers are devising novel ways to collect and disseminate information to voters. In 2018, for example, a coalition of criminal justice reform groups based in Philadelphia joined forces to organize the Judge Accountability Table, an organization dedicated to educating Philadelphians about candidates in the city's judicial races. Ahead of the Democratic primaries this past year, the group held a series of virtual public forums with candidates running for the city's municipal and common pleas court and invited candidates to answer a public questionnaire about their judicial philosophy and approach to key issues facing the judiciary. The questionnaire included questions such as, "Do you feel that implicit bias plays a role in our courts? If so, how do you think it should be addressed?" and "What role should judges play in making courts more transparent and accessible to members of the community? What will you commit to do if elected judge?"

"One of the largest parts of this work is educating people [about] who these candidates are—not just telling them who to vote for, but educating them on how to vote based on their values and if their values are aligning with these individuals who are running," said Brandi Fisher, the president of the Alliance for Police Accountability and one of the main organizers behind the "slate of eight" campaign in Allegheny County. "People are ready to make more informed decisions, but with these judicial races, you can't just expect everyone to be aware of who these people are when they decide to run, or even what their job is."

But changing voters' ingrained indifference toward judicial elections requires regular and sustained engagement, not just election-year canvassing—a difficult task for even the most organized local activist groups.

"This work is all year round, not election per election," Fisher said. "You have to keep people engaged all year round, and you have to keep people educated all year round."

Activists are also having to contend with skepticism from would-be judicial candidates. Many attractive candidates are current or past public defenders who have spent the majority of their careers facing off with judges, and few even considered that their careers could lead them to the other side of the bench.

"Running for judge one day is not something talked about between people who are public defenders," said Katia Pérez, an organizer with Reclaim Philadelphia and the lead coordinator of the Judge Accountability Table. "Most people that run for judge have either been folks that have been in the private sector, and maybe they made a lot of money and this was like a seat they can get, or they have worked as prosecutors before or in the D.A.'s office. So it's difficult [to recruit candidates] because it doesn't really seem to be a career path that's established within circles of public defenders."

To overcome these deficits, reformers have been working to win the backing of local Democratic Party organizations, whose endorsements have historically been the decisive factor in partisan judicial elections. In some cities, the party has endorsed reformist candidates even without significant pressure from activist groups, part of the party's broader shift to the left on criminal justice reform issues. But in large cities such as Philadelphia and New Orleans that have long been run by entrenched political machines, winning over local Democratic Party organizations hasn't been easy.

"There's definitely been pushback from the Democratic establishment," Pérez said. "There is a lot of [pressure] to continue to do politics the same way they've been done in Philly . . . but the problem with that is that the system prioritizes 'How many favors have been done?' and 'When do I get my payback for the favors that I've done?'"

There are some preliminary signs that activists have been able to counteract the influence of local Democratic Party organizations where they have not been able to benefit from it. During the Democratic primary for the court of common pleas in Philadelphia, for example, all six candidates endorsed by both the Democratic City Council (DCC) and Reclaim Philadelphia advanced to the general election, in addition to one candidate who was endorsed only by the DCC and one candidate who was endorsed only by Reclaim. But more notably, the only candidate endorsed by Reclaim who didn't advance to the general election, the former public defender Caroline Turner, beat out the party-backed incumbent Mark Moore by about 8,500 votes, suggesting that reformers successfully convinced voters to support their preferred candidates over the candidates endorsed by the DCC.

Finally, there is the stubborn fact that tough-on-crime rhetoric continues to play extremely well in the vast majority of judicial elections outside of major metropolitan areas. The solution, Pfaff says, is for reformers to focus their attention on specific counties that are demographically predisposed to support criminal justice reform.

"[The places] where we have our most progressive D.A.s are not just a random collection of more liberal cities," Pfaff said. "They're almost all elected in liberal cities where the city and the county are the exact same jurisdiction"—cities such as San Francisco, where the city is coterminous with the county, or Boston, where the population of urban Boston makes up over 85 percent of the total population of Suffolk County. The key, Pfaff explained, is that this quirk of geography effectively neutralizes the electoral influence of suburban voters, who tend to support tough-on-crime candidates over their more reform-minded challengers.

Although this dynamic automatically limits the possible scope of a broader judicial reform movement, it also presents a potential strategic benefit: reformers can concentrate their efforts on the areas where they are most likely to find receptive voters. And fortunately for reformers, these areas tend to have relatively high rates of crime, and therefore account for a disproportionately high percentage of criminal cases that wind up in courts.

"Crime is really, really concentrated, and therefore the costs of both punishment and the cost of good or bad responses to crime are all born in very geographically dense places . . . and those places we see came to be the areas that most favor reform," Pfaff said. "[People from these areas] understand that tough-on-crime [policy] doesn't work well, because it's their families that are being needlessly arrested and detained in harmful kinds of ways."

Ultimately, Holbrook said, the success of the movement will have to be measured not only by its scope but also by the longevity of its impact.

"The next step is to realize that what we're trying to build are legacy prosecutors and legacy judges that will last the next twenty, thirty, or forty years," Holbrook said. "We want to build legacies."

Reimagining Judging*

Nancy Gertner
2021

What does it take to turn this system, with these pressures and influences, around? Given judicial resistance to changing the habits of mass incarceration, how can we provide institutional support for meaningful change? A few suggestions follow.

JUDICIAL SELECTION

An important first step is to change whom we select for the bench. It is not simply a question of racial, ethnic, or even gender diversity. A bench can be racially diverse, diverse in terms of gender and sexual preference, and still come from the same sociocultural background as most judges have for decades. The issue is diversity of experience, not just demographic diversity. The vast majority of judges are former prosecutors and government civil attorneys, rather than defense or civil rights attorneys. And if they are not prosecutors, they are corporate lawyers. Eighty-five percent of former president

* Nancy Gertner, "Reimagining Judging," The Square One Project, January 2021.

Barack Obama's appointees were in either category. And recent selections have also done little to change the gender or racial makeup of the bench. They may well be extraordinary legal thinkers, they may well have the appropriate temperament, but they represent a narrow swath of attitudes and experiences— and that matters to the thousand decisions, big and small, that they must make on the bench.

JUDICIAL TRAINING

Judicial training, at least in the federal courts, is largely about rules, as if the only measure of a fair sentence is whether it is lawful, within statutory limits. While the Federal Sentencing Guidelines are now supposed to be advisory, judges are primarily trained in their application. The slide deck used by the United States Sentencing Commission is almost completely about the guidelines, their application, and their interpretation, save for the last slide, which announces that the guidelines are advisory. There is no analysis of how to deal with that new discretion, or what programs and considerations might be relevant. It is no small wonder federal judges continue to default to the guideline analysis; there is no framework for anything else.

Training about the impact of trauma and exposure to violence, poverty, and lack of access to schools, health care, employment, etc., should be required. They should hear from scientists about the neuroscience of trauma, addiction, and adolescent neurodevelopment; from sociologists about the social and cultural contexts of men and women they are sentencing; from health professionals about the social determinants of health.

As I have described, this information—not likely a part of the world view of the majority of judges—informs how a judge sees a case, how carefully they will question the parties, how deeply they will delve into the issues, and how much time they will give to it, as well as what he or she may do in the final decision. That discussion needs to be paired with a sophisticated understanding of the risk of pathologizing defendants from Black and Latinx communities, the danger being that the problems appear so complex that they are beyond a judge's consideration at all.

One of the many factors that ushered in mandatory sentencing in the 1980s was an article by sociologist Robert Martinson which seemed to suggest that nothing worked to rehabilitate people who have committed harm. We know that "nothing works" is wrong in many contexts related to crime, violence, and harm.

We need training programs that include information about other countries' criminal legal systems in order to enable judges to envision approaches other than the usual ones, and other than the assumptions of thirty years of judging. Judges often believe that what they are doing is the only way criminal legal work can be done, as if U.S. penal practices reflect the natural order of things. They do not.

SENTINEL EVENT AUDITS

In medicine, doctors hold "sentinel event" reviews whenever there is a death or serious physical or psychological injury to a patient or patients. Too often, the only outcome that matters to judges is a reversal by a higher court or press criticism. For the police, we have discussed changing incentives from arrests and convictions to more substantial measures of a community's health and safety. Likewise, we need to change the incentives for judges, and in so doing change their deliberative processes. Judges (and other players in the system) could hold a retrospective review when there is a wrongful conviction, when there is recidivism, or when there is an unexpected tragic event. What happened? What could be changed? What did we miss? What program worked or did not work? Should recidivism even be the measure of success or some other criterion—family, job, reintegration into a supportive community? What about accountability for wrongful or disproportionate sentences? What if judges were obliged to review case studies of what has happened to the defendants sentenced to lengthy retributive sentences, reexamining them, critiquing them, and considering alternatives? Did a thirty-year sentence, or twenty years, or ten, make sense in this case, in a humane, or even rational, sentencing system? How much did it disrupt the defendant's life course? Was it justified? What else could have—or should have—been done?

STATISTICAL REVIEWS

One way to address racial bias in policing is an after-the-fact, thorough statistical analysis of arrests to examine the extent to which they correlate with the race of the defendant. To be sure, this requires a commitment to accurate data collection and periodic reviews. Judicial decisions are rarely subject to that kind of analysis, except by scholars; even then, the analysis happens on a group, not an individual, level. Fearful of public criticism, judges are reluctant to allow scrutiny of their sentencing decisions. The fear is well-founded in a world in which press coverage of criminal matters is more parody than fact. Still, there is no other way to address unexamined bias.

I am working to submit my seventeen-year record to a statistical analysis to identify my racial bias. When I proposed such a program while I was still on the bench, there was considerable resistance; judges feared that the analyses would become public, that they would be criticized in the media, that Congress would swoop in with additional mandatory minimums. But without a statistical examination of sentencing, even if only for the internal review of the courts and individual judges, there is a risk that a judge will see racial bias as an abstraction; it applies to other judge's decisions, not their own. And for the public, such reports could well enhance the court's legitimacy, suggesting "we have nothing to hide," even "we are trying."

COMMUNITY ENGAGEMENT

Federal judges are too often removed from the communities they serve. The community's voice is filtered through the prosecutor and occasionally the victims, who pass on only the information that is most advantageous to seeking harsh sentences. [Boston's] Black community had broadly supported police-driven efforts to deal with crime in their communities, but their attitudes began to change as more and more young men were sentenced to extraordinarily long sentences and as police practices in stopping and frisking young Black men were exposed. That support dissipated, and they sharply criticized the government, when the U.S. Attorney decided to seek the death penalty in a case before me involving the murder of a man, allegedly by a local gang.

Concerns about judicial neutrality should not impede meaningful, unfiltered engagement with the community, an understanding of its needs and resources, what it takes to make a community flourish, and the role that courts play in doing so. That engagement should count as important—indeed more important—than the usual engagement with bar associations or law schools.

Judges are rarely held accountable in a meaningful way for their criminal legal decisions. They may be appealed, but that is not real accountability. That is only about conformance with rules and procedures, not necessarily justice. Judges may be criticized in the press, but that is rarely a dispassionate review and is often discounted. In fact, judges are likely to be criticized for sentencing too little, never too much; held responsible when someone they sentenced commits another crime, no matter what the cause, and not when someone they sentenced succeeds in reconstructing (or constructing) a good life. It results in a one-way ratchet, rewarded for overpunishing, for adopting whatever sentence the prosecutor requests, but rarely for their humanity and compassion.

NARRATIVE CHANGE

The questions I grapple with are, how can that narrative be reflected in the work of judging, and perhaps more critically, how do we incentivize judges to do so?

Opinion writing is the way for judges to reflect new narratives, to shine a light on the humanity of the defendants, and the inhumanity of the criminal legal system. In "Do Judges Cry? An Essay on Empathy and Fellow-Feeling," the authors cite the dissent of Justice John Harlan in *Plessy v. Ferguson* (1896), which they describe as "lamenting the sterile formalism by which the majority found nothing wrong with a railroad ordinance that required separate seating for white and black passengers"; the opinion of Judge David Bazelon of the D.C. Circuit in *United States v. Alexander* (1973), who discussed the ways in which a "rotten social background," including child abuse, violence, and maltreatment, should figure into the court's understanding of a defendant; and my opinion in *United States v. Leviner* (1998), which rejected the consideration of prior convictions that were for "driving while Black." Other examples might include my opinion in *United States v. Haynes* (courts should consider the ways in which the failed experiment in mass incarceration has disrupted families and communities) or Judge Jack Weinstein's decision in *United States v. Bannister* (warning that mandatory minimum sentencing "impose[s] grave costs not only on the punished but on the moral credibility upon which our system of criminal justice depends"). Or perhaps the most compelling narrative was in *United States v. Burudi Faison*, which begins a sentencing memorandum with a quote from Shon Hopwood in *Law Man: My Story of Robbing Banks, Winning Supreme Court Cases, and Finding Redemption*: "As we neared the prison, I saw its razor-wire fences, towers, and lights. . . . Our bus pulled up to the gate. Again, we faced a reception line of guards with shotguns and automatic assault rifles."

Even in situations in which a judge must impose a mandatory sentence, when the opinion is nothing but a cri de coeur, a judge should write if only to decry the unfairness of the result. In *United States v. Vasquez*, Judge John Gleeson began:

> When people think about miscarriages of justice, they generally think big, especially in this era of DNA exonerations, in which wholly innocent people have been released from jail in significant numbers after long periods in prison. As disturbing as those cases are, the truth is that most of the time miscarriages of justice occur in small doses, in cases involving guilty defendants. This makes them easier to overlook. But when they are multiplied by the thousands of cases in which they occur, they have a greater impact on our criminal justice system than the cases you read about in the newspapers or hear about on *60 Minutes*.

The goal is explicit: to speak not simply to the litigants and possibly the appellate courts, but to the public.

Chief Justice Warren was clear that the majority decision in *Brown v. Board of Education*, reversing *Plessy*, should have the public in mind: "[The opinion outlawing separate but equal education] should be short, readable by the lay public, non-rhetorical, unemotional, and above all, non-accusatory." During my time on the bench, I tried to make the first three or four pages of any opinion the functional equivalent of a press release.

Judges speak through their opinions—to the lawyers, to other judges, to the media, to the people before them. They can speak in the antiseptic language of the law, the language of guidelines and rules. They can pretend that what they are doing is fair when it is not. Or they can change the narrative.

The habits of mass incarceration die hard, helped by the insularity of the courts, by its composition, and by factors I have only begun to address. But these habits are not impenetrable. The goal is to engage the courts in the wider discussion about the unfairness of the system and its impact on poor communities and especially communities of color. The goal is to invite judges to reimagine what community safety really looks like, not with police, prosecutors, and exorbitant mandatory minimums—and the role that judges can play in facilitating it.

The way to change is to hold all of the players in the criminal legal system accountable—including judges—to effect a true reckoning.

Part V

Prisons

Prison is commonly thought of as the last step in the system we've been describing in this book. (Although, as we'll see in the next part, punishments can continue for years after prison.) After the police have arrested, the lawyers have argued, and the courts have sentenced, prison is the end of the line. What does the end look like? It's enormous—the American prison system is the world's largest. It's also harsh, degrading, and sometimes deadly. When the U.S. Department of Justice released a fifty-three-page report in 2019 documenting grotesque violence in Alabama's prisons, few experts were shocked. In fact, a common reaction was, "Sure, Alabama is terrible, but it's not just an Alabama problem." And while violence and brutality garner the most attention, conversations with incarcerated people reveal a long list of other problems: tedium, arbitrary visitation and phone restrictions, overcrowding, inadequate health care, nonexistent mental health and addiction services, substandard educational programs, chronic noise, and cruel guards. These disparate injustices cohere to send a consistent message: society deems you expendable.

This bleak state of affairs has not gone unchallenged. This part explores some of the efforts by activists, organizers, everyday people, and forward-thinking government officials both to shrink our prison system and to render it less cruel to those currently in it. As we did in the part on policing, we organize these efforts under two broad categories: abolition and reform. It turns out, though, that the boundaries between the two are often blurry.

Prison abolitionism refers to the theory and practice of working toward a society without prisons, grounded in the belief that prisons are ineffective, unnecessary, and destructive. Prison abolition came to the fore of mainstream political discourse in the summer of 2020 as millions protested police brutality and systemic racism. Abolitionism, however, has deep roots in leftist and Black political thought. This part opens with four pieces examining the merits of prison abolition.

Angela Y. Davis, perhaps the most influential prison abolitionist, introduces abolitionist theory in her seminal text, *Are Prisons Obsolete?* The public, Davis argues, has come to take prisons for granted. "It is as if prison were an inevitable fact of life, like birth and death," she writes. Yet as Davis points out, America's prison expansion is a recent phenomenon. There were relatively few prisons in the United States until the 1980s, when Reagan-era "tough on crime" politics launched a prison explosion. California, for example, had only nine prisons in the

1970s; that number grew to more than thirty in the 1980s and 1990s. While the prison population grew dramatically, Davis argues that putting more people behind bars did not make communities safer. Instead of prisons, Davis calls for decarceration measures, such as decriminalizing drug use and pursuing "restorative rather than exclusively punitive justice." Such measures remain central to abolitionism today.

Following Davis, we include an excerpt from the 1976 classic *Instead of Prisons: A Handbook for Abolitionists*, written by Quaker activist Fay Honey Knopp and a group of authors who called themselves the Prison Education Advocacy Project. In an opening statement titled "Nine Perspectives for Prison Abolitionists," the handbook outlines what abolition is, what it isn't, and how it differs from the dominant thinking of that time. For readers unfamiliar with abolitionist theory and language, the "Nine Perspectives" excerpt offers an excellent introduction.

Abolitionism is more than a collection of ideals. It is a practice and vision for a different kind of society—one in which incarceration is unnecessary. In "Can Prison Abolition Ever Be Pragmatic?," the journalist and political commentator Nathan J. Robinson examines whether abolition is utopian. He grapples with a question that arises early and often in many abolition discussions—if we abolish prison, what will we do with society's most dangerous offenders? While acknowledging the force of that question, Robinson concludes that abolition remains appealing even if it fails to offer a complete answer. In Robinson's view, one of abolition's ultimate objectives is to transform social and political relationships in such a way that heinous offenses occur less often—or perhaps never. This, says Robinson, could be abolition's greatest promise: its determination to build a world free of prisons *and* serious harm.[1]

In a world so dependent on prisons, debating whether to

abolish them can feel a bit theoretical. In "The Case for Abolition," longtime abolitionists Ruth Wilson Gilmore and James Kilgore urge us to turn toward the practical. Gilmore and Kilgore argue that, far from being utopian dreamers, most abolitionists are pragmatic organizers and activists working locally to create caring communities. Yes, abolitionists fight to close prisons and jails—but just as crucially, they fight for robust social welfare guarantees, including housing, jobs, education, and health care.

Alongside local organizing, prison abolitionists have long been concerned with the language we use to describe prisons and the people we lock inside them. The 1976 handbook *Instead of Prisons* was groundbreaking in this regard as well, arguing for what the authors called honest language (e.g., "prison," not "reformatory"; "prison guard," not "correctional officer"; "criminal (in)justice system," not "criminal justice system").[2] Since debates over language will never end, some of the words we use today (including, undoubtedly, in this book) will be challenged by future generations—if not sooner. We illustrate this point with a Twitter thread by the poet Reginald Dwayne Betts, who argues against referring to prison cells as "cages." This term has seen a recent resurgence among some critics of mass incarceration. While sympathetic to their intention—to avoid sanitizing inhumane conditions—Betts argues that the term does more harm than good. In his words, "the very thing being done to point out dehumanization is dramatically more dehumanizing."

If prison abolition is one front in today's struggle against mass incarceration, a companion set of efforts—which we gather together under the label "reform"—seeks to change how incarcerated people are treated on the inside. One way to do that is by adopting incarceration practices long common in

Northern Europe. "North Dakota's Norway Experiment," by the journalist Dashka Slater, explains how a visit to Norway's Halden prison (often called "the world's most humane prison") prompted North Dakota officials to make a series of changes, including limiting their use of solitary confinement, allowing some incarcerated people to wear civilian clothing instead of prison garb, and offering others day passes to visit their homes.[3] North Dakota is a deeply conservative state, but its racial homogeneity and lower-than-average incarceration rate have made these changes politically viable. Similar initiatives have taken root in Massachusetts, South Carolina, and Connecticut.[4]

These articles show that there are a variety of approaches to improving prison conditions. Among the most important is to provide incarcerated people with educational opportunities. Studies show that investing in prison education programs is highly cost-effective because it reduces recidivism.[5] But more importantly, argue the authors included here, it is the moral course of action. Imprisonment is, itself, deeply punitive. We should not impose additional punishments such as isolation, violence, or denial of the chance to read, write, and learn.

But, as the poet and *Atlantic* writer Clint Smith underscores, denying people the opportunity to learn is exactly what we have long done. In "Restoring Pell Grants—and Possibilities—for Prisoners," Smith explains that the federal Pell Grant program was once the most important initiative supporting prison education. In the early 1990s, there were more than 770 college programs in 1,300 prisons across the country. In 1994, however, Congress eliminated Pell Grant eligibility for currently and formerly incarcerated people. Almost overnight, college education in prison disappeared, since the mostly low-income incarcerated population could not pay for classes. By 1997, there were only eight prison college programs in the United States; each had to secure its own funding without the federal government's support. After years of activism and lobbying by people inside and outside prison, in 2020 Congress finally reversed its 1994 decision, making Pell Grants available once again to currently and formerly incarcerated individuals.[6] Drawing on his own experience teaching in prison, Smith powerfully explains why providing Pell Grants to incarcerated students is so important.[7]

One of the most prominent efforts to bring university classes inside prisons is the Inside-Out Prison Exchange Program, which trains professors to teach classes that bring students from their university together with people incarcerated in a local prison or jail. Started at a single prison in 1995, the program now partners with more than 200 correctional facilities and 150 universities to bring courses to 60,000 students across the nation. In "The Inside-Out Prison Exchange Program: Its Origin, Essence, and Global Reach," founder Lori Pompa describes the program's success in prompting students to engage in dialogue across various types of difference, and in giving people from the "outside" direct exposure to prisons, where they see "who is there, who's not there, and what is going on (or not) on the inside."

Just as they lack college courses, most prisons lack something even more fundamental: books. Reginald Dwayne Betts, whose objection to calling prison cells "cages" appears earlier in this part, is trying to change that through his nationwide Freedom Reads program. He has curated a collection of five hundred books that he hopes to place in every prison in the United States. Among the first locations to receive the collection are the notorious Louisiana State Penitentiary in Angola and MCI-Norfolk in Massachusetts, where Betts has housed the books in the cell that once held Malcolm X.

In the opening essay, Angela Y. Davis documents California's unprecedented prison expansion in the 1980s and 1990s. In the final essay, "A Future for Susanville," Piper French asks what it will take to shrink the number of prisons—in California and across the country. French reports on the response to California governor Gavin Newsom's promise to close the California Correctional Center in Susanville. Governor Newsom's pledge came in the midst of a sustained pressure campaign led by Californians United for a Responsible Budget (CURB), a coalition of more than eighty grassroots organizations. As is the case in so many small towns across America, Susanville's prisons anchor the local economy. (In the 1990s, a new prison or jail opened its doors in rural America every fifteen days.[8]) Many of Susanville's free residents have substantial political power and fought hard to keep the California Correctional Center open—but on June 30, 2023, it was deactivated.[9]

In presenting writing on prison abolition alongside writing on improving life inside prisons, we hope to prompt reflection on whether these approaches are in tension. Angela Y. Davis warns they might be: "Debates about strategies of decarceration, which should be the focal point of our conversations on the prison crisis, tend to be marginalized when reform takes the center stage." Yet many prison abolitionists support meaningful reforms such as ending solitary confinement and improving educational opportunities inside prisons.

Wherever you land on the abolition-reform spectrum, one of this book's unifying themes is the role ordinary people can play in creating change. Gilmore and Kilgore say that efforts to eliminate the need for prisons don't come from on high but are rooted in "clubs, political organizations, faith communities, unions, and neighborhood associations." The same is true of prison education. While it is crucial for legislators and prison officials to support this work, nothing can happen without teachers willing to design courses and offer them to incarcerated students. In the Inside-Out program, as Pompa shows, university students can participate in and help shape these courses. Everyday people from all walks of life, churches, and nonprofits can donate books, school supplies, and other resources. And we can all learn about more humane ways to hold people accountable for harm without destroying them and our communities in the process. So, as you consider the various initiatives described here, we encourage you to reflect on the following questions: Which of these approaches appeals to my sense of justice? Which offers a path toward liberation and equality? And if you are moved to act, we encourage you to ask an additional question: Which do I want to fight for? Then, whatever your answer, find a few allies (you only need a few) and get to work!

From *Are Prisons Obsolete?**

Angela Y. Davis
2003

In most parts of the world, it is taken for granted that whoever is convicted of a serious crime will be sent to prison. In some countries—including the United States—where capital punishment has not yet been abolished, a small but significant number of people are sentenced to death for what are considered especially grave crimes. Many people are familiar with the campaign to abolish the death penalty. In fact, it has already been abolished in most countries. Even the staunchest advocates of capital punishment acknowledge the fact that the death penalty faces serious challenges. Few people find life without the death penalty difficult to imagine.

On the other hand, the prison is considered an inevitable and permanent feature of our social lives. Most people are quite surprised to hear that the prison abolition movement also has a long history—one that dates back to the historical appearance

* Angela Y. Davis, From *Are Prisons Obsolete?* (New York: Seven Stories Press, 2003).

of the prison as the main form of punishment. In fact, the most natural reaction is to assume that prison activists—even those who consciously refer to themselves as "antiprison activists"— are simply trying to ameliorate prison conditions or perhaps to reform the prison in more fundamental ways. In most circles prison abolition is simply unthinkable and implausible. Prison abolitionists are dismissed as utopians and idealists whose ideas are at best unrealistic and impracticable, and, at worst, mystifying and foolish. This is a measure of how difficult it is to envision a social order that does not rely on the threat of se-questering people in dreadful places designed to separate them from their communities and families. The prison is considered so "natural" that it is extremely hard to imagine life without it.

It is my hope that this book will encourage readers to ques-tion their own assumptions about the prison. Many people have already reached the conclusion that the death penalty is an outmoded form of punishment that violates basic princi-ples of human rights. It is time, I believe, to encourage similar conversations about the prison. During my own career as an antiprison activist I have seen the population of U.S. prisons increase with such rapidity that many people in black, Latino, and Native American communities now have a far greater chance of going to prison than of getting a decent education. When many young people decide to join the military service in order to avoid the inevitability of a stint in prison, it should cause us to wonder whether we should not try to introduce bet-ter alternatives.

The question of whether the prison has become an obso-lete institution has become especially urgent in light of the fact that more than two million people (out of a world total of nine million) now inhabit U.S. prisons, jails, youth facilities, and immigrant detention centers. Are we willing to relegate ever larger numbers of people from racially oppressed communities to an isolated existence marked by authoritarian regimes, violence, disease, and technologies of seclusion that produce severe mental instability? According to a recent study, there may be twice as many people suffering from mental illness who are in jails and prisons than there are in all psychiatric hospitals in the United States combined.

When I first became involved in antiprison activism during the late 1960s, I was astounded to learn that there were then close to two hundred thousand people in prison. Had anyone told me that in three decades ten times as many people would be locked away in cages, I would have been absolutely incredulous. I imagine that I would have responded something like this: "As racist and undemocratic as this country may be [remember, during that period, the demands of the Civil Rights movement had not yet been consolidated], I do not believe that the U.S. government will be able to lock up so many people without producing powerful public resistance. No, this will never happen, not unless this country plunges into fascism." That might have been my reaction thirty years ago. The reality is that we were called upon to inaugurate the twenty-first century by accepting the fact that two million people—a group larger than the population of many countries—are living their lives in places like Sing Sing, Leavenworth, San Quentin, and Alderson Federal Reformatory for Women. The gravity of these numbers becomes even more apparent when we consider that the U.S. population in general is less than five percent of the world's total, whereas more than twenty percent of the world's combined prison population can be claimed by the United States. In Elliott Currie's words, "[t]he prison has become a looming presence in our society to an extent unparalleled in our history or that of any other industrial democracy. Short of major wars, mass incarceration has been the most thoroughly implemented government social program of our time."

In thinking about the possible obsolescence of the prison, we should ask how it is that so many people could end up in prison without major debates regarding the efficacy of incarceration. When the drive to produce more prisons and incarcerate ever larger numbers of people occurred in the 1980s during what is known as the Reagan era, politicians argued that "tough on crime" stances—including certain imprisonment and longer sentences—would keep communities free of crime. However, the practice of mass incarceration during that period had little or no effect on official crime rates. In fact, the most obvious pattern was that larger prison populations led not to safer communities but, rather, to even larger prison populations. Each new prison spawned yet another new prison. And as the U.S. prison system expanded, so did corporate involvement in construction, provision of goods and services, and use of prison labor. Because of the extent to which prison building and operation began to attract vast amounts of capital—from the construction industry to food and health-care provision—in a way that recalled the emergence of the military industrial complex, we began to refer to a "prison industrial complex."

Consider the case of California, whose landscape has been thoroughly prisonized over the last twenty years. The first state prison in California was San Quentin, which opened in 1852. Folsom, another well-known institution, opened in 1880. Between 1880 and 1933, when a facility for women was opened in Tehachapi, there was not a single new prison constructed. In 1952, the California Institution for Women opened, and Tehachapi became a new prison for men. In all, between 1852 and 1955, nine prisons were constructed in California. Between

1962 and 1965, two camps were established, along with the California Rehabilitation Center. Not a single prison opened during the second half of the sixties, nor during the entire decade of the 1970s.

However, a massive project of prison construction was initiated during the 1980s—that is, during the years of the Reagan presidency. Nine prisons, including the Northern California Facility for Women, were opened between 1984 and 1989. Recall that it had taken more than a hundred years to build the first nine California prisons. In less than a single decade, the number of California prisons doubled. And during the 1990s, twelve new prisons were opened, including two more for women. In 1995 the Valley State Prison for Women was opened. According to its mission statement, it "provides 1,980 women's beds for California's overcrowded prison system." However, in 2002, there were 3,570 prisoners and the other two women's prisons were equally overcrowded.

There are now thirty-three prisons, thirty-eight camps, sixteen community correctional facilities, and five tiny prisoner mother facilities in California. In 2002 there were 157,979 people incarcerated in these institutions, including approximately twenty thousand people whom the state holds for immigration violations. The racial composition of this prison population is revealing. Latinos, who are now in the majority, account for 35.2 percent; African-Americans 30 percent; and white prisoners 29.2 percent. There are now more women in prison in the state of California than there were in the entire country in the early 1970s. In fact, California can claim the largest women's prison in the world, Valley State Prison for Women, with its more than thirty-five hundred inhabitants. Located in the same town as Valley State and literally across the street is the second-largest women's prison in the world—Central California Women's Facility—whose population in 2002 also hovered around thirty-five hundred.

If you look at a map of California depicting the location of the thirty-three state prisons, you will see that the only area that is not heavily populated by prisons is the area north of Sacramento. Still, there are two prisons in the town of Susanville, and Pelican Bay, one of the state's notorious super-maximum security prisons, is near the Oregon border. California artist Sandow Birk was inspired by the colonizing of the landscape by prisons to produce a series of thirty-three landscape paintings of these institutions and their surroundings. They are collected in his book *Incarcerated: Visions of California in the 21st Century.*

I present this brief narrative of the prisonization of the California landscape in order to allow readers to grasp how easy it was to produce a massive system of incarceration with the implicit consent of the public. Why were people so quick to assume that locking away an increasingly large proportion of the U.S. population would help those who live in the free world feel safer and more secure? This question can be formulated in more general terms. Why do prisons tend to make people think that their own rights and liberties are more secure than they would be if prisons did not exist? What other reasons might there have been for the rapidity with which prisons began to colonize the California landscape?

Geographer Ruth Gilmore describes the expansion of prisons in California as "a geographical solution to socio-economic problems." Her analysis of the prison industrial complex in California describes these developments as a response to surpluses of capital, land, labor, and state capacity.

California's new prisons are sited on devalued rural land, most, in fact on formerly irrigated agricultural acres . . . The State bought land sold by big landowners. And the State assured the small, depressed towns now shadowed by prisons that the new, recession-proof, non-polluting industry would jump-start local redevelopment.

But, as Gilmore points out, neither the jobs nor the more general economic revitalization promised by prisons has occurred. At the same time, this promise of progress helps us to understand why the legislature and California's voters decided to approve the construction of all these new prisons. People wanted to believe that prisons would not only reduce crime, they would also provide jobs and stimulate economic development in out-of-the-way places.

At bottom, there is one fundamental question: Why do we take prison for granted? While a relatively small proportion of the population has ever directly experienced life inside prison, this is not true in poor black and Latino communities. Neither is it true for Native Americans or for certain Asian American communities. But even among those people who must regrettably accept prison sentences—especially young people—as an ordinary dimension of community life, it is hardly acceptable to engage in serious public discussions about prison life or radical alternatives to prison. It is as if prison were an inevitable fact of life, like birth and death.

On the whole, people tend to take prisons for granted. It is difficult to imagine life without them. At the same time, there is reluctance to face the realities hidden within them, a fear of thinking about what happens inside them. Thus, the prison is present in our lives and, at the same time, it is absent from our lives. To think about this simultaneous presence and absence is to begin to acknowledge the part played by ideology in shaping the way we interact with our social surroundings. We take prisons for granted but are often afraid to face the realities they produce. After all, no one wants to go to prison. Because it would be too agonizing to cope with the possibility that anyone, including ourselves, could become a prisoner, we tend to think of the prison as disconnected from our own lives. This is even true for some of us, women as well as men, who have already experienced imprisonment.

We thus think about imprisonment as a fate reserved for others, a fate reserved for the "evildoers," to use a term recently popularized by George W. Bush. Because of the persistent power of racism, "criminals" and "evildoers" are, in the collective imagination, fantasized as people of color. The prison therefore functions ideologically as an abstract site into which undesirables are deposited, relieving us of the responsibility of thinking about the real issues afflicting those communities from which prisoners are drawn in such disproportionate numbers. This is the ideological work that the prison performs— it relieves us of the responsibility of seriously engaging with the problems of our society, especially those produced by racism and, increasingly, global capitalism.

What, for example, do we miss if we try to think about prison expansion without addressing larger economic developments? We live in an era of migrating corporations. In order to escape organized labor in this country—and thus higher wages, benefits, and so on—corporations roam the world in search of nations providing cheap labor pools. This corporate migration thus leaves entire communities in shambles. Huge numbers of people lose jobs and prospects for future jobs. Because the economic base of these communities is destroyed, education and other surviving social services are profoundly affected. This process turns the men, women, and children who live in these damaged communities into perfect candidates for prison.

In the meantime, corporations associated with the punishment industry reap profits from the system that manages prisoners and acquire a clear stake in the continued growth of prison populations. Put simply, this is the era of the prison industrial complex. The prison has become a black hole into which the detritus of contemporary capitalism is deposited. Mass imprisonment generates profits as it devours social wealth, and thus it tends to reproduce the very conditions that lead people to prison. There are thus real and often quite complicated connections between the deindustrialization of the economy—a process that reached its peak during the 1980s—and the rise of mass imprisonment, which also began to spiral during the Reagan-Bush era. However, the demand for more prisons was represented to the public in simplistic terms. More prisons were needed because there was more crime. Yet many scholars have demonstrated that by the time the prison construction boom began, official crime statistics were already falling. Moreover, draconian drug laws were being enacted, and "three-strikes" provisions were on the agendas of many states.

In order to understand the proliferation of prisons and the rise of the prison industrial complex, it might be helpful to think further about the reasons we so easily take prisons for granted. In California, as we have seen, almost two-thirds of existing prisons were opened during the eighties and nineties. Why was there no great outcry? Why was there such an obvious level of comfort with the prospect of many new prisons? A partial answer to this question has to do with the way we consume media images of the prison, even as the realities of imprisonment are hidden from almost all who have not had the misfortune of doing time. Cultural critic Gina Dent has pointed out that our sense of familiarity with the prison comes in part from representations of prisons in film and other visual media.

> The history of visuality linked to the prison is also a main reinforcement of the institution of the prison as a naturalized part of our social landscape. The history of film has always been wedded to the representation of incarceration. Thomas Edison's first films (dating back to the 1901 reenactment presented as news reel, *Execution of Czolgosz with Panorama of Auburn Prison*) included footage of the darkest recesses of the prison. Thus, the prison is wedded to our experience of visuality, creating also a sense of its permanence as an institution. We also have a constant flow of Hollywood prison films, in fact a genre.

Some of the most well-known prison films are: *I Want to Live!, Papillon, Cool Hand Luke*, and *Escape from Alcatraz*. It also bears mentioning that television programming has become increasingly saturated with images of prisons. Some recent documentaries include the A&E series *The Big House*, which consists of programs on San Quentin, Alcatraz, Leavenworth, and Alderson Federal Reformatory for Women. The long-running HBO program *Oz* has managed to persuade many viewers that they know exactly what goes on in male maximum-security prisons.

But even those who do not consciously decide to watch a documentary or dramatic program on the topic of prisons inevitably consume prison images, whether they choose to or not, by the simple fact of watching movies or TV. It is virtually impossible to avoid consuming images of prison. In 1997, I was myself quite astonished to find, when I interviewed women in three Cuban prisons, that most of them narrated their prior awareness of prisons—that is, before they were actually incarcerated—as coming from the many Hollywood films they had seen. The prison is one of the most important features of our image environment. This has caused us to take the existence of prisons for granted. The prison has become a key ingredient of our common sense. It is there, all around us. We do not question whether it should exist. It has become so much a part of our lives that it requires a great feat of the imagination to envision life beyond the prison.

This is not to dismiss the profound changes that have occurred in the way public conversations about the prison are conducted. Ten years ago, even as the drive to expand the prison system reached its zenith, there were very few critiques of this process available to the public. In fact, most people had no idea about the immensity of this expansion. This was the period during which internal changes—in part through the application of new technologies—led the U.S. prison system in a much more repressive direction. Whereas previous classifications had been confined to low, medium, and maximum security, a new category was invented—that of the super-maximum security prison, or the supermax. The turn toward increased repression in a prison system, distinguished from the beginning of its history by its repressive regimes, caused some journalists, public intellectuals, and progressive agencies to oppose the growing reliance on prisons to solve social problems that are actually exacerbated by mass incarceration.

In 1990, the Washington-based Sentencing Project published a study of U.S. populations in prison and jail, and on parole and probation, which concluded that one in four black men between the ages of twenty and twenty-nine were among these numbers. Five years later, a second study revealed that this percentage had soared to almost one in three (32.2 percent). Moreover, more than one in ten Latino men in this same age range were in jail or prison, or on probation or parole. The second study also revealed that the group experiencing the greatest increase was black women, whose imprisonment increased by 78 percent. According to the Bureau of Justice Statistics, African Americans as a whole now represent the majority of state and federal prisoners, with a total of 803,400 black inmates—118,600 more than the total number of white inmates. During the late 1990s major articles on prison expansion appeared in *Newsweek*, *Harper's*, *Emerge*, and *Atlantic Monthly*. Even Colin Powell raised the question of the rising number of black men in prison when he spoke at the 2000 Republican National Convention, which declared George W. Bush its presidential candidate.

Over the last few years the previous absence of critical positions on prison expansion in the political arena has given way to proposals for prison reform. While public discourse has become more flexible, the emphasis is almost inevitably on generating the changes that will produce a *better* prison system. In other words, the increased flexibility that has allowed for critical discussion of the problems associated with the expansion of prisons also restricts this discussion to the question of prison reform.

As important as some reforms may be—the elimination of sexual abuse and medical neglect in women's prison, for example—frameworks that rely exclusively on reforms help to produce the stultifying idea that nothing lies beyond the prison. Debates about strategies of decarceration, which should be the focal point of our conversations on the prison crisis, tend to be marginalized when reform takes the center stage. The most immediate question today is how to prevent the further expansion of prison populations and how to bring as many imprisoned women and men as possible back into what prisoners call "the free world." How can we move to decriminalize drug use and the trade in sexual services? How can we take seriously strategies of restorative rather than exclusively punitive justice? Effective alternatives involve both transformation of the techniques for addressing "crime" and of the social and economic conditions that track so many children from poor communities, and especially communities of color, into the juvenile system and then on to prison. The most difficult and urgent challenge today is that of creatively exploring new terrains of justice, where the prison no longer serves as our major anchor.

Nine Perspectives for Prison Abolitionists*

Fay Honey Knopp

1976

Perspective 1: Imprisonment is morally reprehensible and indefensible and must be abolished. In an enlightened free society, prison cannot endure or it will prevail. Abolition is a long-range goal, an ideal. The eradication of any oppressive system is not an easy task. But it is realizable, like the abolition of slavery or any liberation, so long as there is the will to engage in the struggle.

Perspective 2: The message of abolition requires "honest" language and new definitions. Language is related to power. We do not permit those in power to control our vocabulary. Using

---

* Fay Honey Knopp, "Nine Perspectives for Prison Abolitionists," *Instead of Prisons: A Handbook for Abolitionists*, ed. Mark Morris (New York: Prison Action Research Project, 1976).

"system language" to call prisoners "inmates" or punishment "treatment" denies prisoners the reality of their experience and makes us captives of the old system. Our own language and definitions empower us to define the prison realistically.

Perspective 3: Abolitionists believe reconciliation, not punishment, is a proper response to criminal acts. The present criminal (in)justice systems focus on someone to punish, caring little about the criminal's need or the victim's loss. The abolitionist response seeks to restore both the criminal and the victim to full humanity, to lives of integrity and dignity in the community. Abolitionists advocate the least amount of coercion and intervention in an individual's life and the maximum amount of care and services to all people in the society.

Perspective 4: Abolitionists work with prisoners but always remain "nonmembers" of the established prison system. Abolitionists learn how to walk the narrow line between relating to prisoners inside the system and remaining independent and "outside" that system. We resist the compelling psychological pressures to be "accepted" by people in the prison system. We are willing to risk pressing for changes that are beneficial to and desired by prisoners. In relating to those in power, we differentiate between the personhood of system managers (which we respect) and their role in perpetuating an oppressive system.

Perspective 5: Abolitionists are "allies" of prisoners rather than traditional "helpers." We have forged a new definition of what is truly helpful to the caged, keeping in mind both the prisoner's perspective and the requirements of abolition. New insights into old, culture-laden views of the "helping relation-ship" strengthen our roles as allies of prisoners.

Perspective 6: Abolitionists realize that the empowerment of prisoners and ex-prisoners is crucial to prison system change. Most people have the potential to determine their own needs in terms of survival, resources, and programs. We support self-determination of prisoners and programs which place more power in the hands of those directly affected by the prison experience.

Perspective 7: Abolitionists view power as available to each of us for challenging and abolishing the prison system. We believe that citizens are the source of institutional power. By giving support to—or withholding support from—specific policies and practices, patterns of power can be altered.

Perspective 8: Abolitionists believe that crime is mainly a consequence of the structure of society. We devote ourselves to a community change approach. We would drastically limit the role of the criminal (in)justice systems. We advocate public solutions to public problems—greater resources and services for all people.

Perspective 9: Abolitionists believe that it is only in a caring community that corporate and individual redemption can take place. We view the dominant culture as more in need of "correction" than the prisoner. The caring communities have yet to be built.

Can Prison Abolition Ever Be Pragmatic?*

Nathan J. Robinson

2017

"While there is a lower class, I am in it, while there is a criminal element I am of it, and while there is a soul in prison, I am
not free."

There are a couple of reasons why I love Eugene Debs's "I
am not free" quote, spoken upon his conviction for violating
the Sedition Act in 1918. To begin with, it's a good first principle for leftism: so long as there is injustice and suffering in
the world, you should feel deeply troubled by it. It also does
something extremely difficult: it empathizes with the despised,
encouraging us to care about all of humanity, even those who
have done horrendous and cruel things. It's an exhortation to
universal compassion: you have to care about *everybody*, without exceptions.

But Debs's statement also contains a radical, even extreme,

* Nathan J. Robinson, "Can Prison Abolition Ever Be Pragmatic?," *Current Affairs*,
August 3, 2017.

view of prisons: so long as there is *a single person* left in prison, Debs feels that freedom is impossible. It's clear the kind of world Debs wants: a world without social classes, without a division between criminals and noncriminals, and without prisons. And Debs doesn't seem to believe this is some impossible dream: he wants it to actually happen, because it's the precondition of his own freedom.

"Prison abolitionism," the belief that prisons should not just be reformed but abolished entirely, has a long tradition within the left. Early socialists believed strongly that because the causes of crime were social, a fair society could eliminate the existence of crime, and therefore the need for prisons. As Peter Kropotkin wrote in a pamphlet:

> The prison does not prevent anti-social acts from taking place. It increases their numbers. It does not improve those who enter its walls. However it is reformed it will always remain a place of restraint, an artificial environment, like a monastery, which will make the prisoner less and less fit for life in the community. It does not achieve its end. It degrades society. It must disappear. . . . The first duty of the revolution will be to abolish prisons—those monuments of human hypocrisy and cowardice.

Clarence Darrow actually gave an address to a group of inmates at the Cook County Jail in Chicago in which he called for the total abolition of imprisonment:

> There should be no jails. They do not accomplish what they pretend to accomplish. If you would wipe them out, there would be no more criminals than now. . . . They are a blot upon civilization, and a jail is an evidence of the lack of

charity of the people on the outside who make the jails and fill them with the victims of their greed.

(Afterward, it was reported that prisoners who were asked what they thought of Darrow's speech had said they found it a bit too radical.) The prison abolitionist strain in left-wing thinking has continued: Angela Y. Davis's 2003 *Are Prisons Obsolete?*, which laid out an uncompromising case against confinement, has attracted a following on the left, and even CNN contributor Marc Lamont Hill has pushed prison abolition, concluding that "if the system was fair, there would be no prison."

The arguments made by prison abolitionists are straightforward: prisons make the world worse rather than better. They are inhuman places, and in many cases do not operate very differently from conditions of enslavement. They do not address the root causes of crime, and they encourage recidivism by hardening criminals. Or, as Emma Goldman colorfully put it in "Prisons: A Social Crime and Failure":

> Year after year the gates of prison hells return to the world an emaciated, deformed, will-less, ship-wrecked crew of humanity, with the Cain mark on their foreheads, their hopes crushed, all their natural inclinations thwarted. With nothing but hunger and inhumanity to greet them, these victims soon sink back into crime as the only possibility of existence.

The case made by prison abolitionists has rhetorical force, and I think a certain persuasive power. It makes both emotional and logical appeals: emotionally, it invokes the human love of liberty and hatred of coercion, while logically, it proposes that the costs of prisons outweigh their benefits.

It also, to a large majority of the population, almost certainly sounds completely insane.

As Gene Demby notes, while people agree that liberty is great and all, they quickly remember the "What About My Cousin?" question: they remember a person they knew who was genuinely violent and dangerous, and realize that they feel far safer knowing that person is locked up. Then, they remember all of the crimes that were *worse* than those committed by their cousin, and the abolitionist position begins to seem even loopier. *Never mind my cousin, what about Ted Bundy?* What about serial rapists and armed robbers and hedge fund managers? Are you saying that they should be left free to roam about society perpetrating their evil deeds on the unsuspecting and upstanding? How naïve can you possibly be?

And, indeed, I think the historical prison abolitionists *have* often been naïve, or at least misleading. In response to questions about the worst kinds of offenders, they point to the factors that drove such people to their crimes. Very few people on death row, for example, had ordinary, prosperous, and stable early lives. And those crimes that do not occur for obvious social reasons can be treated as manifestations of mental illness, with treatment rather than punishment being the goal. Prison abolitionists frequently point to restorative justice approaches that try to bring both victims and offenders together to figure out a way that the wrong done by the crime can be undone.

But none of this actually addresses the *question*. All of it sounds good in theory, but it describes an ideal society rather than the society in which we actually live. In the real world, there are people who have committed serious violent crimes, like serial domestic abusers. If those people were all suddenly freed one day, they would likely resume the pattern of abuse, because it's very hard to transform a person overnight. If you are concerned not just with the injustice inflicted on defendants by a brutal prison system, but on victims by violent aggression, then prison abolition just amounts to blindly focusing on stopping one injustice while ignoring the potential consequences for increasing the amount of another injustice. That's what's meant by naïveté: instead of asking the question "In which cases can restorative justice approaches work, and are there others in which they would not?" prison abolition adopts an extreme position and says, "Punitive justice is wrong and restorative justice is right, therefore we must end punitive justice." Prison abolitionists advocate all kinds of sensible measures, like decriminalizing marijuana use and sex work, increasing community services that help people find jobs, and having courts rely more heavily on creative forms of restitution and community service than prison sentences. That still doesn't get us a straight answer to the question, though, which is: When *is* prison justified and acceptable? If abolitionists really see prison as being akin to slavery, that question is absurd: it's like asking when slavery is justified. Holding the abolitionist position must mean that murderers would be set free, regardless of the possible consequences. We can see this kind of difficulty in the rousing tracts of people like Goldman and Darrow: both of them said jails were in and of themselves a crime, but neither was willing to confront the problems that flow from such a view.

Because prison abolition seems an untenable position, then, most progressive people are advocates of prison "reform" instead. They subscribe to a position like the ACLU's: decriminalize certain offenses, emphasize rehabilitation, improve prison conditions, and stop using the prison system as a way of warehousing the mentally ill. They believe that while there will always be some need for punishment, the goal should be to make the U.S. prison system a lot more like those of the Scandinavian countries: humane and reform-oriented, and with a focus on keeping the perpetrator from harming society again rather than exacting revenge on them by depriving them of comfort. (Florida's Department of Corrections, for example, proudly states that most of its state-run facilities are not air-conditioned, even in the blistering summer heat. Louisiana has its mostly black inmates picking cotton.) Recently, a socialist acquaintance who opposes prison abolitionism told me that he thought the left's aim should be for all prisoners to have conditions like those afforded to Norwegian mass murderer Anders Breivik. Showing me a photo of Breivik's cell, he said that if we could make prisons look like this, it's hard to think there would be any serious injustice left:

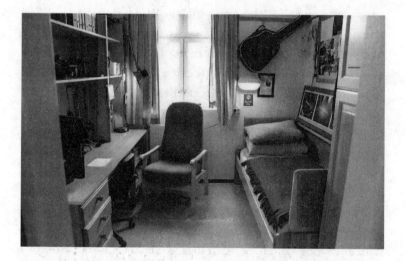

I think many people would be tempted to agree. Anders Breivik murdered dozens of children. He did it with deliberation and planning, and he is totally unapologetic. Giving him conditions essentially no different from (probably better than) the average college dorm room instinctively seems totally unobjectionable, possibly even too lenient. And Norwegian prisons are, in general, intentionally not much different from living on the outside. As one prison governor said, they follow the "normality principle," meaning that "daily prison life should not be any different than ordinary life, as far as this is possible." As a result, the lives of Norwegian prisoners sound almost idyllic:

> Inmates on the prison island of Bastoey, south of Oslo, are free to walk around in a village-style setting, tending to farm animals. They ski, cook, play tennis, play cards. They have their own beach, and even run the ferry taking people to and from the island. And in the afternoon when most prison staff go home, only a handful of guards are left to watch the 115 prisoners.

If this is what prison life could be like, then why adopt an abolition framework at all? Surely, even if we are romantic utopians, the Norwegian system ought to satisfy us.

And yet: I cannot help but feel that the abolitionist principle is actually the right one. As I looked at the photo of Breivik's cell, at first I thought to myself, "Well, there doesn't seem anything wrong with this. Surely this is the ideal." But then I realized that using the word "ideal" to describe what I was seeing seemed perverse. After all, the photo I was looking at existed because seventy-seven people were dead. I was not just looking at a comfortable room. I was looking at the place where a racist mass murderer was kept, and being asked to evaluate whether it was a sensible and fair place to keep such a person. This is the question around which prison reform asks us to frame our discussions: What is the humane way to treat a person who commits an atrocity? And the answer, for seriously committed reformers, is that photograph.

What I like about abolition, though, is that it rejects the premise of the question. It says that, if we are assuming that in our ideal society, the Anders Breiviks would be given Ikea furniture and Ping-Pong tables, we are still assuming the existence of Anders Breiviks. But the kind of society we are aiming for should *not* be the one in which "criminals are well-treated." It should be a society in which we do not have white supremacists murdering dozens of children.

Now, once again this sounds profoundly naïve. I can feel the eyes rolling. Well, of *course* we'd all *love* a world without crime, but that's *not going to happen*, which is why the important question is about what we do here and now. However, this misses the point: what the abolitionist is actually saying is that, while it's good to improve prison conditions, it's vital to remember that "prison conditions" are not the real issue, just as if we mainly targeted "improving conditions for prisoners of war" rather than "stopping war" or "improving support given to the families of people who die in mining accidents" rather than "stopping mining accidents," our focus would be too narrow in a way that led us to fail to appreciate the true problem.

Prison abolitionists, ironically enough, sometimes seem more committed to stopping crime than those who criticize them for being naïve about crime. Some approaches to criminal justice focus on things like improving public defender services, improving prison health care, ensuring freedom from police harassment. But what the abolitionist socialists have always said is that, while these are valuable and should be done, it's equally important to try to understand why crime happens in the first place. In Clarence Darrow's speech to the Chicago prisoners, he said:

> The only way in the world to abolish crime and criminals is to abolish the big ones and the little ones together. Make fair conditions of life. Give men a chance to live. Abolish the right of private ownership of land, abolish monopoly, make the world partners in production, partners in the good things of life. Nobody would steal if he could get something of his own some easier way. Nobody will commit burglary when he has a house full. No girl will go out on the streets when she has a comfortable place at home. The man who owns a sweatshop or a department store may not be to blame himself for the condition of his girls, but when he pays them five dollars, three dollars, and two dollars a week, I wonder where he thinks they will get the rest of their money to live. The only way to cure these conditions is by equality.

Now, Darrow might have been thinking simplistically in believing that nobody would steal if they were rich already (see, e.g., Wall Street). But note that he is thinking about how to get rid of crime itself. The reason he would be uncomfortable saying that "the goal is to make American prisons more like Norwegian ones" is that for Darrow, the elimination of violent crime is inextricably tied in with the entire point of socialism, which is to create a society in which people are prosperous and happy and don't hurt one another. Abolition is a useful way of thinking about things, because it says "The task is to make a world in which prisons are unnecessary" rather than "The task is to make a world in which prisons are comfortable."

Of course, people think such a world is impossible. Prisons

will always be necessary, they believe, because *some people* will always be warped and cruel. But I object to this way of looking at things: it accepts an erroneous chain of reasoning often held by conservatives, namely that human nature is prone to violence and viciousness and this is an ineradicable part of us. The reason I call this view "erroneous" is that I don't think it's a correct inference: the argument is that because humans *have* always been a certain way, they *must* always be a certain way. This is no more logical than if, in 1900, I had said "there has never been a successful man-made aircraft, thus there will never be a successful man-made aircraft." Or if I had said (as I did) in 2016, "America has never elected a president who has openly bragged about committing sexual assault, thus America will never elect a president who has openly bragged about committing sexual assault." When we assume we can judge the full range of possibilities for the future from the evidence we have about the past, we can end up cramping our ambition through self-fulfilling prophecies, or underestimating certain risks.

The truth is that we don't *know* the degree to which crime can be controlled by addressing social causes. We don't know it, because we've never seriously tried it. But we do know that there are cities in the United States that have *incredibly* low crime rates, where violent crime hardly ever occurs and property crime is incredibly infrequent. We are far from understanding why that's the case. Since we know that it *is* the case, though, we know that it's possible to create places in which crime is almost nonexistent. Violent crime has consistently been dropping in the United States despite the public perception otherwise (not helped by Donald Trump's demagogic attempts to terrify people). It is impossible to know how much further it could be made to drop. (Nor is that because we've been locking up all of the criminals. States with low crime rates can also have very low incarceration rates, whereas states like, for example, Louisiana have both incredibly high crime rates and incredibly high incarceration rates.) Since very low-crime societies are possible *already*, even when they consist entirely of perfectly ordinary human beings, it does not actually seem especially naïve to believe that both crime and prisons can essentially be eliminated from the world. I refuse to see Anders Breiviks as an inevitability; I believe he is the product of a perverse racist ideology, one that can be countered and eradicated.

Prison abolition and prison reform can actually be reconciled fairly easily. The ultimate goal is prison abolition, because in a world without hatred and violence there would be no need for prisons, and the goal is a world without hatred and violence. In the interim, prisons must be made better and more humane. It's not that you should, in the world we live in now, open the prison gates and give murderers probation. It's that you should always remember that even if you think prison is a *necessary evil*, that still makes it evil, and evil things should ultimately be gotten rid of, whatever their short-term necessity. You can be both pragmatic and utopian at the same time. One should always adopt the "utopian" position, because it helps affirm what our ideal is and serves as a guiding star. But you can simultaneously operate with the real-world political constraints you have. As Angela Y. Davis says, "the call for prison abolition urges us to imagine and strive for a very different social landscape." It's useful because it gets us thinking about big questions, picturing what very different worlds might be like and then beginning to plot how we might get from here to there.

To me, one of the most moving pieces of writing on prison

is Oscar Wilde's "Ballad of Reading Gaol." I find it a far more persuasive indictment of the concept of prison than any number of abolitionist tracts or policy papers about restorative justice. Wilde, destroyed by an unjust and bigoted Victorian criminal court system, wrote that no matter how we felt about the justice of particular laws, the very existence of prisons was a stain on humanity:

> *I know not whether Laws be right,*
> *Or whether Laws be wrong;*
> *All that we know who lie in jail*
> *Is that the wall is strong;*
> *And that each day is like a year,*
> *A year whose days are long.*
> *But this I know, that every Law*
> *That men have made for Man,*
> *Since first Man took his brother's life,*
> *And the sad world began,*
> *But straws the wheat and saves the chaff*
> *With a most evil fan.*
> *This too I know—and wise it were*
> *If each could know the same—*
> *That every prison that men build*
> *Is built with bricks of shame,*
> *And bound with bars lest Christ should see*
> *How men their brothers maim.*

Eugene Debs's principle is an essential one, then. You can't rest until the prisons are gone, because only then will injustice have been banished from the world: While there is a soul in prison, I am not free.

The Case for Abolition*

Ruth Wilson Gilmore and
James Kilgore
2019

Our belief in abolition is first and foremost philosophical. It grew from watching, experiencing, and opposing decades of reliance on concrete and steel cages as catch-all solutions to social problems. We want a society that centers freedom and justice instead of profit and punishment.

Locking people up does not provide adequate housing, proper mental health treatment or living wage jobs, nor does it make us safe in any other way. Moreover, reforms that embody electronic monitoring or other forms of e-carceration, build gender-responsive jails, or broaden the scope of parole and other forms of carceral control only deepen our conviction that fundamental change is the only path.

While we value philosophy, we have also grown weary of worn-out debates over the feasibility of a world without prisons

* Ruth Wilson Gilmore and James Kilgore, "The Case for Abolition," *The Marshall Project*, June 19, 2019.

and whether we would like to abolish prison for Dylann Roof. We prefer to talk about what we do.

Ultimately, abolition is a practical program of change rooted in how people sustain and improve their lives, cobbling together insights and strategies from disparate, connected struggles. We know we won't bulldoze prisons and jails tomorrow, but as long as they continue to be advanced as the solution, all of the inequalities displaced to crime and punishment will persist. We're in a long game.

Authors of reforms claim expertise about what "the public" will accept, as if it were a single entity that's already made its mind about everything. But people frequently broaden their commitments because they learn about, and link to, previously unfamiliar struggles. These are not *the* public experts invoke but *a* public resolved to pursue policies and plans to realize their goals.

In other words, a public is made. How do we know? Experience.

To forge such a public, for decades abolitionists have been doing everything we can imagine to bring about change. We stand on the frontlines to oppose all forms of state violence.

We work with communities sited for prisons to fight expansion, while organizing to secure decent wages and housing in the regional economy. We work with Republican ranchers worried about the water table, and with undocumented agricultural workers vulnerable to pesticides and Immigration and Customs Enforcement. We work with city managers and residents of prison towns disappointed in lockups touted for economic development that never deliver.

We document the cultural and environmental degradation resulting from cities of incarcerated people deprived of their civil rights, write handbooks and advise rural and regional development experts on alternative projects. We work with unions on strategy to develop long-term goals for job protection, environmental justice, and membership growth—especially because half the U.S. labor force has some record of criminalization that makes employment insecure and depresses wages.

We were prompted to write by reading Bill Keller's essay last week in *The Marshall Project* asking "What Do Abolitionists Really Want?" We took issue with many of his points and felt, by not quoting abolitionists, he echoed historical precedents of white people asking what Black people want, or men debating *Roe v. Wade.* But he got one thing right: Abolition is thriving, something he can't quite figure out.

Abolition is thriving because our organizational energies draw on local and international infrastructures of mutual assistance like clubs, political organizations, faith communities, unions, and neighborhood associations, previous and ongoing rounds of long-term organizing, and widespread desires for greater democratic participation. Our ranks increasingly include those directly affected by incarceration and all forms of violence and trauma.

Our work thrives because we recognize that reform has assumed new, troubling shapes. From New York City to Los Angeles, and across rural America, jail expansion has been chugging along largely because law enforcement continues to absorb social welfare work—mental and physical health, education, family unification. To imagine a world without prisons and jails is to imagine a world in which social welfare is a right, not a luxury.

Every U.S. delegation that jets off to Scandinavia to study prisons comes back declaring they've seen a future they didn't actually look at. As career criminal justice experts, they thought they could isolate a prison system from its context: tax, housing, health care, education, transportation, immigration, and other policies. Everyone who says it's unrealistic to demand more willfully ignores the fact that to use law enforcement, as the U.S. does, to manage the fallout from cutbacks in social services and the upward rush in income and wealth is breathtakingly expensive, while it cheapens human life.

Abolitionists have brought to the struggle against what came to be called "mass incarceration" an array of experiences in which we learned how to fight on many fronts at once: how to organize, promote ideas, and bargain in the political arena. In other words, we work the entire ecology of precarious existence that shapes, but is not bounded by, the aggrandizing "criminal justice system," including housing, jobs, education, income, faith, environment, status. Far from being starry-eyed idealists, we are specialists in the daily grind of the deliberate, patient, and persistent work necessary for what we want—freedom and justice.

"On Cages"
Twitter Thread*

Reginald Dwayne Betts

2019

On cages—people should immediately stop calling prison cells cages. The very thing being done to point out dehumanization is dramatically more dehumanizing.

———

Imagine spending twenty years in prison and having an activist reduce your life to a cage. As if the first man you told that you love, you didn't meet in prison. As if you didn't learn to be willing to bleed to protect someone else in prison.

———

As if you didn't learn a generosity that defies expectation in prison.

———

* Reginald Dwayne Betts, "On Cages" Twitter Thread, October 22, 2019, 5:33 PM, https://twitter.com/dwaynebetts/status/1186757383361568770?s=20.

As if you didn't mourn in prison. The loss of your parents, your friends, your youth. And all the while as if you didn't live a life.

Replete with all the shit. From running Bostons to trying to get anybody to call you their sweetheart.

I am a fucking convict, ex-convict. A felon. Was an inmate. But was in a cell and not a cage.

North Dakota's Norway Experiment*

Dashka Slater
2017

Late one night in October 2015, North Dakota prisons chief Leann Bertsch met Karianne Jackson, one of her deputies, for a drink in a hotel bar in Oslo, Norway. They had just spent an exhausting day touring Halden, the maximum-security facility *Time* has dubbed "the world's most humane prison," yet neither of them could sleep.

Halden is situated in a remote forest of birch, pine, and spruce with an understory of blueberry shrubs. The prison is surrounded by a single wall. It has no barbed wire, guard towers, or electric fences. Prisoners stay in private rooms with en suite bathrooms and can cook for themselves in kitchens equipped with stainless-steel flatware and porcelain dishes. Guards and inmates mingle freely, eating and playing games and sports together. Violence is rare and assaults on guards are unheard of. Solitary confinement is almost never used.

---

* Dashka Slater, "North Dakota's Norway Experiment," *Mother Jones*, July/August 2017.

By this point, Bertsch had been in charge of North Dakota's Department of Corrections and Rehabilitation, which includes four adult prisons and one juvenile facility, for more than a decade, and Jackson had spent seven years as director of correctional practices. They'd left Bismarck feeling pretty good about their system, which prided itself on its humane practices and commitment to rehabilitation. But now, sitting in the glassed-in bar of the Radisson hotel with its view of the Oslo fjord, Bertsch began to cry. "We're hurting people," she said.

It is worth noting that Leann Bertsch is no pushover. With her ivory skin, flaxen hair, and chiseled cheekbones, she comes across as stoic and cool. She grew up on a farm in the eastern part of the state and served twenty-one years in the National Guard (retiring as a major) and eight years as a state prosecutor. She has run the prisons in this deep-red state under three Republican governors, and she moonlights as president of the Association of State Correctional Administrators. "No one who has met Leann or seen her in action would consider her a softie," says John Wetzel, the association's vice president and Pennsylvania's secretary of corrections. "I would describe her as ballsy. Corrections has historically been a really misogynistic field, so when you see a woman in charge of a corrections system, and in charge of one of the more influential organizations in corrections, you know she's got to be strong."

But in Oslo that evening, Bertsch was uncharacteristically emotional. "It was definitely one of those moments where you're rethinking everything," she recalls. "I had always thought that we run a good system. We're decent. We don't abuse people. We run safe facilities with good programs. It was just like, 'How did we think it was okay to put human beings in cagelike settings?'"

The Norway sojourn was the brainchild of Donald Specter, executive director of the Prison Law Office, a California public-interest law firm. In 2011, while visiting European prisons with a group of Maryland college students, Specter was struck by how profoundly the experience altered their views on incarceration. He decided to use some of the legal fees his office had won in its lawsuits against California prisons to bring state corrections chiefs, judges, and lawmakers on similar journeys.

Scandinavian prisons tend to elicit eye rolls from law-and-order types weaned on the punitive American model. Yet a growing number of state corrections officials are coming to the realization that our approach is ineffective, costly, and cruel. Fred Patrick, director of the Center on Sentencing and Corrections at the Vera Institute of Justice, cites the nation's staggering recidivism rate—77 percent of inmates released from state prisons are rearrested within five years. "Once you realize that this system isn't working well," he says, "it's fairly easy to pivot to: 'How do we do something different?'"

That's where Specter's field trips come in. "To be so fricking optimistic that you think you can take some knuckle-dragging corrections guys like me over there and it's going to change their perspective—you have to be a hippie to think that!" says Wetzel, who toured German prisons with Specter in 2013. But Specter's ploy worked. "It really screws you up, because it changes you," Wetzel adds. "I joke around with Don Specter. I'm like, 'Fuck you, man! I can't believe you did this shit to me!'"

And so, when Bertsch and Jackson returned home, it was with a radical new goal: "to implement our humanity."

Along the highways of North Dakota, drivers are greeted by billboards advising people to "Be Nice" or "Be Kind." Fittingly, the state's incarceration rate of 240 prisoners per 100,000 residents is among the lowest in America, where the national average is 670. (Norway's rate is 75.) And North Dakota's prison

population of about 1,821 is less than half that of its neighbor
to the south. But the "be nice" ethos has come under strain in
recent years as rising crime associated with the state's fracking
boom has provoked a new wave of tough-on-crime measures
by the Legislature. The number of inmates in North Dakota
prisons has increased by 28 percent since the end of 2011. A
new 430-bed penitentiary complex built in 2013 was filled to
capacity in six months.

By 2015, Bertsch was ready to ship excess prisoners to a private facility in Colorado. In Norway, though, she learned that
the farther a prisoner is removed from his home community,
the less likely he is to have visitors. And that's a problem, because multiple studies suggest that inmates who have regular
visitors are less likely to reoffend later. So instead of sending
prisoners away, Bertsch seized on a suggestion from one of
her maintenance employees and leased a ready-made "man
camp"—the same portable modular units used to house rough-
necks in the Bakken oil fields. The accommodations weren't
nearly as charming as the inmate cottages she and Jackson had
toured at Norway's Bastøy prison, a minimum-security facility
located on a picturesque island. But they were a cheap way to
ease overcrowding and give the men a dose of self-sufficiency.

I went with Jackson to see the trailers at the Missouri River
Correctional Center, a minimum-security facility nicknamed
"the Farm." Located on the rural outskirts of Bismarck, it is
surrounded by cottonwood trees and backs onto the river for
which it is named. There are no fences. The day I visited, the
grounds were swaddled in a sparkling blanket of snow; prisoners strolled along walking paths in puffy orange jackets, their
breath steamy in the cold. Some of the men were placed here
for lesser crimes; others are approaching the end of lengthy
sentences that began in the maximum-security state prison.

Warden James Sayler and Joey Joyce, his deputy, were quick to embrace the Norway philosophy. They immediately began devising ways for inmates to earn more freedom—shopping excursions, day passes home, and even the right to wear civilian clothes on-site. They also scaled up an existing work-release program so more men could take real jobs. "Everybody down here is going to be out of here in a short amount of time," Sayler says. "So how do you want 'em?" This is the crux of Norway's approach: Once you accept that these people will one day be your neighbors, you might feel more invested in making sure they have the skills to get by on the outside.

Each of the Farm's preexisting housing units packs eight to sixteen men into side-by-side berths in a space about the size of a subway car. But provided he is well behaved, an inmate approaching his release date can secure one of thirty-six private rooms, each of which shares a toilet and shower with just one other room. The chambers are modest—bed, desk, bulletin board—but for men unused to privacy, they're pure luxury. More than one resident told me he couldn't sleep the first few nights after moving in. The quiet was unsettling, and so was having a real mattress. "Kind of neat and kind of spooky at the same time," says Rod Hegle, who was transferred to the Farm after more than two decades in the state penitentiary. Here Hegle has a room he can lock with his own key. He drives a forklift in the commissary and has a job in the welding shop. He's eager to be approved for work release.

But I also heard stories of prisoners so acclimated to confinement that even small freedoms were too much for them. This was particularly acute in the state penitentiary's administrative segregation (solitary confinement) unit, one of the first places Bertsch and Jackson set out to reform. The seg unit was previously viewed, as it still is in many states, as a catchment for the most difficult prisoners—not just those who assaulted guards or fellow inmates, but also the crazy or defiant ones. A prisoner might get thrown in the hole for tattooing, mouthing off, or repeatedly refusing to tuck in his shirt. Getting in was easy, getting out hard.

That all changed after Norway. Throughout the prison system, Bertsch and Jackson are winnowing the list of minor infractions that earn prisoners a "shot." As Jackson puts it, "Why is this a rule? Why is that important? Is the juice worth the squeeze?"

Now the only way you'll land in the hole is by endangering somebody, Bertsch says. Solitary stints are short, with clear expectations for how to get out, and the emphasis has shifted from punishment to treatment. Long-isolated prisoners are no longer dumped back into the general population—a new behavioral therapy unit gives them time to adjust to being around people.

Upon her return from Oslo, Jackson, a feisty, bighearted woman whose warmth provides the counterpart to Bertsch's cool demeanor, immediately set to work combing through the solitary rolls, flagging candidates for transition into the general population: "I was like, 'Here's all the mental illness. Here's who's in here for chronic failure to follow rules.'"

Over in the behavioral modification unit, I meet Jeremy Isaac Rodriguez Rios, a twenty-year-old with a shaved head, dark eyes, and finger tattoos. He's two years into a forty-five-year bid for a double murder and has spent more than half that time in segregation, locked down twenty-two to twenty-three hours a day. Rios admits he's quick to throw a punch, but he says the prison counselors are helping him learn to defuse potential conflicts. "You have to bring yourself in first: 'I feel anxious and disrespected when you say that,'" he explains.

"Those situations where they say 'bitch' or 'punk' to me, I try to verify—am I in danger? Or can we talk it out?"

Another twenty-year-old, Michael Taylor, just arrived here after a month in the highly restrictive "acute intervention" wing. His hands won't stop shaking. "I'm super paranoid," he tells me. He's hoping he can stay in the behavioral unit another month or two. "Even though it sucks being back here," Taylor says, he likes the therapy sessions—and the "treatment ladies."

The day-to-day population of the seg unit is now less than one-third of its pre-Norway peak. Since the new policies were put in place, prison officials report sharp declines in inmate violence and threats against staff, and also in the use of force by staff against inmates. "When the environment feels less aggressive and contentious," Jackson says, "you're safer."

North Dakota has advantages as a laboratory for correctional reforms. Like Norway, it is sparsely populated and relatively homogeneous—race-based prison gangs hold little sway here. Another advantage, Don Specter told me, is simply that the state government is sufficiently small that it can be responsive to the exertions of a visionary leader. Yet Bertsch and Jackson have no illusions about transforming their system into a corrections utopia overnight. "You have to pace yourself," Bertsch says.

The Norwegian principle of "dynamic security" posits that warm relationships between inmates and staff reduce the potential for violence. American prisons typically try to create safe conditions by means of oppressive rules, random searches, and the threat of additional punishment. Transitioning from one approach to the other requires a profound paradigm shift and the ability to sell front-line prison workers on a brand new mindset. "How do you get somebody who thinks they're in law enforcement to figure out you need to be more of an empath, more of a social worker, a friend, and a mentor?" Jackson asks.

The correctional officers I met at the state penitentiary, ex-military all, weren't outwardly hostile to the idea of cultivating relationships with prisoners, but it clearly didn't come naturally to them. For that reason, perhaps, the brass created a mandate: Guards in the segregation unit must have at least two conversations per shift with each of the inmates under their supervision. "It's worth a shot," a corrections officer named Josh Hedstrom told me. "Because what we were doing before wasn't working."

That sentiment came up often in my conversations with corrections officials. "Those of us who are in the system are just tired of the mass incarceration," says Rick Raemisch, Colorado's prisons chief. His system of roughly twenty thousand adult inmates phased out solitary confinement almost entirely "in less than a year and a half," he told me. "You can put what we've done in any system." In fact, roughly a third of state prison systems have embarked on plans to cut back on solitary.

Even some notoriously punitive states, such as South Carolina, Mississippi, Georgia, and Texas, are slashing incarceration rates after concluding that the old lock-'em-up policies are a pricey failure. In North Dakota, where falling oil and grain prices have put the state government in belt-tightening mode, I watched Bertsch shame state senators for the tough new criminal penalties they'd enacted. "I would say that you've handed the checkbook over to the judiciary," she told them.

Across the nation, the sheer number of men and women behind bars is at the root of most of the problems faced by corrections officials. "We're not able to devote the resources to treatment," explains Marc Levin, the executive director of Right on Crime, a Texas-based criminal justice reform initiative championed by the likes of William Bennett, Newt Gingrich, Grover Norquist, and Ralph Reed. While Attorney General Jeff Sessions may be nostalgic for 1990s-style criminal justice policies, these conservative luminaries have done an almost complete one-eighty on the topic. "There's some point where the public appetite for punishment has been satisfied, and now we need to look at public safety with some kind of measurable data," Levin says.

Whether this perspective survives the Trump era remains to be seen, but several people I spoke with credited the opioid epidemic for the conservative change of heart. "Incarceration and the criminal justice system are touching a lot of people, including poor people in rural areas, a lot of whom are white," Levin says. One scenario, given Sessions's pursuit of maximum penalties for federal crimes, is a growing divide between reform-minded state facilities, which hold more than half the nation's 2.3 million prisoners, and an intransigent federal system.

Bertsch and Jackson are convinced that their quest to treat prisoners like human beings jibes well with their state's conservative goals: Be nice. Be fiscally responsible. Be a good neighbor. "The most I can do with the Legislature," Bertsch tells me, "is get them to understand that incarcerating more people is not a good investment. If we had the same incarceration rate as Norway, we would have the resources to do a really good job with the people in our system."

"I'm not a liberal," she adds. "I'm just practical."

Restoring Pell Grants—and Possibilities—for Prisoners*

Clint Smith

2021

During the winter months, the small classroom smelled of wood and heat. Three rows of desks faced the door, and before class began I would rearrange some of them into a circle. Different shades of forest green hugged the walls, the remnants of years of paint jobs done with varying levels of proficiency and care. On bright mornings, the sun sliced through two large windows and bathed the classroom in the day's new light. During thunderstorms, rain sang along the windows' glass, and I would turn on the lights so that everyone in the class would be able to read the books in front of us. The lights would hum and crackle, the air still in anticipation of the bodies that would fill it.

---

* Clint Smith, "Restoring Pell Grants—and Possibilities—for Prisoners," *The Atlantic*, March 11, 2021.

I have been teaching in prisons and jails for several years now, but I have not forgotten those first weeks at a Massachusetts correctional center in my early years as a graduate student: feeling the linoleum underfoot as I was made to remove my shoes, raising my arms and being patted down, having the pages of my books and notebooks examined for any contraband that might have been snuck into its creases, listening as a heavy steel gate slid across the floor and closed behind me after I entered each room, the eyes and cameras—so many cameras—watching as my body moved from one location to another.

In that prison and in that classroom, I read and discussed books—novels, plays, essays, poems—with a group of five men who were serving life sentences, most of them three or four decades into their time. I was changed by those men and by that class—a class in which I was less a teacher and more a guest welcomed into an intellectual community they had already created. My time with those men led me to focus my graduate research on the relationship between education and incarceration, particularly for those serving life sentences. What did it mean to learn or to pursue an education, I wondered, when you've been told you will spend the rest of your life in a cage?

Over the course of my teaching and research, I learned that while education was transformative for many incarcerated people, the opportunities for people in prison to obtain formal educational credentials, specifically college degrees, were painfully limited. Almost none of the courses I taught could be used by the men to obtain any higher-education credit.

In 1994, Congress put a new impediment in their way, removing Pell Grant eligibility for incarcerated people as part of that year's crime bill. But last December, after twenty-seven years, the $900 billion stimulus package—passed by both chambers of Congress and signed into law only a few weeks before President Joe Biden was sworn into office—reversed that decision. That bill has the potential to reshape the educational landscape inside prisons, providing a set of possibilities for incarcerated people across the country that has not existed in decades.

In 2001, eighteen years after he was first incarcerated, Vincent "Sharif" Boyd received his GED. He had been in prison since he was sixteen. "I was so happy," he told me when we spoke in 2019, as I was conducting interviews for my dissertation. A huge smile stretched across his face, but it faded into disappointment as he told me how he'd never had the chance to continue his education through college. By the time he had decided to pursue the opportunity, Pell Grants had been taken away from people in prison, and he could not afford to pay for college on his own.

"I tell you like this, I got a degree in *penitentiaryology*," he told me. "I got a degree, you know what I mean? But I ain't got no paperwork for it."

The Higher Education Act of 1965, which expanded college access across the country, triggered a surge of requests from incarcerated people who wanted the opportunity to take college courses. Then the 1971 Attica prison uprising brought new support for the rights of incarcerated people, increasing correctional departments' willingness to incorporate higher-education programs. By 1982, 350 college-prison programs enrolled twenty-seven thousand people—9 percent of the nation's prison population. By the early '90s, more than 770 programs were operating in nearly 1,300 prisons nationwide. And because incarcerated people are disproportionately poor, the students in these programs were particularly dependent on Pell Grants for higher-education funding.

But in 1994, everything changed. Determined to show that he was tough on crime, President Bill Clinton signed the Violent Crime Control and Law Enforcement Act, which, among other things, stripped Pell Grant eligibility from people who are incarcerated. That provision had been added to the bill by Representative Bart Gordon, a Democrat from Tennessee, with the support of almost all House Republicans and a majority of Democrats. The bill itself was championed by then-Senator Biden—who now says that he regrets supporting the Pell Grant provision—and a bipartisan group of legislators and activists, many of whom, like Biden, say that they did not foresee the full impact the bill would have on accelerating mass incarceration.

In a 1994 floor speech, Gordon said:

> Just because one blind hog may occasionally find an acorn doesn't mean many other blind hogs will. The same principle applies to giving federal Pell Grants to prisoners. Certainly there is an occasional success story, but when virtually every prisoner in America is eligible for the Pell Grants, national priorities and taxpayers lose.

From the other side of the aisle, Republican Representative Jack Fields pushed a similar message:

> Every dollar in Pell Grant funds obtained by prisoners means that fewer law-abiding students are eligible for that assistance. It also means that law-abiding students that meet eligibility criteria receive smaller annual grants.

These attacks were not grounded in reality. In the 1993–94 academic year, those in prison received just $35 million of the $5.6 billion in overall Pell Grants—less than 1 percent. And no applicant who was eligible for a Pell Grant ever lost that grant to someone who was incarcerated, according to the Government Accountability Office. The grants are awarded on the basis of merit, and any costs above the yearly appropriation come out of the next year's budget.

Nonetheless, the bill decimated the formal educational infrastructure in prisons across the country, as university after university withdrew their programs because of a lack of financial support. Making matters worse, individual states followed the lead of the federal government, cutting off their financial support. By 1997, only eight college-prison programs were left, all of which had to find their own funding, as Gerard Robinson and Elizabeth English noted in a 2017 report from the American Enterprise Institute.

According to the Prison Policy Initiative, without federal aid, the rate of college-course participation dropped by about a half. In 1991, 13.9 percent of people in state prisons and 18.9 percent of people in federal prisons had taken at least one college-level course since being incarcerated. By 1997, according to the Bureau of Justice Statistics, 9.9 percent of people in state prisons and 12.9 percent of people in federal prisons had taken a college-level course. In 2004, only 7.3 percent of those surveyed in state prisons had taken a college-level course since they became incarcerated.

Now that people in prison could not access college courses, degrees proved out of reach. A 2014 study of incarcerated people by the National Center for Education Statistics found that just 2 percent had completed an associate's degree while they were incarcerated, and only 1 percent had completed a bachelor's degree or higher. Fully 58 percent of those surveyed said they had not completed any formal education programs since they entered prison.

I found that, among the people I interviewed for my dissertation research, the crime bill was a watershed: There was life in prison *before* the bill, and there was life in prison *after* it.

John Pace has smooth, black hair with thick waves coursing across his scalp. He has a calm disposition, a wide grin, and a pair of reading glasses that he doesn't wear as much as he uses them to keep his hands busy. We met at a Subway in downtown Philadelphia in the fall of 2018, and he told me about how the withdrawal of Pell Grants had shaped his life in prison.

When he was seventeen, Pace pleaded guilty to second-degree murder after mugging a man who later died from his injuries. He was sentenced to life in prison, serving thirty-one years in a Pennsylvania prison before a 2012 Supreme Court ruling said that mandatory life sentences without the possibility of parole were unconstitutional for children; a 2016 Supreme Court case made that ruling retroactive.

While he was incarcerated, Pace desperately wanted a college degree, and he was taking as many classes as he could when the crime bill went into effect. Without Pell Grants for people in prison, any university in Pennsylvania that wanted to serve incarcerated students had to cover the costs itself, often through grants received for that purpose. This meant fewer teachers, smaller classes, and less space.

"When they took away the Pell Grants, essentially they eliminated lifers," Pace told me. People serving life sentences were at the bottom of the priority list for classes, and there weren't enough slots to go around. "The state still continued to provide education, particularly for nonlifers. And the idea was that lifers will spend the rest of their life in prison; why invest in them?" he said. "If you wanted to participate as a lifer, you had to pay for your own course."

But Pace wasn't willing to simply accept that he could no

longer take college classes, not when he had already worked hard to accumulate credits, so he persuaded his sister to pay for his education. While Pace was grateful, he also knew that his sister had a limited income; paying for these classes was a significant strain on her finances. She had two kids. He needed to figure out another way.

Pace befriended an incarcerated man who had earned a Ph.D. in the early '80s, who told Pace there might be another way he could get money for his education. Together, they wrote to churches, businesses, and organizations, explaining Pace's story and requesting financial sponsorship so that he could complete his college degree. After sending out more than fifty letters, Pace finally heard back from a small Lutheran church that was willing to pay for his remote courses at Penn State University.

Pace was transferred to a different prison in 1997, where courses from Villanova were available. At first, he was only able to audit classes. "I guess that they was trying to determine who's serious, who's not," he said. "But once I took a couple of audit classes, then they started giving me credit." The process was extremely slow; Pace took thirteen years to graduate. But when he was released, in 2017, he said, he felt far more ready than he otherwise would have been to step back into the world.

In 2015, the Obama administration announced a pilot program known as "Second Chance Pell," an initial effort to make amends for the damage wrought in 1994. According to the Vera Institute of Justice, over the course of its first three years, the program reached more than seventeen thousand students in twenty-eight states, who earned 4,500 certificates, postsecondary diplomas, associate's degrees, and bachelor's degrees.

Research has begun to identify some of the benefits of providing access to education in prison. Such programs can reduce violence inside prisons, as well as recidivism rates. Among incarcerated people who earned a GED, recidivism rates within three years decreased 14 percent for those under twenty-one, and 5 percent for those over twenty-one. But when people took college-level courses, there was an even stronger correlation: a 46 percent lower rate of recidivism compared with those who did not.

"The cost-benefit of this does not take a math genius to figure out," then-Secretary of Education Arne Duncan said when the pilot program was announced. "We lock folks up here, [$35,000]–40,000 every single year. A Pell Grant is less than $6,000 each year."

Duncan is correct, of course, but what I found in my research and in my time teaching in prisons was that the benefits of education in prison are far greater than what can be captured in financial figures. Classes inside prison give people a sense of community, a sense of purpose, a sense of identity, and a sense of hope. These are not the sorts of things that are easily quantifiable, or entered into a spreadsheet that can be presented to policy makers, but they play a profound role in shaping both the time people spend in prison and their life after being released.

A lot of incarcerated people have an acute sense of the possibilities that education offers them while they are incarcerated. That gives many with long-term or life sentences hope that educational attainment, along with good behavior, might lead to a lessening of their sentence and a chance of going home. As another one of the men I interviewed told me, "You always had the feeling that, the more you learn, the more you stay outta trouble; the more you educate yourself, the greater your chances of actually becoming free."

Pell Grants being taken away was part of a larger effort

during the tough-on-crime era in which many states made incarcerated people pay for services and programs themselves. "They would find a way to get money from incarcerated people rather than giving money," Pace told me. "We were in that particular period of time where they were just stripping things away. Pell Grants are one of those things. So you got a large population competing for the little resources that are available."

Pace recalled that whenever the man who ran the Villanova program came to the prison to gauge interest and register prospective students, there was never enough space, either on the registration form or in the room where the introductory session was held. "The whole class is filled up," he said, recalling the scene. "People hanging out the doors . . . people can't get into the room, because they trying to sign up for college classes. But he couldn't take everybody." But with Pell Grant eligibility being restored to incarcerated people, Pace said, more colleges should be able to come into prisons to provide these much-desired classes.

I recently asked Pace why he thought that providing college courses, and educational opportunities more generally, was important for incarcerated people. He thought for a moment, then responded. "There's times when you're in dark spaces, particularly if you're facing a lot of time," he said. "But if you're engaged—and for me, college was one of those things that I was engaged in—it provides you with tools to be able to express your thoughts [and] what it is that you're going through. It's transformative in that regard, because many of us came to prison without a voice and didn't know how to articulate ourselves. And I think college provides that opportunity to be able to express yourself in a constructive way, and to be able to help yourself. It really provided me with that tool where I could advocate for myself."

Pace took classes in philosophy, history, and sociology—courses that helped clarify his sense of the world around him and his place in it. In his sociology class, for example, he remembers reading Jonathan Kozol's *Savage Inequalities*, and learning more about how the racial inequities in contemporary society have come to manifest themselves. The neighborhood he grew up in was saturated with poverty and violence, he began to understand, not because anything was wrong with the people in the community, but because of things that had been done to his community.

Pace also read books on his own, but it was in his college classes, he told me, that he was able to discuss, wrestle with, and make sense of what he was reading in a community of other learners. "It gave me an [understanding] in terms of the social context in which Black folks encounter America," he said.

"When I think about what college does, here it is you read diverse books, many different books—I call it 'old knowledge,'" he told me. "You're trying to make sense of these different perspectives. And you're trying to construct your own to make sense of their thoughts. And that's challenging, but it's a good challenge."

We will need some time to better understand the full impact that reinstating Pell Grant eligibility will have on the prison-education landscape (the bill's provisions don't go into effect until 2023). And right now, educational programs in most prisons across the country have either halted or gone virtual because of Covid-19. The writing workshop I teach at a Washington, D.C., jail has been suspended for a year now, with tablets currently serving as the most manageable substitute. Even when in-person programming finally resumes, it may take some time to restore higher-education opportunities to the levels that existed before the pandemic, much less prior to 1994. Making sure that happens swiftly isn't just an economic imperative, but a moral one.

The Inside-Out Prison Exchange Program: Its Origin, Essence, and Global Reach*

Lori Pompa

2021

It began by chance—an idea tossed into the universe—and then it took hold. It has been unstoppable ever since.

This article provides a description of, and reflection on, the Inside-Out Prison Exchange Program, a unique, groundbreaking initiative that brings people together for in-depth dialogue about issues of social justice.

Here is how it started. I have been going into prisons and jails several times a week since 1985 as a volunteer, a social worker, and, finally, as an educator. In 1992, I began teaching in the Criminal Justice Department at Temple University in

* Lori Pompa, "The Inside-Out Prison Exchange Program: Its Origin, Essence, and Global Reach," in *Giving Voice to Diversity in Criminological Research*, eds. Orla Lynch, James Windle, and Yasmine Ahmed (Bristol: Bristol University Press Digital, 2021), 253–266.

Philadelphia, PA, taking my students into correctional facilities multiple times each semester. In 1995, I took one of my
classes to the state prison in Dallas, PA, for a tour, and we met
with a panel of men who were incarcerated there.

What ensued was a surprisingly nuanced, complex conversation about crime and justice, race and class, philosophy,
psychology, and social issues—generating a sense of depth that
belied its forty-five-minute length. This astonishing moment in
time inspired one of the men on the panel, Paul Perry, to suggest that we do this as a semester-long class. While we couldn't
do it at the prison in Dallas (it's three hours from campus), I
told him that I would think about it, and did so immediately
upon returning home from the trip. I began to consider what
the class would look like, what we would study, and how it
would operate.

I decided to call the class the Inside-Out Prison Exchange
Program, since it would be an exchange among "inside" (incarcerated) and "outside" (campus-based) students, held inside of
prison. I identified what seemed to be some of the most central
issues in criminal justice (for example, what prisons are for,
why crime happens, victims and victimization, punishment
vs. rehabilitation, etc.) and that became the course content.
Since I imagined that it would be uncomfortable bringing inside and outside students together, I found several icebreakers
that would decrease the anxiety in the room. It also seemed
important for us to sit in a circle, to emphasize the equality of
voice of everyone who shared the space.

DISTINCT ASPECTS OF INSIDE-OUT

From the beginning, it has been important to make clear what
Inside-Out is—and is not. As outside people, we are not going

in to "study" the men and women on the inside or to "help" them in any way. It is also not about advocacy or activism; we are not pushing a particular agenda. And it is not an opportunity for people to develop relationships that exceed the boundaries of the classroom. At the same time, there are three distinct aspects of the program, each of which, it should be noted, many other sorts of groups are engaged in. Nonetheless, Inside-Out is the only program that has interwoven all three of these dimensions simultaneously.

First, we provide higher educational opportunities for men and women who are incarcerated. In recent years, increasing numbers of colleges and universities have been offering classes in correctional facilities. The importance and impact of these opportunities are well-documented and cannot be overstated. Inside-Out has played an important role in that expansion since the program's inception.

> Inside-Out is a platform. One of many stepping stones I'm utilizing to make myself a better person. I'm finding that I can do the work of college level courses and even do well. This is an empowering feeling and I'm grateful to all those who've made this opportunity possible. (Inside student)

Second, we engage in dialogue across many levels of difference as we explore issues together.

> The Inside-Out Program made me realize how people can come together to answer tough issues. Our society can solve problems if we could only have a dialogue. (Inside student)

At first blush, it may seem that, in a class that combines incarcerated and nonincarcerated participants, the issue of each group's social location would be the major distinguishing factor. Actually, the kinds and levels of difference far exceed that single feature.

> What a motley crew we made in that little program room at [the prison]. I often think about the incredible dynamic of our group and wonder what we must look like to the people outside that room. People of different colors, sexes, ages, education levels, social classes and opinions in a circle, laughing, talking, arguing, and respecting each other for hours at a time. It has to make it difficult for anyone who watches to hold on to the status quo. The status quo says that doesn't happen. It says that people are different and that some things are never going to change. For two and a half hours every Thursday this semester, we proved that untrue. (Outside student)

Third, and of vital importance, we take people from the outside into prison—to see who is there, who's not there, and what is going on (or not) on the inside. One of the first people I met in prison in 1985 was Tyrone Werts, who was serving a life sentence in Graterford Prison (Tyrone was granted a commutation of his sentence several years ago, after serving over thirty-six years, and has been on our staff since his release). At some point during his incarceration, while meeting with a group that included outside participants, Tyrone offered this simple, yet profound, observation. Referring to the thirty-foot wall surrounding the prison, he said: "That wall isn't there just to keep me in, but to keep you [the public] out." Exactly. It is this ignorance of the reality of imprisonment and everything that leads to it that has allowed mass incarceration (in the United States) to reach such egregious levels in the past forty years.

THE INSIDE-OUT APPROACH TO LEARNING

Once the syllabus, methodology, and logistics were determined, I conducted the first Inside-Out class in a Philadelphia maximum-security facility for men in 1997. That first class involved fifteen students from Temple University and fifteen students from the jail. We sat in a circle each week, sitting alternately (inside student, outside, inside . . . and so on) and entered into dialogue in the large group and smaller subgroups.

> I entered this program without knowing what to expect. I imagined that it would be a bunch of white college students basically coming to observe convicts first hand. From the first moment I came into contact with the students it was an experience out of the ordinary. I felt like a saltwater fish moving into freshwater. Years of conditioning by brutality, anger, hatred, mistrust, and guarded emotions, left me unprepared for the reception and humanness with which the . . . students greeted me. (Inside student)

As the instructor, I served as a facilitator of the learning process, guiding the exploration of the group. Gone was the conventional didactic style of teaching that is too often used in our classrooms, that frequently renders participants mere passive observers.

> My brain never stopped processing information as each student was able to add a piece to the steadily growing mosaic. For me, this is what a college class is all about. I left class with my mind racing to place all of the pieces discussed into their proper places. (Inside student)

Most college courses are lectures and readings which, later on, we are supposed to apply to real-life situations. This class was a real-life situation itself. The readings gave all of us facts, statistics, and the opinions of the "experts," but the class itself was what gave the course an additional meaning and another dimension. The students in the class gave it life—we taught each other more than can be read in a book. (Outside student)

I have found this approach to teaching and learning to be a very humbling experience. What has been most surprising to me are the multiple levels of learning that take place—all of us learning about ourselves, about other people, about how we are both different and alike, about communication and working through conflict, and about the systems that impact our lives and our relationship to those systems, as individuals and as a community. Deep, multilayered, lasting learning.

The initial meeting . . . brought home to me the extent to which I've been isolated and socially deprived. . . . While you're isolated, you do not realize how much you lose psychologically. This is the first time in thirteen years that I've been exposed to such an environment. . . . It made me consider how much I may have lost touch with humanity. Emotional centers were stirred within me that I thought had long since been atrophied. I guess it's because this was the closest I've been to society in thirteen years. (Inside student)

REALIZATIONS FROM PARTICIPATING IN INSIDE-OUT

Two of the most profound, albeit unexpected, insights that I have gained over these years of going in and out of prison and meeting thousands of people behind the walls are the following: I have come to realize that, though some of us may be incarcerated, all of us are imprisoned, in some way(s), at some level, and how important it is to recognize that reality in our own lives, as well as in the lives of others. That simple truth is core to an empathic way of living.

The second realization is something that I have come to understand about myself and, by extension, about human beings in general. Here is how I would explain it. I know that I could have the capacity to do terrible things, possibly to even, given the right (or wrong) circumstance, take the life of another person. But I also know that I am capable of doing tremendous things in the world—and everything in between. And from the many people I have met over the years, for whom both ends of the spectrum are true, I have begun to reframe how I understand a dimension of what it means to be human—that each of us has a continuum of potentialities. We are all so much more than the worst (or best) thing that we have ever done.

I continued to teach in the Philadelphia jails each semester for the next five years, on the men's side of the facility in autumn, and on the women's side in the spring. Gradually, two professors from Temple came to me with ideas for classes they were interested in teaching using the Inside-Out pedagogy, asking me to help them get started. I was both surprised and gratified that anyone else was interested in doing something like this that was so out of the ordinary. Little did I know, at that point, where this would all go.

EXPANDING THE PROGRAM

In 2002, I expanded the program to Graterford Prison, a very large maximum-security facility for men near Philadelphia, with the help of Tyrone (mentioned previously), who was serving as the president of the Lifers' Association. Tyrone was able to secure the approval of the prison administration and developed an ad hoc committee of men on the inside to work out the logistics to make this course happen inside the institution. One of the men who was asked to be on that committee was Paul Perry, who, unbeknownst to me, had been transferred from Dallas to Graterford in the intervening years from when he had first suggested the idea for such a course. It was a perfect full-circle experience to have Paul be instrumental in getting the class up and running at Graterford—and everything else that has followed.

The first course held at Graterford (in which both Tyrone and Paul took part) was light-years beyond the Inside-Out experience in the jails, in part due to the length of time that most of the inside students had been incarcerated. In fact, that first Graterford class was so powerful that the inside and outside students together decided that they wanted to keep meeting each week, voluntarily, after the semester was over, to continue exploring and working on issues of social justice.

We got permission from the administration and began meeting in October 2002. Amazingly, that group (which we called the "Think Tank") has met weekly ever since for the past eighteen years. Though many of the group's original participants have changed over time, there have been some very long-term members (including Paul) who have been involved since its inception.

The Think Tank determined early on that Inside-Out was too good an idea to keep at just one university, that we needed to make it into a national model. With the help of a Soros Justice Fellowship, we were able to make that happen. We spent the academic year 2003–2004 developing what we needed to replicate the program (materials, a curriculum for a seven-day intensive training for professors, outreach and fundraising strategies, etc.). We held our first national training in July 2004, which, to our great surprise, was attended by twenty academics from throughout the United States. Clearly, there was interest. We were off and running.

We have completed seventy-eight intensive training sessions between July 2004 and August 2021. More than 1,200 educators have attended these trainings and have offered classes in disciplines spanning the social sciences, the arts and humanities, education, social work, business, health, and law. So far, approximately sixty thousand inside and outside students have taken part in these classes, and Inside-Out has partnered with more than 150 universities and colleges and about 200 correctional facilities. And along the way, quite organically, the program became international, involving academics from a dozen other countries besides the United States (for example Australia, Canada, Denmark, Mexico, the Netherlands, the United Kingdom, and others).

CONCLUSION

My hope is that the impacts of the program are illustrated, to some degree, through the voices of the inside and outside students and instructors that are included here. It is often difficult to adequately measure, in a quantitative way, the effects of a program of this kind. However, the amount of qualitative and anecdotal information that we have gathered over the years speaks volumes. Additionally, we have watched as the program has expanded, in the numbers of instructors who have taken our training, the number and kinds of classes offered throughout our network, the number of prisons and universities involved, as well as in the countless initiatives that have been spawned, in think tanks and otherwise, by the Inside-Out experience.

The most powerful and enduring impact has come from the ongoing work of the two men mentioned throughout this piece, Paul Perry and Tyrone Werts. Their contributions over these many years have served as the thread that ties together the many disparate strands that have coalesced to create the Inside-Out gestalt. We believe in what we do very deeply and plan to keep expanding and developing dimensions of this cutting-edge program in the years to come. People who get involved in the program often talk about Inside-Out as a movement, that it is blazing a trail. As Tyrone often says: "Inside-Out is more than just a program—we are changing the world." I hope that is true in some small way.

Inside-Out moves through the walls—it is an exchange, an engagement—between and among people who live on both sides of the prison wall. It is through this exchange, realized in the crucible of dialogue, that the walls around us (and within us) begin to crumble. The hope is that, in time, through exchanges of this kind, these walls will become increasingly permeable and, eventually, extinct—one idea, one person, one brick at a time.

Reginald Dwayne Betts on His Groundbreaking Prison Library Project*

Adrian Horton

2021

When Reginald Dwayne Betts fell in love with poetry as a young man, his reading options were limited. He could not spend aimless hours in the library, nor have access to boundless titles, nor browse shelves at will. Convicted at sixteen, in 1997, of carjacking with a pistol in Fairfax County, Virginia, Betts was serving eight years in prison when an unknown person slipped a copy of Dudley Randall's *The Black Poets* under his cell door.

The book opened his mind, showed him things he didn't know were possible. It provided the entryway to a writing practice, a portal to a world outside his cell, a model to envision a future beyond prison.

---

* Adrian Horton, "'It Feels Like the Start of Something': Reginald Dwayne Betts on His Groundbreaking Prison Library Project," *The Guardian*, October 8, 2021.

Betts, now forty, a Yale-trained lawyer and a recipient last month of the prestigious MacArthur "genius grant," now endeavors to offer incarcerated people a similar experience with one thousand micro-libraries in prisons across the country through his nonprofit, Freedom Reads.

The group's name derives from the notion that "freedom begins with a book." [Works of literature], especially books which represent a wide array of experiences, "give you access to possibility, they reveal worlds to you," said Betts. The multilayered project has shipped over fifteen thousand books to prisoners across the United States piloted forty-nine reading circles in fourteen states, and begun development of curated reading lists for Freedom Libraries. Through partnerships with literary ambassadors such as the journalist Nikole Hannah-Jones, essayist Kiese Laymon, and novelist Marlon James, Freedom Reads has also brought numerous authors into prisons to meet inmates, many of whom have never met a professional writer before.

"It's something about presence that signals love, and prison is one of those places where it's hard to know people love you, even when they do," Betts said. The visits put a tangible, dynamic face on the process of writing, unvarnished by editing, part of one of Freedom Reads's guiding beliefs: it is very difficult to become what you can't see. "I'm proud of having writers return to prisons as a statement of love and tenderness," said Betts. "It's nice to see the sort of mess of a human that somebody presents, in addition to the really curated and perfected artistic portrayal of whatever they're talking about."

It's something Betts wished he had seen more as an inmate in the Virginia state correctional system, when the idea of writing as a profession seemed beyond remote. "Naming myself as a writer was a destination of sorts," he said of his early determination to hone a writing practice. "There was something powerful in that because it was really based on what I wanted to do, not what I wanted to be, it wasn't connected to anything. It wasn't connected to an expectation to write a book, it wasn't connected to an expectation to be an educator, it was just connected to an expectation of: I could do this tomorrow."

Betts kept at it—over eight years, he lived in five prisons; his reading was voracious, his writing instinctive. By the time he was freed in 2005, at twenty-four, he had read all of John Steinbeck and Richard Wright, tore through poetry by Lucille Clifton, Etheridge Knight, and Wanda Coleman, completed a paralegal course, and written, as he called it in a searing 2018 essay for the *New York Times Magazine*, "1,000 bad poems."

Betts went on to earn a bachelor's degree from the University of Maryland and a master's in fine arts in poetry from Warren Wilson College, and published the poetry collections *Bastards of the Reagan Era* and *Shahid Reads His Own Palm* and the memoir *Question of Freedom: A Memoir of Learning, Survival, and Coming of Age in Prison*. His path from felon to attorney and PhD candidate at Yale Law School has been both remarkable and deeply against the odds in a nation which saddles rehabilitation from prison with unnecessary, arbitrary roadblocks.

The United States leads the world in incarceration, with two million people behind bars. The numbers are staggering, if usually faceless—one out of every five prisoners in the world is incarcerated in the United States, 0.7 percent of America's population, one in one hundred working-age adults. Betts, and the guiding purpose of Freedom Reads, has a clear vision of life in prison, usually tucked out of view—the drudgery, degradation, untapped potential. The MacArthur Fellowship provides critical visibility for the day-to-day experiences behind the statistics of mass incarceration. "I'm so glad that we're having a nationwide conversation about mass incarceration, but we don't talk enough about the conditions of people's lives in prison," he said. "I'm just trying to insert Freedom Reads and the Freedom Library into a broader conversation about that."

What does he wish we talked more about now? "All of it, that people inside are coming home, and what does that mean to be coming home? What does that mean to prepare folks for coming home? I wish people understood the lack of opportunities and the need to make space for more opportunities," he said

It's something Betts understands well—when he was first released from prison, employment opportunities were heavily circumscribed by his record. He was one of the lucky ones—he got a job at a paint store in Maryland, as he recalls in the *Times* essay, by lying about his lack of employment history. In some states, a felony conviction remains an automatic dismissal on job applications or occupational licenses. A handful of states still enforce bans on convicted felons from receiving food stamps or housing assistance—potentially crucial steps on the ladder to re-entering civilian life. As of 2020, according to the Sentencing Project, 5.2 million Americans were prohibited from voting due to laws that disenfranchise citizens with felony convictions.

Part of the project, as well, is encouraging writers still behind bars. Betts requested John J. Lennon, a journalist who is one of the very few incarcerated people to become a professional writer while in prison, to pen the foreword for an edition of John Milton's *Paradise Lost* to be placed in Freedom Libraries. Lennon, serving twenty-eight to life for a 2004 second-degree murder conviction, doubles the confessional analysis of Milton's hell as a letter to the New York governor, Kathy

Hochul, who, like governors across the nation, has the power to grant clemency to inmates at her "sole discretion." "This is really a letter to all governors, even the president," he writes, "because you all have so much power over prisoners, yet you can never truly know us."

Betts hopes Freedom Reads will help communicate this "day-to-day existence . . . of being incarcerated. Just thinking: man, you can't open your cell door. It's a lot of imposition on your brain to understand, for years and years and years, that at some point, somebody's going to tell you to go into that cell and they're going to close the door behind you.

"It's so deeply, deeply, deeply brutal as an existence, and I think people should know that so that we only use it when absolutely necessary," he added. "And right now, we don't live in a world where we only use it when absolutely necessary."

Even with so much behind him—a law degree, the Connecticut bar exam, a poetry practice, starting a family, one of the most renowned intellectual honors in the nation—Betts still sees a long road ahead. "It obviously feels great," he said of the $625,000 MacArthur Fellowship grant, which he intends to put toward Freedom Reads, his two kids' college funds, and lingering student debt. "But it still feels like the start of something." With Freedom Reads, "I know there's still so much more to do."

A Future for Susanville*

Piper French
2022

If you drive into Susanville, California, from the southwest, one of the first things you will see coming over the mountains and beginning the descent into town is a green road sign declaring the population of this remote outpost in the state's rural northeast. The sign says that 17,500 people live in Susanville, an outdated number from the 2010 census; today, it's more like 13,000. It does not specify that nearly one third of those residents are not free citizens but incarcerated people: around four thousand men locked inside two facilities a few miles farther down the valley.

All of Susanville's residents are in a way tied to these prisons. The construction of the two facilities, completed in 1963 and 1995, has created a sort of forced dependency for the town's free residents. The prisons drive the local economy; they have even shaped the physical landscape of the city, bringing new businesses and driving out others. Counting incarcerated people in the city's official population helps boost everything

---

* Piper French, "A Future for Susanville," *Inquest* and *Bolts*, May 5, 2022.

from healthcare funding to money for local schools. Susanville is a prison town, a label that sits uneasily with its residents but a fairly accurate description of a place where half of the city's free population labor behind prison walls. Everybody on the outside has a brother, cousin, or friend who works inside—as an office tech, nurse, janitor, guard.

Last April, California Governor Gavin Newsom disrupted that strange balance by announcing that Susanville's California Correctional Center would cease to operate by June 30, 2022, fulfilling an earlier pact to close two of the state's thirty-three prisons. The governor has framed these closures as a fiscally sensible response to California's shrinking prison population: closing the CCC would, in the state's estimation, save $122 million out of an approximately $14 billion prison system budget. State officials offered to transfer guards to other prisons, though they acknowledged there would be layoffs, and stressed to the public that closures did not mean early releases. *Don't worry*, they seemed to imply, *nobody's getting out*.

Newsom's plan to close the CCC appears in line with many Californians' demands for a state less reliant on prisons and policing. However, the state has charted a course over the past year that seems to have satisfied no one: neither the free nor the incarcerated residents of Susanville, and not even the activists who fought for prison closures in the first place.

In the months following Newsom's announcement, Susanville officials filed a last-ditch lawsuit against the state that sought to halt the CCC's closure, alleging a series of procedural violations. The closure, the lawsuit claimed, would "cause the City of Susanville to suffer massive economic loss." It quoted Lassen County representatives who said the planned closure "proves yet again that the leaders of our state agencies couldn't care less about the livelihood of residents of the North State."

The statewide coalition Californians United for a Responsible Budget (CURB) supported the prison closures, but it was also demanding more. The coalition argues that the state must close ten prisons by 2025, targeting the most decrepit, dangerous, environmentally hazardous facilities; use the closures to advance the release of elderly and sick people as well as those serving very long sentences; and invest the money saved back into communities whose members are likely to be highly policed and imprisoned in the first place.

Central to this ambitious agenda is a belief that California cannot leave behind all the people who have been bound up in its decades-long prison expansion project. CURB likes to invoke the notion of a "just transition"—a phrase popularized by climate activists and labor unions to describe a shift away from reliance on fossil fuels that doesn't abandon that industry's workers—to invoke a vision of decarceration that pairs prison closures with a reinvestment in communities, workers, and people.

"We don't agree with the argument that a prison should stay open—human cages should stay open—because that's the only way to run an economy," Courtney Hanson, an organizer with the California Coalition for Women Prisoners, a CURB member, told me. "But we do believe that the state of California and the California Department of Corrections has a responsibility to work with those on the ground in these communities, and particularly those incarcerated in those communities, to envision and implement alternatives." In Susanville, that might look like retraining programs for former prison workers to do forest management or firefighting, work that has become ever more critical as the risk of wildfires in the region continues to mount.

Susanville made me wonder about the potential for overlapping aims, solidarity even, between the people who wanted to close the prison—close *all* prisons—and the people in town fighting for it to stay open. There were obvious political and cultural rifts to bridge. The official demographic count for Susanville denotes one of the Blackest cities in Northern California, but its free residents are mostly white, though there is also a sizable Native community in town. Many residents are conservative; Lassen County voted overwhelmingly for Newsom's recall last September. CURB is a progressive, multiracial coalition of activists, many of them abolitionists, and many of whom have felt the sting of incarceration themselves.

But there was one commonality between groups advocating for the free and incarcerated people of Susanville: neither was satisfied by the state's plans for closing the prisons. And in the activists' calls for a better world, I saw a glimpse of possibilities that might suit the residents of Susanville as well—an economy that didn't revolve around a prison, a country where losing your job wasn't tantamount to ruin, a future that looked brighter than the past.

Driving up to Susanville from Los Angeles at the end of February, I thought of the bus journey from LA to Sacramento that the scholar and abolitionist Ruth Wilson Gilmore depicts at the outset of *Golden Gulag*, her definitive account of prison expansion in California. The passengers, a diverse crew of prison reform advocates, "embodied 150 years of California history and more than 300 years of national anxieties and antagonisms," in Gilmore's telling. The final stretch of my brutal, eleven-hour voyage up the 5, the interstate connecting Southern and Northern California, ran through a desolate valley filled with the dead husks of trees that the Dixie Fire had incinerated the summer before.

In 1963, when the number of people incarcerated in state prisons in California was just over twenty-six thousand, the state had conceived of the CCC as "the world's first correctional conservation center." It was a prison with no cells, no guard towers, no bars on its windows, where people held in minimum-security lockup would be trained in firefighting and land stewardship. But in the late 1980s, a Level III unit was added, along with ominous, high-voltage electric fences. The expansion was part of a massive prison building boom that occurred both in California and across the nation in the 1980s and 1990s, just as laws like California's Street Terrorism Enforcement and Prevention Act (1988) and Three Strikes Law (1994) and their federal analogues significantly lengthened sentences. More people were going to prison, and for longer periods than ever before. Between 1982 and 2000, California's prison population more than quadrupled.

Over the course of the 1990s, according to the scholar and filmmaker Tracy Huling, a new prison opened its doors in rural America every fifteen days. In California, large tracts of former farmland were becoming available, and as a plan to build a new prison in East Los Angeles collapsed under unexpected community opposition, state prison officials decided to focus instead on rural areas.

CDCR began to dispatch employees—mostly women—around the state to convince rural residents of the benefits of placing prisons in their backyards. Lillian Koppelman was one of them. "I had a script," she told me. "We would say that we intended to hire predominantly locally—which, as a matter of fact, wasn't the case. You can't really open a prison with brand new people."

Lillian and her colleagues promised rural residents money, local contracts, economic "rejuvenation." In the early 1990s, when the state sought to place a second prison in Susanville after nearby Plumas County rejected it, 57 percent of residents voted yes. High Desert State Prison opened its doors in 1995. Susanville had become a company town, and the business was incarceration.

The prisons brought prosperity to many of Susanville's residents, but their presence had also produced a stratified economy: One class of people lived well while the other struggled, working hard for little pay. After High Desert was built, a Walmart came to town, and many local businesses folded, unable to compete.

"You could see the little shops just closing," Lillian recalled. Chain stores at the east end of town, which had proliferated in the years after the second prison's construction, paid very little. City council member Quincy McCourt told me that many of his friends had master's degrees but made barely over minimum wage. Plenty of them worked for the government, too—the Bureau of Land Management or the Forest Service or the Department of Fish and Wildlife. But workers outside the prisons didn't have the benefit of the California Correctional Peace Officers Association, the state prison guards' union, which Gilmore has called "the most powerful lobby group in California." In 1998, the union spent $2.3 million helping elect Governor Gray Davis. Four years later, he gave them a 33.67 percent pay raise over five years.

Those wages went further in Susanville than they did in LA or San Francisco. I met Tim Nobles at his prefab construction company, one of the biggest nongovernmental employers in Lassen County, which he operates out of one of Susanville's former sawmills. A strong believer in unions, Tim spent over $50,000 a month on his employees' health insurance; still, he had trouble competing with the prison for workers. "If I tried to match some of the wages out there, I wouldn't be in business," he told me.

It frustrated Tim how the money people made at the prison didn't seem to translate to a vibrant community or thriving local economy. "We have these prisons which create really good jobs, especially for our area," he said. "But our town just seems to just be dying. I can go to towns that are half the size of Susanville that have more dining, more restaurants, more bars." To Tim, it felt like a self-perpetuating cycle: Locals were less likely to take a chance on starting up their own business when the prisons offered stability and a comfortable retirement; there were few options for dining or entertainment; people with money to spend went to Reno to spend it; and so on. All the shuttered storefronts uptown started to make sense.

Tim also saw a link between vanishing economic opportunities across the U.S.—stagnant wages, the destruction of organized labor—and California's incarceration rates. "Private sector unions have been destroyed since Ronald Reagan," he told me. "I think we do lock up way too many people—but there's no good jobs out there anymore!" It was all connected: Fewer good jobs meant that more people ended up in prison, but it also made prison labor artificially attractive, because it was some of the only work left that came with great benefits, a living wage, and an early, comfortable retirement.

When he announced his plan to shutter two state prisons by 2025, Governor Newsom called prison closure a "core value" of his administration. But in communicating the decision to close the CCC to the residents of Susanville, the state hadn't presented a vision of prison closure that affirmed life, community, a healthy economy—that offered anything other than a sudden lack. Why would anybody in Susanville, especially people whose jobs were tied to the prison, support that?

CURB organizers had tried to reach out to Susanville residents to discuss their competing vision for the town's future.

"I think it's really important to meet people where they're at," Courtney Hanson told me. "We all have a limited understanding based on our unique perspective and what experiences we've had or haven't had." But they hadn't succeeded in reaching many people—nobody I spoke to in Susanville had been contacted by an organizer or even really knew about the group—and they hadn't gotten very far with the people they did reach. Most residents didn't return their emails, and locals sympathetic to the cause of prison closure didn't want to rock the boat; the prison would go or stay, but they had to keep living alongside their neighbors.

When I asked people in Susanville about CURB's argument that the state of California had a responsibility to provide a better alternative for prison-dependent towns facing closures, most seemed to think the idea was too fanciful to even consider. Arian Hart, the chair of the local tribal council, seemed skeptical of the notion that state government owed Susanville a just transition. "Yeah, I mean, I really can't . . . like, you're talking reparation type of stuff," he said, laughing.

"The state has the power to do whatever they want," Mike McCourt, Quincy's father, told me. Mike moved away from Susanville in 2020, but he still felt invested in the place that he had called home for so long. He had fond memories of Susanville—he recalled how, after he first moved to town in 1967 at just seventeen, the woman who owned the Grand Café kept him fed, selling him soup for a quarter. Mike felt like the state government didn't really care about what happened to Susanville. "You can have all the injunctions you want, but if it's made its mind up and it's not efficient for the state's budget, you're history," he told me.

This pessimism, I thought, could be linked to any number of things: a deep-seated suspicion of the state in communities that have long been disenfranchised; the feeling of political alienation common in rural areas; the general sense of most people living in America that government is not really working for them. These sorts of feelings couldn't be uprooted by a single conversation with an organizer—it might take a lifetime of listening and arguing. Ultimately, Courtney told me, CURB was focused on the big picture. The office of the Legislative Analyst had determined back in 2020 that, given declines in the state prison population, California could save money by closing at least five prisons by 2025. There was only so much their coalition could do. "We're very concerned with what's going on on the ground in Susanville, and at the same time, we're fighting more broadly for the state to commit to closing ten prisons by 2025," she said.

Quincy saw that the prisons had not been "the end-all-be-all savior of our city—it's clearly not, otherwise we'd be better off than we are." But he never had the chance to talk with CURB organizers about their ideas. Quincy was also elected to represent the people of Susanville, and the majority of the city's residents—at least, those who had any say in the matter— wanted the CCC to stay open, and so he was supporting that effort.

In August 2021, a Lassen County superior court judge found that the CDCR had skipped over a number of bureaucratic steps in trying to shutter the CCC, and delayed the closure until an environmental review and other measures take place. In the meantime, Quincy was looking for other solutions. He had been working on an economic development plan for the city, which more and more people were starting to take seriously as the threat of prison closure loomed. For the first time anyone could remember, thanks to Quincy and Arian, the city, the county, and the tribal council were all working together.

Despite the prisons, the city's budget is threadbare and has been for years—there's no money for major projects, and local government offices remain seriously understaffed. When I asked Quincy what he might do if the state simply gave Susanville the $122 million that closing the CCC had been projected to save, he wrote out a list: a four-year college, a community arts center, a bypass to revitalize the Uptown district. Maybe the CCC could focus solely on reentry, or be converted into a data center.

Quincy believed deeply that people could change, whether they had done something that landed them in prison or were just set in their ways. "I'm probably more of an idealist than anything," he told me. And he believed his town could change too, even if he didn't know for sure what that might look like yet.

True change may require the kind of coalitions that Ruth Wilson Gilmore writes about in *Golden Gulag*. The book concludes with another bus ride, but this time, it's the precursor to an incredible organizing feat: rural residents and urban anti-prison activists coming together for a conference in Fresno about the fight for environmental justice and against prisons. The gathering is an unlikely one—"for quite some time each group imagined that the other, in a general way, was the reason for its struggles," Gilmore writes—which is precisely why it's so powerful.

In Fresno, that solidarity had come about because organizers managed to link the struggles of two groups that seemed impossible to unite. In Susanville, the pandemic and the city's remote location had thwarted organizing attempts. The lawsuit and the state's wall of silence calcified the divisions that already existed, and exacerbated intolerable conditions for the town's incarcerated residents. The free residents of Susanville never saw their fate as tied to the people behind bars. On its own, each group was easy to dismiss: the locals arguing to keep their prison, who would not find much sympathy from liberal, urban California; the incarcerated organizers, battling a system designed to keep them hidden and silenced; and the activists, whose abolitionist aims are constantly being waved away as extreme, unrealistic.

But more prisons will close in California, and those closures will bring with them the same window of possibility, the same choices that Susanville offered. And they will show, once again, how we are all tied to these prisons—free and incarcerated people alike. We may not work at them, we may not be locked inside them, but they were built in our name.

Ed. Note: The editors have, with the author's permission, updated the original piece for publication in this anthology and made minor edits for clarity. It is important to note that the full piece also includes the experience of people at the CCC throughout the closure, including covering in detail the perspective of former CCC workers.

Part VI

Aftermath

Does a person's punishment begin when they enter prison and end when they get out? Most people think so. Once upon a time—before we became public defenders and saw the criminal system up close—so did we.

We couldn't have been more wrong. In fact, when the penitentiary gates open, thousands of opportunities close for the ten thousand people leaving prison every week.[1] After being set "free," formerly incarcerated people are burdened with countless restraints on their civic, economic, and social lives.[2] They will likely face legal discrimination in accessing education, employment, housing, and public benefits. Banks will deny them financing to buy a home or start a business, and they may lose the right to vote, serve on a jury, or hold public office.[3]

The law calls many of these restrictions "collateral consequences." But we think a more accurate term is "lifetime punishments" because they can lurk forever, constraining people for the rest of their lives. According to the American Bar Association, state and federal law contains about forty-five thousand such punishments after conviction.[4] Innumerable decisions by private companies and individuals, such as refusing to hire or rent to somebody with a criminal record, add to these legal exclusions.[5] These discrete choices compound over time and, along with the forty-five thousand laws, condemn people with criminal convictions to a lifetime of second-class citizenship.[6]

Fortunately, we see attempts to roll back the lifetime punishments regime nationwide. In Part IV, we highlighted efforts to curtail pretrial detention, which has a harmful impact on people's lives before conviction. This part focuses on the lifetime punishments that follow conviction, when courts are no longer involved—indeed, when no system actor takes responsibility for the fact that punishment continues, far beyond the courthouse and far beyond the prison.

We begin with a federal district court judge's decision to take collateral consequences into account in determining what sentence to impose on a first-time offender. In *United States v. Chevelle Nesbeth*, federal District Court Judge Frederic Block had to decide what sentence to give Chevelle Nesbeth, who had been convicted of trying to import cocaine from Jamaica. Nesbeth, a twenty-year-old college student with no criminal record, carried two suitcases at her boyfriend's request. An airport search revealed cocaine stuffed in the suitcases' handles. A judge would typically impose a prison sentence in a case like this. But here, Judge Block did something novel—he asked both sides to present him with research describing the collateral consequences Nesbeth would face if convicted.

After reviewing that research, Judge Block sentenced Nesbeth to a year of probation rather than imposing any prison time. The severe collateral consequences of her conviction, he said, were already punishment enough. We include this opinion for its detailed discussion of how far-reaching lifetime punishments can be and because it serves as an example for how judges can mitigate the criminal system's harshness. Though Judge Block's colleagues have not widely cited *United States v. Chevelle Nesbeth*, we uplift it here in the hope that members of the bench will find inspiration in its wisdom.

Most readers of this book are not judges. But many of you may work in a business, nonprofit, or university. You may not realize it, but you too have power to ease the way for people with criminal records. In "A Conversation About Second Chance Employment," Crystal Mourlas-Jaun and Rahsaan Sloan talk to *The Marshall Project*'s Lawrence Bartley about the challenges they faced searching for a job after leaving prison. They each eventually found their way to Dave's Killer Bread, a Portland-based bakery that was one of the first companies to begin hiring large numbers of its employees out of prison. Mourlas-Jaun and Sloan have since received promotions and now direct staff hiring. When asked how it feels to be able to extend the same opportunity he once received to recently released people, Sloan said, "Man, you see I cannot stop smiling, man. That was the goal. To feel it come together and to see the change in people after a few years. It is beautiful."[7]

Dave's Killer Bread is not the only employer that has proven that people with criminal records can be excellent workers. Johns Hopkins Hospital and Health System has become an industry leader for its fair hiring practices. Faced with a labor shortage, Johns Hopkins officials asked themselves: "Who are we overlooking in our communities who would be great candidates for employment?" The answer, they realized, was people who had been convicted of crimes. To recruit more such people, officials took a series of seemingly small steps that together made a big difference. Because research suggests that employers who learn about a criminal conviction *after* getting to know an applicant are less likely to consider the conviction disqualifying, Johns Hopkins delayed background checks until later in the hiring process. And although officials didn't remove all employment restrictions for convicted people, they limited them to specific jobs. After all, while a drug conviction might bar a person from becoming a pharmacist, it shouldn't keep them from joining the accounting department.[8]

In our conversations with people coming out of prison, housing is the only topic that comes up as often as jobs. Formerly incarcerated people are about ten times more likely to be unhoused and twenty-seven times more likely to face housing instability than the general public.[9] Zachariah Oquenda, an attorney with the California nonprofit Root and Rebound, saw these obstacles firsthand as he tried to support his brother Noah after Noah served time on felony drug charges. Oquenda describes the desperate measures that victims of housing discrimination must resort to and the resulting psychological toll: "Like my brother, many people in reentry can feel boxed in with an array of bad options. It's not hard to understand how they can internalize the message society is sending: you don't belong and your life doesn't matter."

Oquenda outlines a series of policy reforms—many of which are being considered in cities, counties, and states across the country—that would make housing more accessible to people like his brother. In California, housing and reentry advocates are pushing the state to increase the amount of "gate money" (so called because you get it at the prison gate) it offers to people upon release. Oquenda also makes the case for "Fair Chance Housing" legislation, which restricts the ability of housing providers to screen applicants based on their criminal records. He explains that while such legislation takes many forms, every version is founded on the same core principle: "Each of our identities cannot be reduced down to the worst thing we've ever done."[10]

While finding a job and a place to live are often the most immediate concerns for those coming out of prison, becoming a full citizen requires more than simply being able to provide for your basic needs. Few rights are more central to full citizenship than the right to vote. According to the Sentencing Project, about 5.2 million people were barred from the polls in 2020 because of a felony conviction, with Black people constituting a disproportionate share of the disenfranchised. If those 5.2 million Americans comprised a state of their own, it would be the twenty-third-largest state in the country. In "D.C. Residents Are Voting from Prison This Week," Kira Lerner canvasses recent efforts in Washington, D.C., and twenty-five states to restore voting rights to people with criminal convictions.

Closely related to the right to vote at the polls is the right to serve (and vote) on a jury. Historically, states have also prohibited people convicted of certain crimes from exercising this right. But this too is beginning to change. In "The Time I Was Called for Jury Duty . . . and What Happened Next," James M. Binnall movingly describes being called for jury duty and learning that his criminal conviction barred him from serving, even though he had completed his sentence long ago and was now a lawyer, practicing in the very courthouse where he was deemed ineligible to be a juror. Binnall used his humiliation to fuel his advocacy for reform. In 2019, California passed a law restoring the right to serve on juries for most people convicted of crimes. Three other states—Louisiana, Connecticut, and Florida—have enacted similar legislation.[11]

While most of the readings in this part focus on regaining a particular right—such as employment, housing, or voting—the final one describes a project that allows people to reclaim all their rights in one fell swoop. In "Rights Restoration Success Stories," Ben Fleury-Steiner introduces us to Delaware's Advancement through Pardons and Expungement (APEX) program, the nation's first publicly funded effort to restore the rights of people convicted of crimes. To date, 70 percent of APEX applicants have regained their civil rights, including voting, serving on a jury, and holding public office. Fleury-Steiner, a professor at the University of Delaware, started an experiential class where students help applicants navigate the process, and he argues that both APEX and his student volunteers could serve as national models. He points out that governors in fifteen states regularly use their pardon power to restore civil rights.[12] Activists elsewhere can push their states to join that list; in those that already provide for rights restoration, students and other volunteers can assist people in preparing their rights restoration applications.[13] As Fleury-Steiner reminds us, "If we are willing to dream—and act on those dreams—nationwide civil rights restoration is within our grasp."

As you consider the readings that follow, we ask that you reflect on the nature of punishment: What constitutes punishment? At how many points in the criminal system is punishment inflicted anew? If punishment is inflicted, how long should it last, and in what form? Ask yourself: Which, if any, post-conviction restrictions fit with my sense of justice? Which, if any, make my community safer?

Each person will come up with different answers to these questions, but we suspect that most of you will find at least some of these punishments unnecessary and harmful. If that is the case, we encourage you to ask another set of questions: What can I do to help eliminate or alleviate any of them? Can I encourage my employer to follow the lead of Dave's Killer Bread or Johns Hopkins and become more welcoming to those with criminal convictions? Can I join with allies in my community to persuade my county or state to make housing more available to people coming out of jail or prison? Can I start or join a rights restoration project like Delaware's?

Of all the parts in this book, this one addresses an area in which ordinary people have perhaps the most influence. While government policy controls life after a criminal conviction, private actors have tremendous power as well. Over the past fifty years, many Americans used that power to be punitive and hostile toward formerly incarcerated people. But we can chart a new course today. When people return from prison, they are coming home. And we have the power to determine what that home looks like. We can work to make it welcoming and restorative. We can open our job sites, schools, housing complexes, and houses of worship. We can choose to be good neighbors.

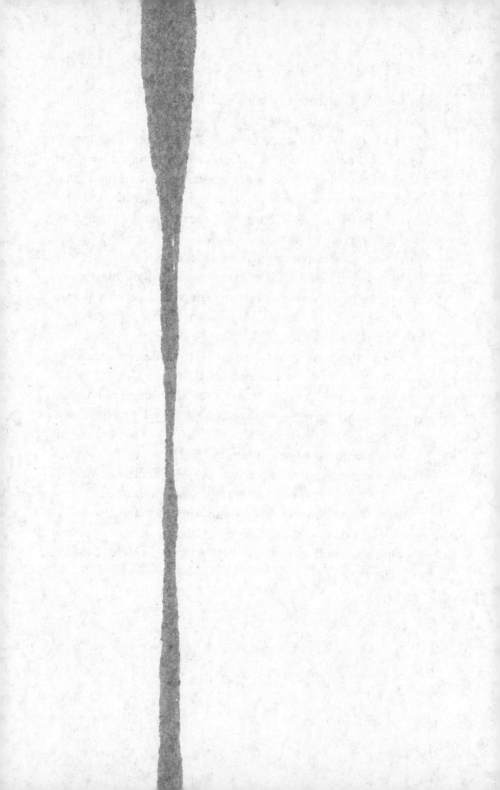

United States v. Chevelle Nesbeth*

Judge Frederic Block
2016

Chevelle Nesbeth was convicted by a jury of importation of cocaine and possession of cocaine with intent to distribute. Her advisory guidelines sentencing range was thirty-three to forty-one months. Nonetheless, I rendered a non-incarceratory sentence today in part because of a number of statutory and regulatory collateral consequences she will face as a convicted felon. I have incorporated those consequences in the balancing of the 18 U.S.C. § 3553(a) factors in imposing a one-year probationary sentence.

I am writing this opinion because from my research and experience over two decades as a district judge, sufficient attention has not been paid at sentencing by me and lawyers—both prosecutors and defense counsel—as well as by the Probation Department in rendering its pre-sentence reports, to the collateral consequences facing a convicted defendant. And I believe

---

* United States v. Chevelle Nesbeth, 188 F. Supp. 3d 179 (E.D.N.Y. 2016).

that judges should consider such consequences in rendering a lawful sentence.

There is a broad range of collateral consequences that serve no useful function other than to further punish criminal defendants after they have completed their court-imposed sentences. Many—under both federal and state law—attach automatically upon a defendant's conviction.

The effects of these collateral consequences can be devastating. As Professor Michelle Alexander has explained, "[m]yriad laws, rules, and regulations operate to discriminate against ex-offenders and effectively prevent their reintegration into the mainstream society and economy. These restrictions amount to a form of 'civi[l] death' and send the unequivocal message that 'they' are no longer part of 'us.'"

I. THE HISTORY OF COLLATERAL CONSEQUENCES

A. From Past to Present

The notion of "civil death"—or "the loss of rights . . . by a person who has been outlawed or convicted of a serious crime"— appeared in American penal systems in the colonial era, derived from the heritage of English common law. The concept of civil death persisted into the twentieth century as an "integral part of criminal punishment." Some commentators express that the continuation of civil death, "[e]ven watered down and euphemistically denominated 'civil disabilities,' . . . functioned after the Civil War to perpetuate the social exclusion and political disenfranchisement of African-Americans." These compelling critiques are not limited to traditional civil death and persist with great force to the modern imposition of collateral consequences to convicted felons.

Today, the collateral consequences of a felony conviction form a new civil death. Convicted felons now suffer restrictions in broad-ranging aspects of life that touch upon economic, political, and social rights. In some ways, "modern civil death is harsher and more severe" than traditional civil death because there are now more public benefits to lose, and more professions in which a license or permit or ability to obtain a government contract is a necessity. Professor Alexander paints a chilling image of the modern civil death:

> Today a criminal freed from prison has scarcely more rights, and arguably less respect, than a freed slave or a black person living "free" in Mississippi at the height of Jim Crow. Those released from prison on parole can be stopped and searched by the police for any reason . . . and returned to prison for the most minor of infractions, such as failing to attend a meeting with a parole officer. . . . The "whites only" signs may be gone, but new signs have gone up—notices placed in job applications, rental agreements, loan applications, forms for welfare benefits, school applications, and petitions for licenses, informing the general public that "felons" are not wanted here. A criminal record today authorizes precisely the forms of discrimination we supposedly left behind—discrimination in employment, housing, education, public benefits, and jury service. Those labeled criminals can even be denied the right to vote.

B. Modern Reform Efforts

The ebb and flow of efforts at reform are tiding back toward dismantlement of collateral consequences and civil death. President Barack Obama, for one, has taken steps by executive order to help felons rehabilitate and reintegrate into society. For example, he has ordered federal agencies to "ban the box," i.e., not ask prospective employees about their criminal histories early in the application process. Additionally, the President has voiced his support for the Sentencing Reform and Corrections Act of 2015, which has received bipartisan support in the Senate. If passed, this bill would, among other things, require the Bureau of Prisons to implement recidivism-reduction programming, expand safety-valve eligibility, and permit a sentencing judge to avoid mandatory minimums in certain circumstances.

Other examples include the Department of Justice's National Institute of Justice's funding of a comprehensive study on the collateral consequences of criminal convictions. The study—which was conducted by the American Bar Association's Criminal Justice Section—has catalogued tens of thousands of statutes and regulations that impose collateral consequences at both the federal and state levels. Based on the results of this study, former Attorney General Eric Holder implored the states to "determine whether [the collateral consequences] that impose burdens on individuals convicted of crimes without increasing public safety should be eliminated."

My former colleague in the Eastern District of New York, Judge John Gleeson, recognized the devastating effects the collateral consequences of conviction had on a defendant who was unable to procure employment due to an offense she had committed seventeen years prior. He explained that he had sentenced the defendant "to five years of probation supervision, not to a lifetime of unemployment." Judge Gleeson determined that district courts in the Second Circuit "have ancillary jurisdiction over applications for orders expunging convictions," and expunged the defendant's conviction. If

Judge Gleeson's opinion is affirmed on appeal, Ms. Nesbeth might—if she could show the "extreme circumstances" necessary for expungement—be a candidate for this form of relief at some future time.

In recent years, the organized bar has again made substantial efforts to alleviate the detrimental effects of collateral consequences. In 2003, the ABA House of Delegates approved Standards on Collateral Sanctions and Discretionary Disqualification of Convicted Persons, which, among other things, prohibited the imposition of a collateral sanction unless "the legislature cannot reasonably contemplate any circumstances in which imposing the sanction would not be justified," and prohibiting "discretionary disqualification" from "benefits or opportunities, including housing, employment, insurance," etc. The Uniform Law Commission released the 2010 Uniform Collateral Consequences of Conviction Act ("UCCCA"), which includes certain procedural protections, such as notifying a defendant who pleads guilty of the various consequences he or she will suffer by so pleading. Vermont has enacted the UCCCA, and bills proposing its adoption are currently pending in New York, Pennsylvania, and Wisconsin.

Notwithstanding these various efforts at reform, felony convictions continue to expose individuals to a wide range of collateral consequences imposed by law that affect virtually every aspect of their lives.

II. MS. NESBETH'S COLLATERAL CONSEQUENCES AND THE BALANCING OF ALL § 3553(A) FACTORS

The Pre-Sentence Report (PSR) was issued on August 17, 2015; it contained no reference to collateral consequences. On September 11, 2015, I instructed counsel to submit in writing

which collateral consequences would likely be applicable in
Ms. Nesbeth's case. They did so on January 26, 2016.

A. The Nature and Circumstances of the Offense and Ms. Nesbeth's Personal Characteristics

There is no question that Ms. Nesbeth has been convicted of
serious crimes. The PSR reports that the net weight of the cocaine she brought into the country was 602 grams. Her criminal conduct is inexcusable.

While visiting Jamaica at the behest of a boyfriend, she was
given two suitcases by friends, who had purchased her return
airline ticket, and was asked to bring them to an individual
upon her arrival to the United States. As disclosed during the
trial, the drugs were in the suitcases' handles. Ms. Nesbeth
"m[et] the profile of a courier," and there was a clear basis for
the jury to reject her claim that she did not know she was bringing drugs into the country, and to render its guilty verdict.

The Probation Department recommended a below-
guidelines sentence of twenty-four months, followed by three
years of supervised release, because Ms. Nesbeth was "a
first-time offender, is enrolled in college," is employed, and
"has otherwise lived a law-abiding life and is at a low risk of
recidivism."

Ms. Nesbeth, who was twenty years old when convicted,
was born in Kingston, Jamaica, has always been single, has no
children, and lives with her mother in New Haven, Connecticut. In 2008, when she was thirteen, she joined her mother in
the United States, who had previously left her with her father
to be raised by him in Jamaica. Ms. Nesbeth is a U.S. citizen.
She has been enrolled in college since 2013, and has helped to

support herself as a nail technician at a children's spa. Between September 2012 and June 2013, she worked as a counselor at a facility that provides services to children in lower-income areas, and during the summers of 2010 through 2012, she held seasonal employment as a parks maintenance worker.

Not surprisingly, Ms. Nesbeth's mother, who is a home-care attendant, was "shocked" by her daughter's arrest and conviction because it was "completely out of character." She described her daughter as an "'excellent' person, who is quiet, nice, caring, and who is both very loving and very loved." The mother also related "that the defendant worries about her future, as she had planned to be a school principal."

In the United States, Ms. Nesbeth was raised under lower-income circumstances, and her family had for a time "required Food Stamp benefits." As for her employment, the name of the facility where she assisted children from lower-income areas was Leap, in New Haven, and she worked as a "counselor" to the children. And her work as a parks maintenance worker was for the Youth at Work agency, where she was "a youth initiative worker."

As for her education, Ms. Nesbeth anticipates graduating from Southern Connecticut State University in 2017. "She was originally studying education," but "due to the instant conviction is now studying sociology."

"The defendant reported no illegal drug use," and to her mother's knowledge, her daughter "has never used illegal drugs, consumed alcohol, or required substance abuse treatment." Ms. Nesbeth was released on January 7, 2015, a day after her arrest, on a $50,000 unsecured bond and has been at liberty ever since. She has been fully compliant with her conditions of release.

B. The Collateral Consequences

The Addendum to the PSR has advised me of the federal collateral consequences Ms. Nesbeth will or may face as a result of her felony drug convictions.

First, the Probation Department has commented:

> Notably, the defendant is a college student and she has held internships working with young children as it was her original intent to become a teacher and eventually a principal. The defendant will be ineligible for grants, loans, and work assistance for a period of two years, the duration of her college career.

The Addendum then sets forth a host of other federal statutory and regulatory proscriptions for drug-related felony convictions:

> Under 21 U.S.C. § 862, for a period of up to one year for drug possession and up to five years for drug distribution, Ms. Nesbeth will be ineligible "for the issuance of any grant, contract, loan, professional license, or commercial license provided by an agency of or appropriated by funds of the United States." Under 42 U.S.C. § 13661 and 24 C.F.R. § 5.855, Ms. Nesbeth and her household may be denied admission to federally assisted housing for a "reasonable time."
>
> Under 21 U.S.C. § 862(a), Ms. Nesbeth "shall not be eligible for assistance under any state program funded under Part A of Title IV of the Social Security Act, or for Food Stamp benefits." And this disability is "permanent," although individual states can grant an exemption, "or can enact a law limiting the period during which the restriction applies." The

Addendum reports that the State of Connecticut, where Ms. Nesbeth resides, "continues to bar felons from receiving Food Stamp benefits."

Under 22 U.S.C. § 2714, Ms. Nesbeth cannot be issued a passport during any period of supervised release. "According to Defense Counsel's submission, this provision is particularly relevant for the defendant, whose father, grandmother, and extended family reside abroad," and "[t]he inability to do so will undoubtedly impact these important familial relationships."

Under 23 U.S.C. § 159 and 23 C.F.R. § 192.4, states are required "to enact a law requiring that any individual convicted of a drug offense have their [driver's] licenses suspended or revoked" for a period of "at least six months."

In addition, "[w]hile a felony conviction does not automatically disqualify a person from federal employment, it can be a factor in determining suitability for a position" on a "case-by-case basis by the specific agency." The Addendum references a number of them:

(i) Child Care

"As to employment in child care services, including teaching, employment is generally subject to a background check for criminal convictions. It also affects employment in child protective services, social services, health care services, residential care, recreational or rehabilitative programs, or correctional or treatment programs." Furthermore, "all individuals seeking employment in child care services to children under 18, including education, must undergo a criminal background check, and the statute provides that a felony drug conviction may be grounds for denying employment."

The Addendum references a host of other restrictions for such things as the mentoring of children of prisoners, a permanent bar from employment with AmeriCorps, and working in a foreign student-exchange program sponsored by the Department of State.

(ii) Pharmaceutical
A felony conviction permanently bars an individual from working for a manufacturer, distributor, dispenser, or reverse dispenser of controlled substances.

(iii) Transportation
A felony conviction bars employment with private transportation companies transporting prisoners or hazardous materials, and as an airport security screener or baggage handler, a flight crew member, and a customs broker.

(iv) Hospice Work
An individual convicted of a felony offense can be barred from working for a hospice if the conviction was within three years and the applicant would have contact with patient records.

(v) Bank or Financial Industry
An individual convicted of a felony offense can be barred from working in an FDIC-insured depository institution within ten years of conviction.

(vi) Armed Forces Enlistment
An individual convicted of a felony offense can also be barred from enlisting in the Armed Forces of this country.

(vii) Labor Union

An individual convicted of a felony offense can be ineligible from working in a labor organization or employee benefits plan.

(viii) Disaster Assistance

Any felony conviction bars an individual from relief for disaster relief, and is permanent.

(ix) Firearm Possession

Any felony conviction bars an individual from possession, sale, shipment, transportation, or receipt of a firearm in interstate and foreign commerce, and is permanent.

(x) Adoption/Foster Care

Any felony conviction bars an individual from adopting a child or serving as a foster parent for five years. Some states, including New York, disqualify prospective adoptive parents or anyone they live with who has been convicted of a drug related offense.

(xi) Jury Service and Voting

A felony conviction in federal and state courts bars an individual from serving as either a grand juror or a petit juror unless the person's civil rights have been restored, which can only be achieved through a pardon.

Ms. Nesbeth has never resided in New York. Any period of supervised release or probation will be administered in Connecticut, where she has always resided. Thus, in addition to whatever federal collateral consequences she will suffer, she will also be subject to collateral consequences under that state's laws. The Addendum did not address them, but I have identified some which are either currently applicable or—given Ms. Nesbeth's history of working with and counseling underprivileged children—may have future relevance:

> She will not be allowed to vote until any probationary or supervised release term has expired.
> She cannot serve on a jury for seven years.
> She is disqualified from receiving a teaching certificate for five years. Afterward, the Connecticut State Board of Education maintains discretion to deny her a teaching certificate.
> She will be ineligible for five years to adopt a child or serve as a foster parent.
> She can be denied a license by the Connecticut Commissioner of Early Childhood to operate or maintain a daycare center or a group childcare home; will be ineligible for employment or to volunteer with an adoptive or foster child placing agency; and may be ineligible to reside in a home that provides family day care services.
> She may be ineligible for Connecticut public housing.

In response to my instructions to counsel to opine on the collateral consequences that Ms. Nesbeth will or is likely to suffer, they have admirably submitted useful information which I have considered. Defense counsel has tracked most of the collateral consequences contained in the Probation Department's Addendum, with the focus on Ms. Nesbeth's limitations on her ability to obtain employment as an educator or a school administrator. Counsel's submission concludes that "the serious consequences that result from her federal drug conviction cannot be overstated. Compacting these consequences with a period of incarceration or even a lengthy period of supervision would be a severe and an unnecessary punishment."

The Government, on the other hand, argues that of the many federal collateral consequences, only a "handful" apply to Ms. Nesbeth and sets forth "a brief list of those that are potentially relevant to the defendant." Nonetheless, the Government asserts that "[t]he obstacles resulting from her crime are by no means insurmountable," and that "[w]hile she may end up choosing a different career path or taking longer to become a teacher than she previously anticipated, if she goes on to prove the instant offense was an isolated and solitary blemish on her record, the defendant can achieve the same level of success in life regardless of her criminal conviction;" thus, it believes that a guidelines sentence is appropriate.

III. THE SHAPING OF THE SENTENCE

Even if I were not to consider collateral consequences, the conventional balancing of the § 3553(a) factors might warrant a non-incarceratory sentence. But I need not make that decision because of the collateral consequences Ms. Nesbeth will suffer, and is likely to suffer—principally her likely inability to pursue a teaching career and her goal of becoming a principal—has compelled me to conclude that she has been sufficiently punished, and that jail is not necessary to render a punishment that is sufficient but not greater than necessary to meet the ends of sentencing.

This surely is not meant to suggest that a convicted defendant's collateral consequences are always likely to result in a non-incarceratory sentence. Each case must, of course, be separately considered, and the balancing of all the § 3553(a) factors may certainly warrant prison—and even significant prison time—for someone else under different circumstances.

I have imposed a one-year term of probation. In fixing this term, I have also considered the collateral consequences Ms. Nesbeth would have faced with a longer term of probation, such as the curtailment of her right to vote and the inability to visit her father and grandmother in Jamaica because of the loss of her passport during her probationary term.

A Conversation About Second Chance Employment*

Lawrence Bartley, Crystal Mourlas-Jaun, and Rahsaan Sloan

2023

Lawrence Bartley: Hello, my name is Lawrence Bartley. I am the director of News Inside for *The Marshall Project*. Today we will be discussing second chance employment. I am here with two brilliant individuals who will talk about companies like Dave's Killer Bread who afford people the opportunity to find employment after incarceration. So, can you all tell me about second chance employment?

Crystal Mourlas-Jaun: Second chance employment to me is an employer giving an individual with a [criminal] background an opportunity for employment for a living

---

* Lawrence Bartley, Crystal Mourlas-Jaun, and Rahsaan Sloan, "A Conversation About Second Chance Employment," 2023.

wage as well as an opportunity for growth personally and professionally.

Bartley: Can you explain how you came to take part in the second chance employment program run by Dave's Killer Bread?

Mourlas-Jaun: I was actually looking for employment. I had just gotten out of prison after spending seven and a half years incarcerated. I had been going to school for dental assisting and I was applying for jobs. I was almost done with schooling and I was not getting any phone calls back. It really made me look at myself like what is going on. Why am I not getting phone calls back? Of course, they are doing background checks, right? I am going to be working in the dental field. I believe it was my cousin who suggested I apply to Dave's Killer Bread.

Rahsaan Sloan: I found out about second chance opportunity while I was finishing up my federal sentence at Sheridan, Oregon. That was the talk of the compound if you were trying to change your life. While I was incarcerated, I made it very clear to myself that I had to give myself an advantage, so I started taking college courses. When I was released from the federal system, it was nothing like I expected. The calls were not coming in. I forgot the part about having to have money to take care of myself while being free. But Dave's Killer Bread had an opportunity; I went and applied, and that became home.

Bartley: There's many formerly incarcerated people that are brilliant, they have skills, but being incarcerated for a number of years they don't have the opportunity to develop the type of experience as their counterparts who aren't formerly incarcerated. When they go to take on jobs a lot of times they are told, you cannot have this job for the lack of experience. How do you think Dave's Killer Bread is handling that?

Mourlas-Jaun: I was given the opportunity to do a marketing course and I never thought in a million years that my employer was going to help me go to school. What employer does that? What about you, Rahsaan?

Sloan: Mainly the one-on-ones with the supervisors and management that have been in the situation that I've been in before or that are understanding of our situations. All these people that believed in us and sat us down and had those one-on-one twenty-minute conversations to be more articulate, to be more presentable, tuck your shirt in, take that frown off your face.

Mourlas-Jaun: I have to definitely agree with you. Teaching us how to be that productive member of society, but also within Dave's Killer Bread community. I was a community outreach coordinator for eight years. That role was very, very big for me. I had never really worked in the office, so I got some office skills. Lots of computer skills that I didn't have and I could walk down the hallway and be like "hey, how's it going?" And everybody pretty much knew who I was. We had that community feel, you know. It is not just, oh, it is another day, it's another job.

Bartley: So tell me what is your current position again, Crystal?

Mourlas-Jaun: Project Coordinator for Dave's Killer Bread Foundation. The Foundation started in 2015 and I have actually been working toward this position, and here I am.

Bartley: What about you, Rahsaan? How long have you been in your current position?

Sloan: It is going on six years now. When that opportunity came up to be production supervisor in Mesa, Arizona, I jumped on it. I had already outgrown Portland, Oregon. That is where I committed my crime at, that is where my old friends were. I knew it was time to take my story somewhere else and to really blossom and to be able to live. I am out here now and doing different speaking engagements because there's a thousand second chance people out there, but who's going to be that person to take that chance to give them that second chance?

Bartley: So Rahsaan, now you have the opportunity to hire formerly incarcerated people? How does that make you feel?

Sloan: Man, you see I cannot stop smiling, man. That was the goal. To feel it come together and to see the change in people after a few years. It is beautiful. Just like I'm pretty sure Crystal feels about talking to me and knowing those talks that we used to have and just seeing that it's worth it.

Mourlas-Jaun: Also, you're teaching hiring supervisors, right there with you. You are teaching them about hiring the right person for the position, not their background. Because there's missed talent out there if you overlook someone with a background.

Bartley: Are there any final words or thoughts any of you would like to say to individuals who are seeking employment and do not know about the second chance employment program?

Sloan: The main thing that I would want to tell people is change is possible, you know, I mean, you give somebody a second chance, they can come out here and be a pillar in their community.

Mourlas-Jaun: My last words I guess would be to know there is hope. Let go of your own shame or doubt and show up every day as yourself, show up and be a hard worker. I can only hope and pray that by me telling my story it is making an impact, whether it is for an employee that needs a job or an employer that wants to see success stories.

The Case for a Fair Chance Housing Act: From a Brother's Perspective*

Zachariah Oquenda
2021

Shelter is a fundamental need for every human being. People with criminal records are no exception. And if housing is a human right, then it must be a right afforded to all, including those who have been arrested and convicted of crimes.

Housing access and stability provides multitudes of benefits beyond simply protecting us from the elements. According to the U.S. Interagency Council on Homelessness, stable housing improves people's outcomes in employment and income, family unity and well-being, mental and physical health, and education success. Most of us take stable housing and its benefits for granted. Basic needs like food storage, hygiene, and sleep

---

* Zachariah Oquenda, "The Case for a Fair Chance Housing Act: From a Brother's Perspective," *Medium*, July 20, 2021.

can be far harder, if not impossible, without stable housing. People convicted of a crime deserve access to housing and its benefits, but they remain the most likely to be denied them.

For formerly incarcerated people who are reentering society, housing stability is also an essential platform for starting fresh, building confidence, and moving forward with their lives. Not only does housing instability disrupt or halt this progress, but also, housing instability increases the odds of recidivism by at least 70 percent for each time the person moves. Our society locks people up, and when they do their time and reenter society, we fail them by providing them too little support and imposing extraordinarily high barriers to housing.

Even formerly incarcerated people who are "doing everything right" still may end up homeless or back in jail for reasons simply beyond their control. That's why, according to reports from PolicyLink and the Prison Policy Initiative, formerly incarcerated people are roughly ten times more likely to be homeless and twenty-seven times more likely to be unstably housed than the general public.

Unlike with housing discrimination based on race or disability, which is prohibited under federal and state laws, housing discrimination based on someone's criminal record is legal. For example, California law currently allows landlords to deny someone housing based solely on their criminal record. However, the California Department of Fair Employment and Housing (DFEH) passed regulations that prohibit landlords from using certain screening practices. Just a few examples of prohibited practices include using blanket bans that deny broad categories of people, like all people with felony convictions; considering an arrest that did not lead to a conviction; or denying housing for convictions that have been sealed or expunged. The regulations also provide guidelines to prevent discrimination, like giving a rental applicant the chance to provide evidence of rehabilitation, but landlords still have the discretion to deny someone for their record even if they provide evidence they have rehabilitated. While helpful for some, these regulations fail to meaningfully increase access to housing for too many formerly incarcerated people. People in reentry and their families require much more support.

A PROXY FOR RACIAL EXCLUSION

On November 19, 2020, the *LA Times* reported on the proliferation of Crime Free Multi-Housing Programs ("Programs") and the disparate impact of these Programs on Black and Brown renters in California. Crime Free Multi-Housing Programs emerged as a tool for landlords and property owners to maintain so-called "crime free" neighborhoods.

Under the Programs, law enforcement provides free training and resources to help property owners and managers create tools to exclude or remove people deemed a nuisance, dangerous, or threatening. Some of the tools are fairly innocuous including training on premise liability and fire safety. However, these Programs tend to center practices for screening applicants and requiring "Nuisance Eviction Provisions" and "Crime-Free Lease Addendums," which grant landlords unchecked discretion to exclude and evict people at will for any perceived nuisance or criminal activity whether on or off the premises. That's a lot of power—too much power.

The *LA Times* found that in communities across California, Black and Brown tenants were far more likely than White tenants to be excluded or evicted from housing due to these so-called "crime free" housing programs. The core reasons for the racial disparity are twofold. First, these Programs tend to be concentrated in neighborhoods where more people of color live, leading to more enforcement in those areas against the very people the provisions claim to protect. This private enforcement just adds to the momentum of gentrification and displacement. Second, the history of racist policies that drive mass incarceration and have disproportionately criminalized people of color make those same people the targets for exclusion and eviction by landlords. Policies to increase access to housing for, and prevent discrimination against, the people most impacted by mass incarceration will promote racial equity.

THE PERSONAL IS POLITICAL

The impact of a criminal record on access to stable housing is personal. My younger brother, Noah Oquenda, twenty-two, has experienced several of the systemic barriers that stem from his arrest and conviction history beginning when he was first incarcerated in a juvenile detention facility for drug possession and burglary at the age of thirteen. Since then he's run up against barriers getting a job, accessing financial aid for education, securing housing, paying off court-ordered debt, fulfilling his duties as a young father, getting public benefits support, and even getting his driver's license.

In late 2018, Noah was facing felony drug charges in Illinois. He'd already been locked up for over a month during pretrial (while his case was pending) because he could not afford bail. Even if he was released on bail, he didn't have a place to go. I flew from California to Illinois to support my brother and make a direct appeal to the judge to recommend a sentence of probation. The goal was to avoid further trauma of incarceration and allow us to apply to transfer Noah's probation to be served out in California, where he could move in with my wife and me. Noah knew having a stable place for him would help his chances of successfully completing his probation. After all, we had both seen the impact of our father's incarceration on our family, and his struggles facing the barriers of reentry.

Family support and relationships can be critical to successful reentry. A report by Human Impact Partners and the Ella Baker Center for Human Rights found that 70 percent of people released from prison believe family is what kept them out, and 82 percent of people leaving prison or jail expect to live with or get help from their families. What can get lost here, however, is that many families aren't necessarily equipped to support their loved one. It has been well documented that many people in reentry rely heavily on loved ones to navigate all the barriers of reentry, and more resources should be provided to empower families who want to support. But even someone like me who is trained in the law found it overwhelming to navigate the many complex systems of barriers my brother faced.

It only took a few months to realize that I simply could not provide the support Noah needed in his reentry and recovery, and social services support from the county probation department was lacking (to put it mildly). Noah decided he wanted a go at independence, and he made the decision to try to take on more responsibility for himself. I was worried, but I also wanted him to feel supported and empowered to do what he felt he needed.

While he had been denied a job in San Francisco because of his record, he did find work sorting plastics at Tri-Ced Community Recycling, which is one of the few employers in the area that proactively hires young people with records to help them gain work experience. He saved money and moved in with his girlfriend (now fiancee), Dache (pronounced Day-sha). It definitely helped that he wasn't required to pass a background check. He seemed to do all right for the next few months before deciding that he did need more structured support to stay on track.

That's when he was lucky enough that a bed became available in a ninety-day rehabilitation program called Second Chance—a program aimed at supporting formerly incarcerated people who struggle with addiction and need housing. Waitlists and demand for supportive housing programs typically make the enrollment process lengthy and unpredictable.

With the support of a case manager, Noah got a better paying job as a lift operator at Living Spaces in Newark, and continued saving money for a rental deposit and first month's rent on an apartment. He had no room to store his stuff at the group house, so he rented a storage unit for less than $100 per month and began gathering some furniture to prepare for his transition to permanent housing. This is exactly the kind of rehabilitative and self-reflective preparation we hope people in reentry and recovery focus on. Noah was trying to do everything right, everything expected of him.

In ninety days, Noah successfully completed the program, kept his job, maintained his sobriety, and even developed an exit plan. He was ready to test his independence again. Two weeks before Noah was to complete his program, Noah and Dache found a place they liked (and could afford) and visited to tour and to meet the property owner. Thinking it better than waiting for rejection after a background check, Noah decided to be upfront about his criminal record and his upcoming completion of the Second Chance program. To his surprise, everything seemed to go smoothly, and the property owner told them they could move in. Things just seemed to be falling into place.

The day before the move, Dache rented a car to take her

stuff to Noah's storage unit in Newark near Second Chance. On a tight budget, they decided to forgo a hotel and to stay for the night in the storage unit, which was outfitted with a bed and some furniture they'd acquired for their move. What they expected to be one night, would turn out to be three months.

That night, my brother messaged the owner to confirm the time he could come pick up the keys, and the owner replied that Noah couldn't move in the next day. My brother shared that he and Dache had already moved their stuff to a storage unit and that's where they were living because his spot in the program was being given to someone else.

"We felt confused and panicked. We didn't have a fall back plan," Noah told me. He had no written lease, and he'd not paid a deposit yet, so there was no record of the agreement. He asked the owner for the reason, and the owner replied that they needed to do some construction on the laundry room of the unit. Noah and Dache explained they wouldn't mind still moving in and could use the laundromat until the renovation was complete. The property owner expressed that she didn't think that would work. The owner told them the work would likely take a couple weeks, so they should look for another place. But it was hard enough to find that place, which checked all the boxes for what they needed. Noah and Dache needed to be close to public transit to get to work without a car. Not to mention, each rental application costs money, which they need to save to be able to afford a deposit and rent.

Feeling like they didn't have any good options, and deciding that a couple weeks wouldn't be so bad, they offered to wait if the owner would agree to let them move in when the renovation was done. The owner agreed. "It felt shady, what she [the owner] was doing, but we felt like we really didn't have a choice. There wasn't a lot of housing available that we could afford," Noah said.

At the end of those two weeks, Noah and Dache checked in again with the property owner, who said that the work hadn't been started and that Noah and Dache should find another place. When I asked Noah what it felt like, he shared, "I think the landlord just didn't want to rent to us because of my credit or my record, but she felt bad because of our situation. Honestly, I felt like she was stringing us along. I would have preferred she just told me that she didn't want us to live there—whatever the reason, whether for my record, or whatever. But the bit about the construction just didn't make any sense to us."

Setting questions of contract law or tenants' rights violations aside, even if the landlord did discriminate against Noah based on his record and recovery efforts, nothing in California law requires her to disclose that. Actually, property owners don't have to disclose any reason for their decision to deny a rental application.

Noah and Dache were left in limbo, biding their time living in the storage unit to save money on a hotel, but ultimately they became discouraged and frustrated. "We tried to make the best of it," Dache said. "We bought some additional things like a wifi hotspot, a dresser, a mini-fridge, and even a stove top. It wasn't so bad for the first week. But after a couple weeks, I began feeling like I was sitting in a metal prison cell—especially when I was there alone. I couldn't get comfortable worrying about safety and other people living in other units with no security around. We were also worried about getting caught because we didn't want to end up on the street."

After the first two weeks, it became clear that the owner was never going to let them stay, and they continued looking for other places. During the search Noah and Dache were constantly denied or deterred altogether from applying. Housing ads on Craigslist and other sources often explicitly ban anyone with a felony from applying—known in reentry advocacy as "blanket bans." As mentioned above, these are illegal in California, but they are prolific.

The California Department of Fair Employment and Housing (DFEH) is still just beginning to target illegal rental screening practices. Just this May, the DFEH took its first step in this effort when it launched a new public complaint portal aimed to combat discriminatory advertisements like blanket bans.

Seeing ads like those and getting questions from landlords about credit history and his felony conviction history, Noah often felt dejected and began accepting the idea that he was stuck and wasn't getting out. Worse, he doubted himself and questioned if he even deserved decent, stable housing.

Noah recounted, "I thought to myself, maybe it's better that we just stay in the storage unit and save money and buy a van to renovate to live in. Honestly, I just started getting used to it." And he's not alone in feeling that. There's a reason why studies estimate that between 25 and 50 percent of people who experience chronic homelessness have a criminal record. Hint: it's not because they want to survive on the street or in a car.

Like my brother, many people in reentry can feel boxed in with an array of bad options. It's not hard to understand how they can internalize the message society is sending: you don't belong and your life doesn't matter. And when you begin to believe that about yourself, it can be hard to envision your life or circumstances being different. Even when I reached out to offer Noah more help, he didn't feel comfortable accepting it.

So they stayed in the storage unit. A little over three months of searching, and in February 2020, Noah and Dache found a room for rent and a landlord who was willing to give them a fair chance. I rented a U-Haul and drove to help them move. It would seem their move came just in time because while the Covid-19 pandemic ramped up in mid-March, they learned Dache was pregnant with their son, Seidon. My nephew was born in late Fall of 2020. And over the last year, Noah has maintained his sobriety, remained stably housed, and, as of May 2021, completed his probation term.

"I did it, bro!" he messaged me the day he got off probation. "I'm in awe. I finally made it. I've dreamed about this day, to be truly free to focus on my future. My son would not be here if it wasn't for that experience or the trials we had to go through, and I wouldn't trade my family for anything."

I love my brother. He'll always be my little brother. He's stronghearted, optimistic, and resilient. He's also a survivor. He has so much to offer the world, if he is only given a fair chance. He and his family deserve more than clinging to survival; they deserve the opportunity to thrive.

No one should have to pass trials to access a basic need like housing. My brother deserves not to be judged for the worst moments of his life. My brother deserves a fair chance to live a full life. My brother deserves housing—like everyone else impacted by the criminal legal system—but not because he has served his time and paid his debt to society. He deserves housing because he is human.

A FAIR CHANCE TO ACCESS HOUSING

The laws, institutions, and attitudes that generate housing barriers and discrimination do not need to exist. We've made these laws and institutions; we can change them. And we must support formerly incarcerated people in leading the way.

Actually, formerly incarcerated people have already begun leading the way to policy solutions to eliminate housing barriers and discrimination. The first solution is funding long-term supportive housing for people who are released from prison. The second solution is passing Fair Chance Housing laws that eliminate background checks in rental housing advertising, applications, or decision making.

FULLY FUND REENTRY HOUSING AND
HOLISTIC SUPPORT SERVICES

Like many of us in California, formerly incarcerated people also face an affordable housing shortage. However, unlike many of us, formerly incarcerated people also carry the stigma of their criminal record, which leads to fewer job opportunities, lower income, and higher rates of housing discrimination. According to the Prison Policy Initiative, people released from prison face the highest risk of homelessness in the first two years of reentry. This means, the first two years of reentry are a critical period to ensure people in reentry have all the right support systems in place to help them succeed.

Unfortunately, reentry support and services, including stable housing, are extremely under-resourced. In California, when people are released from prison, they receive "gate money," which is limited to a $200 debit card. When only 15 percent of incarcerated people get picked up by family upon their release, this $200 is often all that people have to pay for a bus ticket, clothing, housing, food, and other essentials. Even though California is one of the most generous states that offer gate money, $200 is hardly enough to live on for a single day with our high cost of living.

Without new investment now, the gaps in services and

funding in the reentry system are only going to get worse. In 2011, the U.S. Supreme Court found California's prisons were so overcrowded that the conditions violated the constitutional rights of the people inside. Since that decision, California has been slowly reducing its prison population by tens of thousands. In May, Governor Newsom announced that seventy-six thousand incarcerated people, a majority of the prison population, may be eligible for an early release date. All these people and their families will need holistic support, including [access] to secure, stable housing and jobs. This means investing in our reentry infrastructure.

We have the resources to do this. The Legislative Analyst's Office (LAO), which provides expert nonpartisan fiscal and policy analysis on the budget, concluded that projected declines in prison population will lead to five prison closures and savings of $1.5 billion by 2025. The California Department of Corrections and Rehabilitation (CDCR) recently announced plans to close two prisons by July 2022, with projected savings of hundreds of millions of dollars per year.

Root and Rebound, in coalition with dozens of housing and reentry advocacy organizations, is supporting two leading reforms. The first is Senate Bill 1304 (Kamlager), which increases the gate money allowance from the 1973 amount of $200 to an amount equal to the Massachusetts Institute of Technology living wage calculator's average for one month of living across California: $2,589. This money will help people make a safer transition, meeting the essential needs they have immediately upon their release, so they don't end up on the street or back in prison or jail. While we believe more money may be required in certain parts of the state, this is a good start.

The second essential reform to building reentry infrastructure is Assembly Bill 1816 (Bryan), which reinvests savings from prison closures ($200 million over five years) into a Reentry Housing and Workforce Development Program that will be run through the California Department of Housing and Community Development. The program will include, among other things, long-term rental assistance, permanent affordable housing, and comprehensive workforce development.

For investments in reentry housing to have maximum impact, the housing and workforce development opportunities need to be open to all people in reentry. Reentry housing and support services will tend to be most critical for formerly incarcerated people without families to return to, especially during the first two years. However, even the best laid plans can fall through.

When Noah was released from jail, he had a place to live with me. Then plans changed, and when he decided he needed more support, he turned to Second Chance's rehabilitation center to help him stay on track.

Successful reentry requires people to adapt to the challenges that arise. Reentry housing and support services need to be able to meet people where they are and adapt with them. By investing in these programs, we are investing in people. Anytime we invest in people, we make it more likely they invest in themselves to grow and succeed. In that world, we are all better off.

CHALLENGE THE STIGMA AND
ELIMINATE DISCRIMINATION IN HOUSING

Nevertheless, investing in reentry housing and support services is not enough on its own. As Noah's experience shows, even when he successfully completed his ninety-day rehabilitation program, he wasn't given a fair chance to show he can be a good tenant because of the stigma associated with his record and recovery. He was pre-judged as undeserving of housing because of his past, rather than being seen for who he was in the present—let alone being seen as the young man he was working so hard to become.

So what does it mean to give someone a "fair chance" to access housing? According to Just Cities, one of our partner advocacy organizations who led the effort to pass local fair chance housing laws in Berkeley and Oakland, "Fair Chance Housing legislation removes structural barriers to housing and enables landlords to consider the merits of individual housing applications—providing people with a fair chance."

To put it differently, giving a fair chance means recognizing that each of our identities cannot be reduced down to the worst thing we've ever done. We all deserve to be treated with dignity and respect, which means the chance to have access to the same resources and opportunities to thrive.

While a growing number of jurisdictions across the country have passed Fair Chance Housing laws, they can differ in important ways. However, best practices in any Fair Chance Housing legislation will prohibit housing providers from screening the criminal history of rental applicants in advertisements or during the application, selection, or eviction processes. And for the limited offenses which some fair chance housing laws permit landlords to still screen for, those landlords are required to disclose the background check information and all reasons for denying a rental application when considering criminal history information.

A fair chance housing law that includes these components is the best path forward to eliminating stigma and discrimination against people with criminal records. It is also the best path for promoting transparency and accountability. For someone like my brother, the security of a fair chance housing

law would mean less concern about discriminatory advertisements targeting him for his record, no more boxes to check on
the application about his felony record, and increased certainty
about being assessed on his merits as a good tenant.

CONCLUSION

At their core, policies to invest in reentry support services and
to create fair chance access to housing in California would advance racial equity, family unity, and public safety.

By passing a statewide Fair Chance Housing Act in California, we would eliminate so-called "crime-free" housing laws
and programs across the state—reversing the trend of increasing segregation, displacement, and racial exclusion. By increasing reentry support services and fair chance housing access, we
would provide formerly incarcerated people and their families
access to safe, stable, affordable housing they need to reclaim
their lives and re-integrate in the community. Finally, by providing access to stable housing and strengthening family support systems, we would reduce the likelihood that people in
reentry will recidivate or return to prison, while increasing the
likelihood that they will invest in themselves, their families,
and their communities—our communities.

D.C. Residents Are Voting from Prison This Week*

Kira Lerner

2022

Earlier this month, about ten men detained in the Young Men Emerging unit in the Washington, D.C., jail sat around a TV to watch the Democratic candidates for mayor debate issues including affordable housing and gun violence. "It was on a communal TV, and it was loud," said Gregory Barnhart, twenty-five, who is incarcerated in the unit. Barnhart said the men were split in their support for the two Black men challenging current Mayor Muriel Bowser, but all agreed that it was time for a fresh face in the mayor's office. "Everybody who was there was super interested."

For Kortez Trasvant, who is twenty-four and has been detained in the jail since August, it was the first political debate he'd ever watched. Barnhart, who has been in the jail for more

* Kira Lerner, "D.C. Residents Are Voting from Prison this Week," *Bolts*, June 20, 2022.

than three years, said he also watched a presidential debate in 2020. Trasvant, Barnhart, and the other men in their unit were particularly interested in the mayoral debate because all of them can vote, even though they are serving time for felonies.

In July 2020, the District became the third place in the nation to grant the right to vote to people who are incarcerated. Just Maine, Vermont, and the District allow anyone to vote while in prison for a felony.

Neither Trasvant nor Barnhart had ever been registered to vote before their time in the District jail, but both say they now understand the importance of having their voices heard. "People who are incarcerated, we make up a big part of the population and a lot of people who have a lot of strong views [about things] that are happening in our society are incarcerated," Trasvant said. "So if we want to change what's going on and change the narrative, it's important for us to take the initiative to vote."

The Tuesday primary is just the second election in which incarcerated people in D.C. can cast ballots. It is the first in which the D.C. Board of Elections is legally obligated to provide every D.C. resident in the custody of the D.C. Department of Corrections (DOC) and the Federal Bureau of Prisons (BOP) a voter registration application and educational information about their right to vote. Anyone who has registered to vote will receive an absentee ballot.

In November 2020, out of about 4,000 incarcerated D.C. residents, only 562 registered to vote and 264 of them cast ballots. But voting advocates in the District and at the Board of Elections say they're hopeful that number will increase this year. Currently, 650 incarcerated D.C. residents are registered to vote, 355 of them in BOP custody and 295 in DOC custody, according to the Board of Elections.

"There's just a simplicity here," said D.C. Council member

Charles Allen, who was an early supporter of the Restore the Vote Amendment Act of 2020 and who chairs the council's Committee on the Judiciary and Public Safety. "You're not going to lose your right to vote. You may have made a really bad decision, and you may have created harm, and so you're going to lose your freedom, you're going to be incarcerated, but you haven't lost that right to vote."

Still, the District's fragmented correctional bureaucracy is a challenge. As of May, 1,390 D.C. residents are held in the D.C. jail, under DOC custody, and 2,615 are in federal prisons all over the country. The voter registration rate is higher among people detained in the jail, where outreach has been more frequent and consistent.

Trasvant and Barnhart explained in a joint Zoom interview that they're confident that all the detainees in the D.C. jail know they're eligible to vote. The hallways are lined with posters informing them of their eligibility and the Board of Elections has worked with jail staff, giving them pamphlets and information and registration applications to hand out in the jail.

Jail staff has also been trained on how to help people register to vote, something they've been doing for a long time given that people serving time for misdemeanors have always been eligible, said Nick Jacobs, a public information officer with the Board of Elections. But informing D.C.'s federal prisoners, who serve their time in roughly one hundred different federal prisons outside the District because D.C. has no federal prison of its own, has proven to be more difficult.

Federal detainees from the District are often housed far from home and the District has to rely on the staff at each facility to help get the word out to D.C. residents about their eligibility. "We're talking about the entire federal prison system," Jacobs said.

To reach everyone, the Board of Elections was allocated a larger budget this year, which allowed it to hire two staff members dedicated to the effort. One of the new hires, Scott Sussman, joined in February from the Bureau of Prisons, where he worked for twenty-six years. It was important to bring on someone who knows the agency and the best way to work with it, Jacobs said.

According to Sussman, the Board of Elections has mailed BOP facilities registration applications, ballot instructions, and postage paid envelopes and has asked staff at each facility to distribute them to those who are eligible. "There were some packages that got returned as undeliverable, and we had to send them to a different address, but nobody outright said they wouldn't do this for us," he said.

The Board of Elections has also worked with the federal prisons agency to post voter registration applications electronically on an internal prison messaging system to all incarcerated people from the District. "They allow us to post material specifically targeted to D.C. residents," Sussman said. "We also supplied them with an electronic version, a PDF, of the voter registration form and some helpful hints on how to fill out that registration form, which they can print and send back."

The Board of Elections is also trying to work with BOP staff members who help with new prison admissions and orientation, as well as staff members who assist people preparing for release, so everyone is informed of their right to vote. Sussman said that he feels confident the Board of Elections has been able to make contact with every D.C. resident in federal prison custody, whether it's through electronic or physical mail.

But "part of the challenge," Jacobs said, is that prison officials often transfer D.C. residents from one prison to another, and it's hard to track where people may be at any given point.

When a D.C. resident is moved, the burden is on them to update their voter registration so they can receive a ballot at their new prison address, as the BOP does not share transfer information with the Board of Elections to update the rolls.

It's also difficult to know who in BOP custody is a D.C. resident because BOP "is unable to provide a comprehensive list due to privacy laws," Sussman said. "However, they have provided us the number of D.C. residents that are out there. We just have to depend on their staff to distribute material to them." Despite some hurdles, Sussman said he believes that "the Bureau of Prisons is going to great lengths to help us, within their rules and regulations."

In addition to outreach by the D.C. government, the Restore the Vote Coalition—which formed to push toward voting rights restoration in D.C.—has pivoted to voter outreach since the effort succeeded in 2020. The non-profit organizations involved in the coalition, including the Washington Lawyers' Committee for Civil Rights and Urban Affairs and the D.C. chapter of the League of Women Voters, have also helped to distribute voter guides and registration forms.

Allen said he's proud that restoration of voting rights in D.C. passed the council unanimously and was never controversial. "There weren't any games being played," he said. "Everyone just realized it was the right thing to do."

A few other states have also tried in recent years to restore voting rights to people in prison, but the efforts have all failed. A legislative attempt in Oregon stalled earlier this year despite strong support among Democratic lawmakers. And legislation was proposed in Illinois but hasn't made it out of a House committee. Similar unsuccessful bills have also been introduced in Hawaii, Massachusetts, and Virginia. In some cities, including Houston, Los Angeles, and Chicago, people detained in jail for misdemeanors can vote at a polling place inside the jail, but Texas, California, and Illinois all prohibit people convicted of felonies from casting ballots while incarcerated.

Across the country, roughly 5.2 million people were disenfranchised as of 2020 because of a felony conviction, according to the Sentencing Project. The population shut out from elections is disproportionately Black, with one in sixteen Black adults disenfranchised nationally. Rights restoration laws vary from state to state, with twenty states allowing people to vote as soon as they leave prison and sixteen others requiring people to complete periods of probation to get their rights back. In eleven states, certain people with felony convictions lose their right to vote for life.

Despite being incarcerated and not knowing when they will be released, Trasvant and Barnhart both said being able to vote makes them feel more connected to their D.C. community. They said they see no reason why other states shouldn't follow the District's lead.

"I feel like it's something everybody should do across the whole United States because it's imperative that our voices get heard too," Trasvant said. "It should spread across the nation because over two million people are incarcerated at the moment and those are a lot of voices that need to be heard," Barnhart added. "I do believe that Washington, D.C., taking the initiative with Vermont and Maine to allow those incarcerated to vote, they're taking a big step to lay the groundwork for the rest of the nation to follow."

The Time I Was Called for Jury Duty . . . and What Happened Next*

James M. Binnall

2023

In May 1999, at age twenty-three, I made the decision to drive after drinking. That night, I caused a car accident that claimed the life of my best friend, the passenger in my vehicle. For that tragic decision, I spent over four years in a maximum-security prison in Pennsylvania. In October 2001, I took my Law School Admissions Test (LSAT) from my prison cell and subsequently applied to a number of law schools while still incarcerated. Though I was accepted to several, only Thomas Jefferson School of Law would allow me to begin my legal studies while an active parolee. I enrolled in January 2005, six months after my release from state prison.

I finished my law degree and parole in May 2007. In the fall of that year, I began an LL.M. at the Georgetown University

---

* James M. Binnall, "The Time I Was Called for Jury Duty . . . and What Happened Next," 2023.

Law Center. In May 2008, LL.M. in hand, I returned to California to take the bar exam and to finish the moral character determination process to prove that I was fit to become a member
of the State Bar of California. For me, someone with a felony
criminal history who had spent time in prison, the process was
a lengthy one. In November 2008, I was informed that I passed
both the bar exam and the moral character determination. I
was sworn in as an attorney and a member of the State Bar of
California in December 2008.

Immediately after my swearing in, I began to practice law.
Initially, I was a contract attorney for several criminal defense
lawyers in San Diego. As part of that work, I regularly assisted
on criminal trials in both state and federal court. Sitting "second chair" meant that I interacted with clients, opposing counsel, and often judges. All seemingly accepted me as just another
attorney. I rarely disclosed my criminal past, and for those who
knew my history, it was ostensibly a nonissue. Only the quality
of my work was scrutinized. To a point, I felt as though I had
transcended my past.

A year after becoming a member of the State Bar of California, I was summoned to jury service for the first time. Though
the summons meant a day of boredom spent waiting at the
courthouse, I was eager to serve. Finally, I was just "any other
citizen," called to perform my civic duty as a juror. I thought,
as a person with a felony criminal history who is also a practicing attorney, my experiences are diverse and important . . .
assuredly my insights would enrich any deliberation?

When I arrived at the courthouse on my day of service, I
passed through security using the entrance designated "attorneys only," feeling a strange sense of pride and privilege. Soon
after this, courthouse personnel ushered a group of about a
hundred prospective jurors into the juror lounge. Once inside,

a courtroom official charged with overseeing jury selection gave a five-minute speech expressing thanks on behalf of the State of California and San Diego County, all the while emphasizing the importance of our service. He then started a video, narrated by actor Rob Lowe (this is Southern California, mind you), exalting the jury as one of the fundamental pillars of democracy and, again, thanking us for our service.

When the movie ended, we were instructed to complete a juror affidavit questionnaire. On that questionnaire was an inquiry regarding criminal convictions. Question five read: "I have been convicted of a felony or malfeasance in office and my civil rights have not been restored." I checked the box, answering in the affirmative. Moments after turning in this questionnaire, the same man who moments before had thanked us for answering our summons, instructed us to stand and proceed to the back of the jury lounge if we had answered "yes" to question five. I stood, mortified that my criminal record was now on display for all to see. I made my way to the rear of the jury lounge, where court personnel informed me that I was ineligible for jury service because of my prior felony conviction. They called it a "permanent excuse" and assured me that I would never be summoned again.

I protested mildly, explaining that I was an attorney—had used the special attorneys-only entrance—and was looking forward to serving. I explained that it seemed illogical that I was permitted to represent clients in the very courthouse from which I was now being expelled. How could I be "fit" to counsel those facing years in prison or death, but "unfit" to adjudicate even a minor civil matter? Not persuaded by my argument, the clerk told me that I should "write my congressperson" if I was unhappy about California's juror eligibility requirements. I was shocked and disheartened. I had not considered that even as a member of the bar I would still be unable to serve as a juror because of my criminal past. At this time, 2009, California was a permanent exclusion jurisdiction, barring all Californians with a felony criminal history from serving as a juror for life in either criminal or civil matters. Notably, my situation at the time—a barred attorney being banished from jury service for life—was not an uncommon paradox. Twenty-five states and the federal government permit those with a felony conviction to practice law, but banish from jury service for life those same individuals.

In response to my degrading experience with felon-juror exclusion, I chose not to write my congressperson. Instead, I spent the next ten years researching the statutory exclusion of citizens with a felony conviction from jury service. The goal of that endeavor was to both call attention to felon-juror exclusion and to build a body of empirical research on the topic. In particular, I sought to interrogate two questions. First, does research support the justifications for excluding those with felony conviction histories from jury service? And second, what are the consequences of excluding millions of Americans from the jury process—a crucial democratic institution?

What I found was that data strongly suggest that the professed purposes for felon-juror exclusion lack empirical support. Moreover, the consequences of such exclusions may be significant, robbing our legal system of jurors that can improve the adjudicative process while negatively impacting the reentry process for those attempting to rebuild their lives after a felony criminal conviction. In this way, from a utilitarian perspective, evidence clearly suggests that felon-juror exclusion makes little sense, as the costs associated with exclusion certainly exceed the benefits of eliminating the negligible threat those with a felony criminal history assumedly pose to the jury. Normatively, felon-juror exclusion is also inappropriate and undesirable. The practice discounts rehabilitation and redemption in favor of perpetual ostracism, cutting against principles of participatory democracy and shared sovereignty.

WORKING TO CHANGE THINGS . . . TEN YEARS LATER

In June 2019, the Judiciary Committee of the California State Assembly invited me to testify as an expert consultant on Senate Bill 310. Introduced by State Senator Nancy Skinner, Senate Bill 310 would restore juror eligibility to those with prior felony convictions in California. In anticipation of my testimony, I reviewed my research and prepared a statement. In that statement, I briefly recounted my own banishment from jury service, before methodically drawing on empirical evidence disproving, or at least calling into question, the professed rationales for the permanent disqualification then at work in the state. When called, I approached my seat, cleared my throat, and began to read my organized remarks. Three minutes later, I was told my time had expired. In those three minutes, I attempted to brings facts and science to the issue at bar. Though brief, my statement felt comprehensive. It clarified the highpoints of ten years of research and shed light on why felon-juror exclusion is an outdated, discriminatory policy that has no place in a progressive jurisdiction that prides itself on leading the nation on a host of social policies. I felt I had done my job as an objective researcher and the leading expert on the topic.

Much to my dismay, the hearing did not continue as I had hoped. Instead, what followed was testimony eerily reminiscent of tough-on-crime arguments that found fame in the 1980s, when the Central Park Five and Willie Horton dominated the news cycle. That testimony ignored facts, focusing instead on illogical arguments and fearmongering. First to testify was a representative from the California District Attorneys Association. He noted his organization's opposition to active state parolees or probationers being allowed to serve as jurors. At the heart of his argument was a familiar refrain, intimating that those with felony criminal histories pose a danger to their fellow jurors.

This notion is simply nonsensical. Like it or not, individuals with felony criminal convictions in their past exist—we eat at restaurants, go to the movies, attend community meetings, join bowling leagues, and sometimes, become lawyers that must interact with non-felon clients. Such an assertion calls to mind images of Hester Prynne, implying that those with a felony criminal record ought to be readily identified and approved as "safe" by their fellow jurors before we reinstate their right to serve. But his was not the most outlandish claim made in opposition to SB 310.

Second to testify against SB 310 was a representative of the Riverside Sheriffs' Association. In sum, he stated:

> I'd like to concur with the comments made by my colleague from the District Attorneys Association and also note that proper court security requires constant monitoring of the accused, the witnesses, the employees, and all visitors. Members of the Riverside Sheriffs' Association have sworn to protect and serve all who come to court. SB 310 will make our members' job much more difficult by mixing violent felons on parole with dutiful citizens who have willingly chosen to participate in our judicial system—who recognize that our civil and criminal justice systems are not perfect—but having convicted felons and parolees serve as jurors will further un-

dermine the public's safety and trust in our courts, and we respectfully urge a no vote.

At the time he made the above statement, there were no fewer than twenty-five individuals with a felony criminal history in the room, and security that day at the capital was business as usual. To suggest that allowing us to serve would necessitate more manpower and surveillance is both insulting and wildly illogical. Again, we exist and we live among those who have never been arrested. Moreover, nobody is a "convicted felon" until their first felony offense. Surely we cannot guarantee that a non-felon juror will not commit an offense that puts others in the court in danger? His statement is rife with stereotype and scare tactics, it employs the "criminology of the other," and it does so as a tool with which to banish those with a felony criminal history from a fundamental democratic process. The opposition's arguments against SB 310 were appalling and were anything but evidence-based.

Ultimately, SB 310 passed, though the current form of SB 310 is different than it was originally. A few months after my testimony, SB 310 was amended. Those amendments now limit the scope of SB 310 by preserving felon-juror exclusion (1) for those with prior felony convictions who are currently on some form of community supervision and (2) permanently for those convicted of a felony criminal offense of a sexual nature. Notably, the California District Attorneys Association did not oppose SB 310 in its current form.

Surely a step forward, SB 310 moved California into a more inclusive era of juror eligibility. Though by amending the legislation to include carve-outs, lawmakers have unfortunately lent credibility to the flawed, prejudicial arguments made by

opponents of SB 310 that day at the capital. A robust debate on
SB 310, one that draws on facts and science, was the goal of my
testimony. And while we fell short of that debate that day in
Sacramento, data and science eventually won out, prompting
a legislative change nearly a decade in the making and the first
in the nation to make juries more inclusive for those with a
felony criminal history in nearly twenty years.

Given the paucity of research on felon-juror exclusion, the
arguments put forth in opposition to SB 310 are, to a point, not
surprising. Felon-juror exclusion likely conjures up appeals to
emotion, in part because the topic has largely escaped critical
empirical evaluation. Still, existing research makes clear that
the threat posed to the jury by potential felon-jurors is nonexistent and as such, does not warrant record-based juror eligibility restriction in any form. Accordingly, for opponents of SB
310 and other measures that would restore juror eligibility to
those with felony criminal convictions in additional jurisdictions, bad facts easily give way to speculation and hyperbole.

In recent years, criminal justice reform efforts have finally
prioritized the voices of those of us who have direct lived experience with the criminal legal system. We are increasingly
being invited to "sit at the table." I am proud to say—as one
with experiential carceral knowledge—that my research played
even a small role in fostering California's more inclusive juror
eligibility criteria. But I was certainly not alone. Many of my
formerly incarcerated and system-involved brothers and sis-
ters publicized the issue and were in Sacramento that day. They
spoke about the need for juries that represent the communities from which they are drawn. They also spoke about feeling
outcast and living in a jurisdiction that simultaneously championed progressive reform while observing and implementing regressive policies. From an advocacy position, we struck

the perfect balance, coupling rigorous empirical research with compelling narratives. Along with Senator Skinner and other allies, like Brendon Woods (Alameda County Public Defender), formerly convicted and incarcerated men and women did this and we are doing it in other jurisdictions.

In 2020, roughly six months after the implementation of SB 310 in California, the District of Columbia reduced the required juror eligibility waiting period for those with prior felony convictions from ten years to one. In 2021, thanks in large part to the work of Will Snowden and the Jury Project, Louisiana reformed their juror eligibility statute to permit those with prior felony criminal record to serve five years after they have completed their sentence. Louisiana was previously a lifetime exclusion jurisdiction. Similarly, in Connecticut, those with a history of a felony conviction can now serve on a jury three years after the completion of their sentence, reducing this waiting period from the prior seven years. In these instances, changes have been the product of dedicated activists and legislators that recognize the value of diverse perspectives and seek to make our jury system more inclusive. But our work continues in earnest.

My own research now focuses on post-reform implementation strategies in California and beyond. Notifying prospective jurors with a prior felony conviction of their eligibility for jury service has proven troubling in California, as counties have been slow to publicize the legislative change. As of August 16, 2020, a survey of county websites—the most accessible and likely source of information for prospective jurors—revealed that only twenty-two of California's fifty-eight counties had provided its citizenry accurate information on the juror eligibility changes. Conversely, twenty-two counties published misleading information on SB 310 (many incorrectly suggesting that a restoration of civil rights is required to serve—it is not) and fourteen have made no mention of the legislation or falsely reported its effect. Thus, almost seven full months after SB 310's effective date, information about legislative changes in felon-juror exclusion policies was almost certainly not reaching those most impacted in California, who are notably disproportionately Black and Latino.

For those jurisdictions considering legislation eliminating or altering felon-juror exclusion provisions, California should serve as both an inspiration and a cautionary tale. SB 310 did not require mandatory notification at the county level (those charged with administering the jury system). As a result, a crazy quilt of approaches regarding notification and implementation has taken hold. Along this line, jurisdictions weighing reform in this context may do well to consider research on notification provisions, utilizing such provisions and crafting them in empirically informed ways using simple, prominent language that not only informs, but also encourages citizens with a felony conviction to serve when called. In California, and elsewhere, such notifications will help to ensure the efficacy of legislative reform hard won.

We must also be vigilant court watchers. On the ground, SB 310 has the potential to radically alter California's juries in fundamental, progressive ways, moving toward the inclusive vision of the jury the Framers contemplated. But that change requires that we show up and that we hold the State accountable. Continuing to use a prior conviction as the sole barometer of a juror's fitness—either for cause or peremptorily—negates the impact of SB 310 and perpetuates the notion that those who have had contact with the criminal legal system possess irredeemable flaws that somehow undermine their ability to contribute as full members of our democracy.

Going forward, felon-juror exclusion is an issue that can no longer be ignored. Today, twenty million Americans bear the mark of a felony conviction, and in certain communities, they comprise a critical mass of citizens that ought to be eligible for jury service. Surely, if California's recent experience with SB 310 is any indication, reforming felon-juror exclusion laws will draw fierce opposition and demands for exceptions and carve-outs. I argue that on this policy, we ought not waver. To do so will only embolden critics, who argue against felon-juror inclusion using time-tested tactics, ignoring science and embracing fear. Though legislative compromise is often appropriate, I would argue that it has no use when evidence so clearly supports one policy position over the alternative.

Rights Restoration Success Stories*

Ben Fleury-Steiner
2023

On a steamy August day in 2013, Kendra, a petite African American woman in her thirties with multiple felony arrests and misdemeanor convictions from nearly a decade ago, begins the process of restoring her civil rights. She seeks a pardon—an official statement of forgiveness issued by the Delaware governor. Her pardon will neither seal nor expunge her criminal record. But it will restore her right to vote, serve on a jury, and hold public office. It will also make it easier for Kendra to find a job, which is her most pressing concern. When the volunteer helping her file her petition asked why she wants a pardon, Kendra explains as follows:

> I am completing a degree in the human services field and know that there will be background checks when it comes to internships. I believe getting these charges pardoned will

---

* Ben Fleury-Steiner, "Rights Restoration Success Stories," 2023.

allow me to get my record sealed and move on with my life and achieve my employment goals. This will also enable me to become financially stable and raise my son properly under the right conditions. I made some mistakes growing up being a little disobedient and rebellious, but life has helped me to realize that that is not how I want to be and that those behaviors are not going to get me anywhere in life, but in jail. I want the opportunity to give back to my community and show them that you can change and do what is right for you and your family without letting prior convictions or charges hold you down.

Along with a petition explaining why she deserves a pardon, Kendra must submit extensive court records and her official criminal history. The criminal history must be no older than three months. Because it costs $52.50 to obtain an official criminal history, Kendra must submit her pardon application quickly or face a potentially costly ordeal (with each additional three months it takes to complete their applications, the individual must spend another $52.50). But Kendra is determined and swift; within six weeks her application is ready to go to the Delaware Board of Pardons. Approximately eight months later, she appears before the state pardon board. Her hearing lasts approximately ten minutes. The representative from the attorney general's office does not object to her request, and the board quickly rules in her favor. The board's recommendation eventually goes to the governor, and after several months of waiting, Kendra learns that the governor has decided in her favor. Her record of two misdemeanor convictions is now updated with the language "pardoned by the governor."

According to the Delaware Board of Pardons, 3,770 people have been pardoned since 2009. All were crime free for many years. Indeed, on average, successful rights restoration required eleven years without any subsequent criminal justice contact. The most common offenses pardoned are shoplifting and disorderly conduct. Only fifty-seven people with violent felony convictions have had their rights restored—an unfortunately low number that reflects our society's reluctance to offer second chances to those convicted of violent crimes.

One of the biggest challenges to rights restoration is the labyrinthine application process. In addition to presenting a convincing case for pardon, all applicants must both explain every offense on their criminal histories and provide court transcripts. Affidavits must be sent to numerous legal and law enforcement agencies involved. It is easy to make a mistake. For example, applicants cannot challenge their guilt; unless charges were dropped or wrongful conviction occurred, they must take responsibility for their criminal histories. To its credit, in 2012 Delaware responded to these challenges by creating the nation's first publicly funded program to assist people with restoring their rights. Called Advancement through Pardons and Expungement (APEX), the program is open to anybody who has gone at least three years without any criminal justice contacts, finished all their terms of probation, and paid any outstanding fines or court costs. In the past decade, a remarkable 70.4 percent of APEX clients have had their rights restored.

Though APEX is powerful, the program faces resource constraints—in particular, the program lacks sufficient staff to quickly assist everyone seeking to restore their rights. When I learned that APEX could use help, I started an experiential class at the University of Delaware and began supervising undergraduate volunteers. My students assisted the program director's weekly client orientation sessions, prepared applications, and attended numerous pardon board hearings. The experience was profound for my students; Yarissa, a graduating senior, wrote the following on her year-end course evaluation: "Interaction with APEX clients offered insight that I could not have gained in a classroom. Experiencing the process firsthand has broadened my understanding of ex-offenders as resilient and deserving citizens." APEX's remarkable work also sparked my own research interests in the role of rights restoration in the reentry process. Between 2013–2016, I conducted numerous interviews with successful APEX clients like Kendra.

According to the Restoration of Rights Project, there are sixteen states with governors who regularly use their pardon power to restore civil rights: Alabama, Arkansas, Connecticut, Delaware, Georgia, Idaho, Illinois, Louisiana, Missouri, Nebraska, Nevada, Oklahoma, Pennsylvania, South Carolina, South Dakota, and Utah. All of these states provide some form of pardon seeker assistance. In addition, California's Records Clearance Project (RCP) provides peer-to-peer mentoring and assistance to currently incarcerated people with the explicit goal of rights restoration. Started in 1994 by San Jose State University Justice Studies professor, Margaret Stevenson, the RCP employs undergraduate students and formerly incarcerated clients who serve as mentors to people in or recently released from prison. Mentors connect RCP clients with transportation, access to drug or alcohol recovery programs, and legal services to expunge their records. Clearly, rights restoration programs like APEX and RCP serve as model programs to be emulated by other states.

Rights restoration programs like APEX are allied with the national clean slate law movement, whose goal is to make record clearing automatic. As the Restoration of Rights Project explains, the ultimate goal of clean slate reforms "is to extend record clearing to all eligible individuals without requiring them to file a petition and go to court." As of this writing, five U.S. states automatically restore rights for misdemeanor convictions (Oklahoma, Pennsylvania, Utah, South Dakota, and Virginia) and five others (California, Connecticut, Delaware, Michigan, and New Jersey) have recently passed clean slate laws that extend to felony convictions. Both rights restoration service programs and the clean slate movement are some of the most promising developments in a generation. They represent a sea change from the past four decades of punitive excess.

If you doubt for a moment the urgency of this work, consider what Kendra told me years after her rights were restored. She has finished college, works fulltime at an organization focused on youth mental health, and is working on a master's degree. I ask her how she feels about having the "slate wiped clean":

> It's not necessarily wiping the slate clean [laughs], because those blemishes are a part of what makes you. Getting the pardon makes you feel stronger about your character but also a sense of forgiveness. I appreciate my strengths and limitations, and I'm okay with that. I mean there are already enough challenges, and this is just one less thing I feel like I must worry about, and I can just put my energy and my focus into things that are going to keep me moving forward towards my goals. There's a lot of stuff to worry about, you know? This is one less thing that I can say, "You know what? I can remove that from my plate."

The APEX success story in Delaware is an invitation to dream bigger. What if people came together to organize a second Freedom Summer with civil rights restoration as the objective? Imagine it: a mass mobilization of college and law students volunteering to support the many Kendras across the United States. This vision is, in many ways, far less daunting than what students faced in the summer of 1964. Today, students would not be bussed into the hostile and, indeed, deadly, environment of Jim Crow Mississippi. Indeed, several southern states today have governors who are willing to extend civil rights to citizens with criminal histories. But these states lack the infrastructure to assist people in preparing their applications. And most people are unable to complete the daunting process on their own. This is where student volunteers—in partnerships with universities, legal aid organizations, and law firms—could step in. If we are willing to dream—and act on these dreams—nationwide civil rights restoration is within our grasp.

Conclusion

More than fifty years ago, the United States began to expand the criminal system in a way that was so wide-ranging it enveloped whole communities. This expansion punished an ever-increasing number of behaviors for ever-longer periods of time. And it did so while criminalizing particular communities across the country—namely, Black, brown, and poor communities. It normalized constant surveillance of people while they drive to work, bird-watch in the park, or sleep in their homes. In doing so, it created a system in which, in the words of former federal prosecutor and current Supreme Court Justice Sonia Sotomayor, "you are not a citizen of a democracy but the subject of a carceral state, just waiting to be cataloged."[1]

Over the years, this burgeoning system has even received its own identity. In 2000, David Garland referred to it as "mass imprisonment," and the term "mass incarceration" became ubiquitous shortly after.[2] Michelle Alexander dubbed it the "New Jim Crow," and Ta-Nehisi Coates called it the "gray wastes," describing "our carceral state, a sprawling network of prisons and jails."[3]

When we were public defenders, the criminal system grew to include two million people in jails and prisons at any given moment. Millions more have been excluded from participating in public life and community. As lawyers, we have represented clients as they faced decades or even life in prison. We can each too easily recall stories of clients facing mandatory sentences or locked in jail while they lost their children or their partners or their jobs. We remember countless clients whose probation terms resulted in jail time because they failed random drug tests or didn't show up to meet their probation officer. We each have stories of driving our clients all over town in search of that elusive mental health or drug treatment program that accepted poor people.

However, in the three decades since we entered our first courtrooms, we have also witnessed some real changes in the criminal system. We set out in this book to capture some of that change. We looked for hope amidst all the punishment. And we found it.

We found it in people like Lori Pompa, a professor whose experiment bringing college students inside prison to learn alongside incarcerated students has grown from one classroom to a global project. And Reginald Dwayne Betts, a poet and lawyer, who is building libraries inside prison cells and bringing writers behind prison walls because, as he says, "It's something about presence that signals love." And companies like Dave's Killer Bread, who are showing what it means to be a welcoming employer to people returning from prison.

We also found it in people working within the system who are making efforts at change—people like North Dakota prison official Leann Bertsch, who visited a Norwegian prison and brought back a host of ideas to make her state's prisons more humane. And federal judge Frederic Block, who took the unusual step of cataloging the hidden ways the law punishes people with criminal convictions—and decided to spare a defendant the additional punishment of a prison sentence. We found inspiration in the Five Boro Defenders' Voter Guide, showcasing how public defenders can put their deep understanding of the system toward building community education and power.

And we found hope in people like Angela Y. Davis, Ruth Wilson Gilmore, and Derecka Purnell, leading an ongoing national conversation about a world without police and prisons. "Abolition, I learned, was a bigger idea than firing cops and closing prisons; it included eliminating the reasons people think they need cops and prisons in the first place," writes Purnell. She urges us to consider single steps on a "broad stairway," such as cities reducing the size and scope of these institutions, and communities demanding a say in budget decisions.

The contributors to this book recognize that dismantling mass incarceration will take both short-term strategies and long-term vision. It will take the expertise and insights of people from a variety of backgrounds. It will take experimentation. We need legislators passing new laws; lawyers fighting for people within and outside of the system; experts sharing their knowledge; organizers connecting with people in small towns and big cities; teachers and employers and librarians acting creatively and boldly in their fields. There is a role for each of these changemakers. And we hope that in a book that includes a wide range of responses to mass incarceration, you have found something to inspire you.[4]

Though we are hopeful, we aren't naïve. Changing a system as entrenched as this one is hard. Creating durable change is harder still. Here are a few of the challenges presented in this book's pages—many of which we have confronted in our own advocacy.

The first challenge is that people who are comfortable with, or benefit from, the current system aren't going to depart quietly. Their resistance might take a public form, as when New Jersey's bail bond industry fought bail reform in that state, or when a Republican billionaire joined forces with San Francisco's police union to finance the recall campaign of reform-minded district attorney Chesa Boudin. Indeed, as we write these words, backlash is growing across the country— including, in some cities and states, the passage of new laws criminalizing mere protest.[5]

Resistance can also take a quieter form, as when New York judges thwarted bail reform by continuing to set bail amounts that poor people couldn't pay. This type of resistance can be especially threatening because it is barely visible—and therefore hard to combat. Our criminal system is rife with discretion— every day, every actor in the system makes choices that few of us learn about. This discretion presents an opportunity for reform when those actors choose redemption and liberty. But it also presents a threat if they choose harshness and incarceration.

The second challenge presented in these pages is that change almost always requires compromise. But how do you know if you've compromised too much? When does compromise morph into co-optation? These questions arise whether your long-term goals point toward abolition or not. As you try to decide whether a given reform is worth supporting, one yardstick may be how much change it will accomplish in the short term. Another may be whether a given reform is "reformist" or "non-reformist"—whether it strengthens the underlying system or prepares the way for more dramatic transformation in the future. Developed by abolitionist organizers, this framework has been adopted by many as a way to assess and support incremental reforms in the short term while working toward the long-term goal of closing prisons and radically reimagining accountability.[6]

On any path to change, we believe, incremental steps are necessary. For example, contributors to this volume describe efforts to reduce the police footprint in traffic stops, create alternate first responders for mental health calls, change sentencing practices to shrink the number of people entering prison, and pass second-look sentencing laws that allow judges to release people who have spent many years behind bars. To some, these changes may seem inadequate. But as Angela J. Davis argues, if we are about all or nothing, we'll get nothing. Reforms that enable more people to live their lives free of state control are worth pursuing, and they advance the long-term work of dismantling the system itself.

The last challenge we want to highlight here is the difficulty of balancing urgency and patience. On the one hand, mass incarceration is a devastating system that requires passion and resolve to fight. On the other hand, because our current system was built over hundreds of years, it won't be dismantled swiftly. Many take the carceral system for granted, and it can be hard for any of us to see that it isn't inevitable.

Moreover, it will take time to develop and perfect the new approaches that we hope will replace the status quo. This is why Patrick Sharkey argues that his proposed massive demonstration project of community antiviolence programs must be funded for many years, up front. "I'm calling for a ten-year commitment," he says. "Give it a chance to fail. Give it a chance to go through scandals and mishaps and bumps along the way, and know that it's still going to be there in ten years."

We agree. Consider how long the old systems had to entrench themselves. America experimented with slavery for 250 years, Jim Crow for 50, and the war on drugs for another 50.

When opponents of mass incarceration try to undo some of that damage, no one has the right to say that *their* experiment gets two years to prove its impact before it's declared a failure.

Having described these challenges, we should make clear why we remain hopeful. Our optimism is rooted in this volume's countless examples of people in towns and cities across the country overcoming the challenges we've described. Consider Raj Jayadev and the growing participatory defense movement that is changing public defense—person by person, community by community. In the process, these defense hubs are building power and connection with one another.

We are also hopeful because people talk about these issues more than they did ten years ago, or even five years ago. They do so because of the protests, community organizing, and solidarity work that have flourished in recent years.[7] Books about abolition are on bestseller lists, and progressive candidates are running to replace not just prosecutors but also judges and sheriffs around the country.

Finally, we are hopeful because even the backlash is a testament to the movement's strength. It is evidence that the ground is shifting. Those who resist the rising demand for change fear its efficacy. In response, we must continue to organize, intervene, disrupt, pressure, and strategize.

In this handbook, we have not offered a prescription for how exactly you should engage in this work. Instead, we have sought to introduce you to the rich dialogue surrounding each component of the criminal system and provide promising examples of action. Wherever you choose to focus your efforts, we welcome you to the cause.

Notes

Introduction

1. *The Case for More Incarceration*, United States Department of Justice, Office of Policy and Communications, October 28, 1992.
2. Keith Humphreys and Ekow Yankah argue that it is a mistake for opponents of mass incarceration to ignore the "unheard-of decline of Black incarceration." Keith Humphreys and Ekow Yankah, "The Unheard-of Decline in Black Incarceration," *Chicago Tribune*, July 25, 2022.
3. United Nations Office of the High Commissioner of Human Rights, "United Nations Special Rapporteur on torture calls for the prohibition of solitary confinement," October 18, 2011.
4. Jacob Whiton, "In Too Many American Communities, Mass Incarceration Has Become a Jobs Program," Brookings Institution, June 18, 2020.

Part I: Police

1. Leovy's reporting eventually became the basis for a book. Jill Leovy, *Ghettoside: A True Story of Murder in America* (New York: Spiegel and Grau, 2015).
2. For an additional perspective, see Thomas Abt's plan to reduce homicides and save lives through urban violence prevention. Thomas Abt, *Bleeding Out: The Devastating Consequences of Urban Violence—and a Bold New Plan for Peace in the Streets* (New York: Basic Books, 2019).
3. Cynthia Lum, Christopher S. Koper, and Xioyun Wu, "Can We Really Defund the Police? A Nine-Agency Study of Police Response to Calls for Service," *Police Quarterly* 25, no. 3 (2022): 255.
4. Jeff Asher and Ben Horwitz, "How Do the Police Actually Spend Their Time?," *The New York Times*, June 19, 2020.
5. Tahir Duckett, "The Overlooked, Enduring Legacy of the George Floyd Protests," *Time*, July 12, 2023.

6. Bureau of Justice Statistics, *Contacts Between Police and the Public, 2018—Statistical Tables*, Office of Justice Programs, U.S. Department of Justice, December 2020, last modified February 3, 2023.

7. Wesley Lowery, "A Disproportionate Number of Black Victims in Traffic Stops," *The Washington Post*, December 24, 2015.

8. For an extended discussion of these themes, we recommend Charles R. Epp, Steven Maynard-Moody, and Donald Haider-Markel, *Pulled Over: How Police Stops Define Race and Citizenship* (Chicago: University of Chicago Press, 2014), 1–17, and James Forman Jr., *Locking Up Our Own: Crime and Punishment in Black America* (New York: Farrar, Straus and Giroux, 2017), 185–215.

9. See for instance: Nazish Dholakia and Akhi Johnson, *Low-Level Traffic Stops Too Often Turn Deadly. Some Places Are Trying to Change That*, Vera Institute of Justice, February 9, 2022. For a more in-depth argument for replacing police with nonpolice traffic enforcement efforts, see Jordan Blair Woods, "Traffic Without the Police," *Stanford Law Review* 73, no. 6 (2021): 1471–1549.

10. Penny White and Glen Harlan Reynolds offer a similar proposal in "A Simple Solution to Policing for Profit," *The Wall Street Journal*, February 21, 2022.

11. Jamelle Bouie, "The Police Cannot Be a Law Unto Themselves," *The New York Times*, January 31, 2023.

12. For an insider's account of the campaign to elect this sheriff, Susan Hutson, see Sade Dumas, "A New Sheriff in Town," *Inquest*, February 19, 2022.

13. For more about reform-oriented sheriffs and elections, see Maurice Chammah, "Progressive Sheriffs Are Here. Will They Win in November?" *The Marshall Project*, October 22, 2022. And for the perspective that investing time, energy and resources in sheriff elections is misguided, see Jessica Pishko, "There Are No Progressive Sheriffs," *Posse Comitatus* Substack, November 14, 2022.

Part II: Prosecutors

1. In the 1973 decision *Inmates of Attica Correctional Facility v. Rockefeller*, for example, the Second Circuit said: "[T]he manifold imponderables which enter into the prosecutor's decision to prosecute or not to prosecute make the choice not readily amenable to judicial supervision." 477 F.2d 375, 380 (2d Cir. 1973).

2. United States Courts, Federal Judicial Caseload Statistics 2020 Tables, last modified March 31, 2020; Jed S. Rakoff, "Why Prosecutors Rule the Criminal Justice System—and What Can Be Done About It," *Northwestern University Law Review* 111, no. 6 (2017): 1429–36.

3. National Association of Criminal Defense Lawyers, *The Trial Penalty: The Sixth Amendment Right to Trial on the Verge of Extinction and How to Save It*, July 10, 2018.

4. Ram Subramanian, Leon Digard, Melvin Washington II, and Stephanie Sorange, *In the Shadows: A Review of the Research on Plea Bargaining*, Vera Institute of Justice, September 2020.

5. Carissa Byrne Hessick, *National Study of Prosecutor Elections*, The Prosecutor and Politics Project at the University of North Carolina School of Law, February 2020.

6. Hessick, *National Study of Prosecutor Elections.*

7. Reflective Democracy Campaign, *Tipping the Scales: Challengers Take on the Old Boys Club of Elected Prosecutors*, WhoLeads.us, October 2019.

8. Ashley Nellis, *The Color of Justice: Racial and Ethnic Disparity in State Prisons*, The Sentencing Project, October 13, 2021.

9. Gene Demby, "Study Reveals Worse Outcomes for Black and Latino Defendants," *National Public Radio*, July 17, 2014.

10. Cynthia Godsoe and Maybell Romero, "Prosecutorial Mutiny," *American Criminal Law Review* 60, no. 4 (2023): 1403–30; Dennis Romero, "Los Angeles County Prosecutors File Lawsuit Against New District Attorney Over Justice Reform Efforts," *NBC News*, January 1, 2021.

11. Akela Lacy and Ryan Grim, "Pennsylvania Lawmakers Move to Strip Reformist Prosecutor Larry Krasner of Authority," *The Intercept*, July 8, 2019.

12. Benjamin Schneider, "The Republican Billionaire Behind S.F.'s Recalls," *San Francisco Examiner*, September 13, 2022; Shaila Dewan, "The Lessons Liberal Prosecutors are Drawing from San Francisco's Backlash," *The New York Times*, June 13, 2022.

13. Rhonda Stewart, "How Black Female Prosecutors are Challenging the Status Quo and Fighting for Reform," *ABA Journal*, September 10, 2020; Nicole Lewis and Eli Hager, "Facing Intimidation, Black Women Prosecutors Say: 'Enough,'" *The Marshall Project*, January 16, 2020.

14. In 2023, Florida Governor Ron DeSantis also suspended reform-oriented Orlando State Attorney Monique Worrell, alleging neglect of duty. Incarceration rates decreased during Worrell's tenure, and she pledged not to prosecute doctors in abortion cases. Jeff Weiner, "After Filing Lawsuit, Worrell Calls Suspension by DeSantis 'His Latest Abuse of Power,'" *Orlando Sentinel*, September 7, 2023.

15. Kathleen Foody, "Chicago-Area Prosecutor Kim Foxx Won't Seek Third Term," *AP*, April 25, 2023.

16. Samantha Michaels, "The Real Reason People Want to Oust Prosecutor Kim Foxx Has Nothing to Do with Jussie Smollett," *Mother Jones*, March 13, 2020.

17. Akela Lacey, "Why St. Louis's Reform DA Kim Gardner Quit," *The Intercept*, May 6, 2023.

18. Christina Carrega, "The Thwarted Promise of Black Women Prosecutors," *Capital B News*, June 9, 2023.

19. Bureau of Justice Statistics, *2007 National Census of State Court Prosecutors*, U.S. Department of Justice, Office of Justice Programs, December 2011.

Abolitionist Principles and Campaign Strategies
for Prosecutor Organizing

1. Jeremy B. White, "San Francisco District Attorney Ousted in Recall Election," *Politico*, June 8, 2022.

2. Eleanor Klibanoff, "House Passes Bill to Rein In 'Rogue' Prosecutors," *The Texas Tribune*, April 27, 2023; "Florida Court Won't Reinstate Prosecutor Removed by DeSantis for Refusal to Prosecute Abortion Cases," *AP News*, June 22, 2023.

3. Akela Lacy, "17 States Have Now Tried to Pass Bills That Strip Powers from

Reform-Minded Prosecutors," *The Intercept*, March 3, 2023; Emily Bazelon, "The Response to Crime," *The New York Times*, April 7, 2023.

4. "No Such Thing as 'Progressive Prosecutors,'" *Beyond Criminal Courts: Defund and Divest*, https://beyondcourts.org/en/learn/no-such-thing-progressive-prosecutors.
5. "Meet the Candidates," People's Coalition for Manhattan DA Accountability, https://web.archive.org/web/20230201120828/https://peopleforprosecutoraccountability.org/candidate-comparison.
6. Taylor Blackston and Sojourner Rivers, "To Address Gender-Based Violence, First Defund the Prosecutors," *Truthout*, June 17, 2021.
7. Rachel Foran, Mariame Kaba, and Katy Naples-Mitchell, *Abolitionist Principles for Prosecutor Organizing: Origins and Next Steps*, 16 Stan. J. C.R. & C.L. 496 (2021).
8. *Beyond Criminal Courts: Defund and Divest*, https://beyondcourts.org.
9. Survived and Punished NY, *No Good Prosecutors Now or Ever: How the Manhattan District Attorney Hoards Money, Perpetuates Abuse of Survivors, and Gags Their Advocates*, June 2021, https://www.survivedandpunishedny.org/anti-prosecution/no-good-das-zine/.

Part III: Public Defenders
1. Public defenders can include private court-appointed counsel, lawyers in nonprofit organizations, and those in institutional offices. The right to counsel protects people at trial, on appeal, and at certain other stages of the process.
2. Richard A. Oppel Jr. and Jugal K. Patel, "One Lawyer, 194 Felony Cases, and No Time," *The New York Times*, January 21, 2019.

Why Public Defenders Matter More Than Ever in a Time of Reform
1. A *Brady* violation occurs when the prosecution does not disclose to the defense evidence favorable to the accused. *Brady v. Maryland*, 373 U.S. 83, 87 (1963).

Interview with Raj Jayadev, Conducted by Premal Dharia
1. Silicon Valley De-Bug is a storytelling, community organizing, and advocacy organization based in San José, California.

Part IV: Judges
1. Rachel Barkow, "The Court of Mass Incarceration," in *Cato Supreme Court Review* (Washington, D.C.: The Cato Institute, 2022), 11–36.
2. *Terry v. Ohio*, 392 U.S. 1, 30 (1968).
3. *Whren v. United States*, 517 U.S. 806, 806 (1996).
4. Lara Bazelon and James Forman Jr., "Liberals Should Use State Courts to Check the Supreme Court," *New York*, July 5, 2023.
5. *Commonwealth v. Long*, 485 Mass. 711 (2020).
6. *United States v. Salerno*, 481 U.S. 739, 755 (1987).
7. John Matthews II and Felipe Curiel, "Criminal Justice Debt Problems," *Human Rights Magazine* 44, no. 3 (November 2019).

8. "[M]ore than 60 percent of inmates are detained prior to trial due to an inability to afford posting bail." *The Civil Rights Implications of Cash Bail* (Washington, D.C.: The U.S. Commission on Civil Rights, 2022), ii.

9. Léon Digard and Elizabeth Swavola, *Justice Denied: The Harmful and Lasting Effects of Pretrial Detention* (New York: Vera Institute of Justice, 2019); Paul Heaton, Sandra Mayson, and Megan Stevenson, "The Downstream Consequences of Misdemeanor Pretrial Detention," *Stanford Law Review* 69, no. 3 (2017): 711; Will Dobbie, Jacob Goldin, and Crystal Yang, "The Effects of Pretrial Detention on Conviction, Future Crime, and Employment: Evidence from Randomly Assigned Judges" (working paper 22511, National Bureau of Economic Research, 2016); Matt Keyser, "'I Just Felt So Violated': Harvard Researcher's Study Shows 'Devastating' Effects of Jailing People Pretrial," National Partnership for Pretrial Justice (2023).

10. *Rowe v. Kwame Raoul*, 2023 IL 129248 (July 18, 2023).

11. In 2020, in response to political backlash, New York revised its 2019 bail reform law. The law was again revised in both 2022 and 2023.

12. A report on judicial decision-making and pretrial detention in New York was released in 2023: https://www.scrutinize.org/our-work.

13. Mark F. Bernstein, "How New Jersey Made a Bail Breakthrough." *Princeton Alumni Weekly*, November 24, 2020.

14. In fact, some bail reforms may contribute to more surveillance of people through electronic monitoring. Sandra Susan Smith and Cierra Robson, "Between a Rock and a Hard Place: The Social Costs of Pretrial Electronic Monitoring in San Francisco" (working paper series RWP22 014, HKS Faculty Research, September 2022).

15. There is, in criminal system reform, and particularly in bail reform, a constant tension around the short- and long-term implications of policy choices. The stakes are high everywhere—real people's lives and freedom are directly implicated—and political realities are different everywhere. For an example of a slightly different approach, in Illinois, the Coalition to End Money Bond, a coalition of organizers and community members that advocated for the Pretrial Fairness Act, put forth a set of principles that undergirded their approach to bail reform: https://endmoneybond.org/pretrialfairness.

16. Ashley Nellis, "No End In Sight: America's Enduring Reliance on Life Sentences." *The Sentencing Project*, February 17, 2021.

17. On December 15, 2020, the D.C. Council unanimously passed the Omnibus Public Safety and Justice Act of 2020. First introduced in 2019, the law allows a person who committed a crime before the age of twenty-five, and who has served a minimum of fifteen years in prison, to apply to the D.C. Superior Court to have their sentence reviewed.

New Jersey Bail Conversation

1. Marie VanNostrand, *New Jersey Jail Population Analysis: Identifying Opportunities to Safely and Responsibly Reduce the Jail Population* (New York: Drug Policy Alliance, March 2013).

Part V: Prisons

1. Not everyone shares Robinson's definition of abolition. Some abolitionists reject the idea that harm can ever be eliminated. Instead, they see abolitionist practice as one that focuses on developing nonpunitive accountability structures to address the harm that will inevitably arise between people and in communities. For example, Mariame Kaba says, "Some people think the abolitionist horizon is a destination that we reach, where human beings, if they continue to exist as human beings, don't do harm. I don't believe that. I think that humans, as long as we're still humans, are going to harm each other. The difference is we will have other ways of addressing harm that are not prisons, policing, and surveillance." Mariame Kaba, "Abolition Is a Collective Vision: An Interview with Mariame Kaba," interview by Elias Rodriques, *The Nation*, March 29, 2021.

2. Fay Honey Knopp, "The Power of Words," in *Instead of Prisons: A Handbook for Abolitionists*, ed. Mark Morris (New York: Prison Action Research Project, 1976).

3. We should note that while Norway's Halden prison and others like it may be more humane, they are still prisons. As such, they necessarily inflict pain upon those incarcerated within them. For a discussion of Halden's punitive aspects, see Ashley Kilmer and Sami Abdel-Salam, "Pretty and Punitive," *Inquest*, October 20, 2022.

4. Miriam Gohara, "A Prison Program in Connecticut Seeks to Find Out What Happens When Prisoners Are Treated as Victims," *The Conversation*, March 9, 2019; Maurice Chammah, "The Connecticut Experiment," *The Marshall Project*, May 8, 2018.

5. Alexandra Gibbons and Rashawn Ray, "The Societal Benefits of Postsecondary Prison Education," The Brookings Institution, August 20, 2021; Lois M. Davis, Jennifer L. Steele, Robert Bozick, Malcolm V. Williams, Susan Turner, Jeremy N. V. Miles, Jessica Saunders, and Paul S. Steinberg, *How Effective Is Correctional Education, and Where Do We Go from Here? The Results of a Comprehensive Evaluation*, RAND Corporation, 2014.

6. While restoring Pell is a crucial first step, lawmakers, prison officials, and universities need to do much to make higher education in prison a meaningful reality. Abraham Santiago and Norman Gaines outline some of these essential next steps in "A Passport to Freedom," *Inquest*, November 10, 2022.

7. Christopher Blackwell, who is serving a forty-five-year prison sentence in Washington State, offers another compelling reflection on the power of education. "I Grew Up Believing I Was Dumb. A College Education Behind Bars Healed That Wound," *The Marshall Project*, April 4, 2022.

8. Tracy Huling, "Building a Prison Economy in Rural America," in *Invisible Punishment: The Collateral Consequences of Mass Imprisonment*, eds. Marc Mauer and Meda Chesney-Lind (New York: The New Press, 2003), 197–213. As a result of this growth, almost as many people work in the criminal justice system as are employed in the nation's agriculture sector. See Lenore Anderson, *In Their Names: The Untold Story of Victims' Rights, Mass Incarceration, and the Future of Public Safety* (New York: The New Press, 2022), 13.

9. See "California Correctional Center (CCC)," California Department of Cor-

rections and Rehabilitation, last modified June 30, 2023, https://www.cdcr.ca
.gov/facility-locator/ccc

Part VI: Aftermath

1. "Prisoners and Prisoner Re-Entry," United States Department of Justice, ac-
    cessed January 24, 2023, https://www.justice.gov/archive/fbci/progmenu
    _reentry.html.
2. While this chapter focuses on punishment after conviction and release from
    prison, it is important to point that out our system imposes pain and suffering
    long *before* conviction. As chapter four explains, when judges jail someone
    pending trial, that person may lose their home, job, or custody of their chil-
    dren. Even if they are never convicted, their arrest record alone can plague
    them for decades. Laura Appleman, "Justice in the Shadowlands: Pretrial
    Detention, Punishment, & the Sixth Amendment," *Washington and Lee Law
    Review* 69, no. 3 (2012): 1297. In addition to these burdens, people released
    from prison are subject to government supervision in their daily lives through
    probation and parole, which both carry the constant threat of re-incarceration
    for any violation. And violations can include things like missed curfews, failed
    drug tests, failure to get permission to travel or to change homes, and missed
    office appointments, in addition to new law violations. Vincent Schiraldi,
    Mass Supervision: Probation, Parole, and the Illusion of Safety and Freedom
    (New York: The New Press, 2023).
3. In addition, they may have already lost parts of their lives—and mental
    health—that they can never regain. Reuben Jonathan Miller, *Halfway Home:
    Race, Punishment, and the Afterlife of Mass Incarceration* (Boston: Little,
    Brown and Company, 2021); Bruce Western, *Homeward: Life in the Year After
    Prison* (New York: Russell Sage Foundation, 2018).
4. "National Inventory of the Collateral Consequences of Conviction,"
    American Bar Association, accessed January 24, 2023, https://niccc
    .nationalreentryresourcecenter.org/consequences.
5. One of the primary ways in which a criminal record restricts opportunities is
    through the use of background checks, which are used by nearly nine in ten
    employers, four in five landlords, and three in five colleges. Society for Human
    Resource Management, "Background Checking—The Use of Criminal Back-
    ground Checks in Hiring Decisions" (2012): 2; David Thacher, "The Rise of
    Criminal Background Screening in Rental Housing," *Law and Social Inquiry*
    33, no. 1 (2008): 5, 12; Marsha Weissman et al., *The Use of Criminal History Rec-
    ords in College Admissions Reconsidered* (New York: Center for Community
    Alternatives, 2010).
6. Michelle Alexander, *The New Jim Crow: Mass Incarceration in the Age of Col-
    orblindness* (New York: The New Press, 2012).
7. The Dave's Killer Bread Foundation was created to inspire and equip other
    businesses to adopt Second Chance Employment. Jobs for Future has acquired
    the Second Chance Employment programs. These programs will become part
    of the Jobs for Future's Center for Justice and Economic Advancement.
8. Julie Cook Ramirez, "How Companies Are Putting Ex-Offenders Back to

Work," *Human Resource Executive*, October 21, 2019. New York's Greyston Bakery is another industry leader worth studying. Greyston uses an "open hiring" system in which the company doesn't ask about criminal history at all. Instead all applicants get a shot to work as an apprentice. Those who perform well are invited to join the union and become full-time employees with benefits.

9. Amee Chew and Chione Lucina Muñoz Flegal, *Facing History, Uprooting Inequality: A Path to Housing Justice in California* (PolicyLink, 2020); Lucius Couloute, *Nowhere to Go: Homelessness Among Formerly Incarcerated People* (Prison Policy Initiative, August 2018).

10. Just Cities, "Comparison of National North Star Fair Chance Housing Laws;" National Employment Law Project (NELP), "Ensuring People with Convictions Have a Fair Chance to Work."

11. Ginger Jackson-Gleich, "Rigging the Jury: How Each State Reduces Jury Diversity by Excluding People with Criminal Records," Prison Policy Initiative, February 2021.

12. Restoration of Rights Project, "50-State Comparison: Pardon Policy & Practice," October 2022. The eight states that Fleury-Steiner mentions are Oklahoma, Arkansas, Alabama, Connecticut, Delaware, Georgia, Pennsylvania, and South Carolina. As of this book's publication, the count of states has increased to fifteen.

13. The White House, Statement from President Biden on Marijuana Reform, October 6, 2022. President Biden released a statement announcing a pardon for all prior Federal offenses of simple possession of marijuana and explaining that this action will help relieve the collateral consequences arising from these convictions such as lack of access to employment, housing, and education opportunities.

Conclusion

1. *Utah v. Strieff*, 579 U.S. 232, 254 (2016), (Sotomayor, J., dissenting).

2. David Garland, "Introduction: The Meaning of Mass Imprisonment," *Punishment and Society* 3, no. 1, (January 2001): 5–7.

3. Michelle Alexander, *The New Jim Crow: Mass Incarceration in the Age of Colorblindness* (New York: The New Press, 2012); Ta-Nehisi Coates, "The Black Family in the Age of Mass Incarceration," *The Atlantic*, October 2015.

4. There are thousands of excerpts and essays that we did not include in this volume: works that tell the story of how mass incarceration came to be; works that capture our country's history of white supremacy and slavery; works that illuminate the role of capitalism and industry in the growth of the carceral state; or works that describe reforms that, in our view, might actually help entrench mass incarceration rather than dismantle it. Many of these are important contributions. But they are not our focus in this book.

5. In Atlanta, bail fund and legal support workers were recently charged with money laundering and charity fraud in connection with support for protestors challenging the construction of a new police training center dubbed "Cop City." Natasha Lennard, "Atlanta Police Charge Organizers of Bail Fund

for Cop City Protestors," *The Intercept*, May 31, 2023. Other jurisdictions have passed laws, courts have changed interpretations, and prosecutors have changed prosecution practices in such areas as the First Amendment, land use, public nuisance, and much more in response to increased protest. See, for example, Daniel Nichanian, "'Designed to End Protesting': Louisiana Supreme Court Makes Protesters Guilty by Association," *Bolts*, March 28, 2022; Tameka Greer, "Tennessee's Attack of First Amendment Right to Protest Turns Attention Away from Real Issues," *Commercial Appeal*, April 10, 2023; and Alexandria Herr, "'They Criminalize Us': How Felony Charges Are Weaponized Against Pipeline Protesters," *The Guardian*, February 10, 2022 (originally published in *Floodlight*). See also, Jocelyn Simonson, "Forget Trump, the Latest Georgia RICO Case Is a Disaster for Civil Liberties," *Slate*, September 7, 2023.

6. Critical Resistance, *Reformist Reforms vs. Abolitionist Steps to End Imprisonment*, 2021; Critical Resistance, *Reformist Reforms vs. Abolitionist Steps in Policing*, 2020.

7. Derecka Purnell, Olúfémi O. Táíwò, and Keeanga-Yamahtta Taylor, "After the Uprising, What Is to Be Done?" *Hammer & Hope*, no. 1 (Winter 2023).

Acknowledgments

For help with research and editing, we would like to thank Steffen Seitz, Jelani Hayes, Chaka Laguerre, Felisha Miles, Katherine Salinas, Claire Stobb, Jordan Jefferson, Tyler Walls, Taiwo Dosunmu, Pragya Malik, Zoe Li, Amanda Gómez Feliz, Otelo Reggy-Beane, and Caroline Korndorffer.

Thank you to our friends and colleagues who listened, debated, and discussed with us and also read drafts at different stages. That list is long and we can't name everyone here but want to make sure to acknowledge Arthur Evenchik, Chris Kemmitt, Konrad Schlater, Alexa Van Brunt, and Diane Geraghty.

And last but not least, thank you to our tenacious agent, David McCormick, as well as to our thoughtful editor, Alex Star, Ian Van Wye, and the entire team at Farrar, Straus and Giroux.

Notes About the Contributors

The late JEFF ADACHI was the elected public defender of San Francisco. He was also an award-winning documentary filmmaker and an author, and he served on numerous boards and committees focused on racial and criminal justice.

RACHEL E. BARKOW is Charles Seligson Professor of Law at New York University and the faculty director of the Peter L. Zimroth Center on the Administration of Criminal Law. From 2013 to 2019, she served as a member of the United States Sentencing Commission. She is the author of *Prisoner of Politics: Breaking the Cycle of Mass Incarceration*.

LAWRENCE BARTLEY is the publisher of *The Marshall Project Inside*, the organization's publications intended specifically for incarcerated audiences.

EMILY BAZELON is a staff writer at *The New York Times Magazine*, the Truman Capote Fellow for Creative Writing and Law at Yale University, and a cohost of *Slate's Political Gabfest* podcast. She is the author of *Charged: The New Movement to Transform American Prosecution and End Mass Incarceration* and *Sticks and Stones: Defeating the Culture of Bullying and Rediscovering the Power of Character and Empathy*.

KATHERINE BECKETT is a sociologist and a professor at the University of Washington. She helped develop the Rethinking Punishment Radio Project.

MONICA BELL is a professor of law and sociology at Yale University and an author. Her work has been published in law reviews, journals, and outlets such as *Politico*.

NOAH BERLATSKY is a freelance writer and editor whose work has been published in various national publications. He is also the author of *Wonder Woman: Bondage and Feminism in the Marston/Peter Comics, 1941–1948*.

REGINALD DWAYNE BETTS is a lawyer, a poet, and the founder of Freedom Reads.

JAMES M. BINNALL is an associate professor of law, criminology, and criminal justice at California State University, Long Beach, and the author of *Twenty Million Angry Men: The Case for Including Convicted Felons in Our Jury System.*

FREDERIC BLOCK was appointed United States district judge for the Eastern District of New York in 1994.

PAUL D. BUTLER is the Albert Brick Professor in Law at Georgetown University and a legal analyst on MSNBC. He is a member of the American Law Institute and serves on the DC Code Revision Commission. He is the author of *Let's Get Free: A Hip-Hop Theory of Justice* and *Chokehold: Policing Black Men.* He was previously a federal prosecutor.

MATT CALDWELL is a public defender in New York City. He started his career at the Miami-Dade Public Defender's Office in Miami and has worked at The Bronx Defenders, Brooklyn Defender Services, and the Legal Aid Society.

COMMUNITY JUSTICE EXCHANGE develops, shares, and experiments with tactical interventions, strategic organizing practices, and innovative organizing tools to end all forms of criminalization, incarceration, surveillance, supervision, and detention. It is also the host of the National Bail Fund Network.

ANGELA J. DAVIS is Distinguished Professor of Law at American University. She was previously the director of the Public Defender Service for the District of Columbia. She is a member of the American Law Institute and the Council on Criminal Justice and the author of *Policing the Black Man: Arrest, Prosecution and Imprisonment* and *Arbitrary Justice: The Power of the American Prosecutor.*

ANGELA Y. DAVIS is a scholar, an author, an activist, and a Black feminist philosopher. She is a founding member of Critical Resistance, an organization dedicated to the abolition of the prison industrial system.

FIVE BORO DEFENDERS (5BD) is an informal collective of public defenders, civil rights attorneys, and advocates fighting for the rights of indigent New Yorkers.

BEN FLEURY-STEINER is a professor of sociology and criminal justice at the University of Delaware.

PIPER FRENCH is an independent writer and journalist whose work has appeared in many publications, including *The New York Review of Books, The New Republic,* and the *Los Angeles Review of Books.*

NANCY GERTNER is a former United States district judge, a professor at Harvard University, and an author.

RUTH WILSON GILMORE directs the Center for Place, Culture, and Politics at the CUNY Graduate Center and is the author of *Golden Gulag: Prisons, Surplus, Crisis, and Opposition in Globalizing California.*

MARIE GOTTSCHALK is a political scientist, a professor at the University of

Pennsylvania, and the author of several books, including *Caught: The Prison State and the Lockdown of American Politics.*

ALEXIS HOAG-FORDJOUR is a dean's research scholar, assistant professor of law, and codirector of the Center for Criminal Justice at Brooklyn Law School. She is also a legal contributor for CNN and spent more than a decade as a civil rights and criminal defense lawyer, primarily representing capitally convicted clients in federal post-conviction proceedings, with the NAACP Legal Defense and Educational Fund, Inc., and the Office of the Federal Public Defender in Nashville, Tennessee.

ELIE HONIG is a lawyer and legal commentator. He has worked as the deputy director of the Division of Criminal Justice in the attorney general of New Jersey's office. He is an author whose most recent book is *Untouchable: How Powerful People Get Away with It.*

ADRIAN HORTON is the arts writer for *The Guardian* U.S.

ALLY JARMANNING is a senior reporter at WBUR. Her work focuses on criminal justice and police accountability.

RAJ JAYADEV is the cofounder of Silicon Valley De-Bug, which focuses on community organizing, advocacy, and multimedia storytelling, and coordinates the National Participatory Defense Network. In 2018, he was named a MacArthur Fellow.

ROGÉ KARMA is a staff writer at *The Atlantic*, where he covers economics and economic policy. He was previously the senior editor of *The Ezra Klein Show* at *The New York Times.*

BILL KELLER is a journalist and was the founding editor-in-chief of *The Marshall Project.*

JAMES KILGORE is an activist, researcher, and writer who spent six and a half years in state and federal prisons. He is the author of *Understanding Mass Incarceration: A People's Guide to the Key Civil Rights Struggle of Our Time.*

The late FAY HONEY KNOPP was an American Quaker minister, a peace and civil rights advocate, and a prison abolitionist.

LARRY KRASNER is the district attorney of Philadelphia. He was previously a criminal defense and civil rights attorney.

JILL LEOVY worked for more than two decades as a reporter and editor at the *Los Angeles Times.* She is the author of *Ghettoside: A True Story of Murder in America.*

KIRA LERNER is the democracy editor for *The Guardian* U.S.

SAM MELLINS is a senior reporter at *New York Focus.* His reporting has appeared in numerous publications, including the *San Francisco Chronicle.*

CRYSTAL MOURLAS-JAUN is a project manager for Jobs for the Future.

The late CHARLES J. OGLETREE JR. was the Jesse Climenko Professor of Law at Harvard University and the founding and executive director of the Charles Hamilton Houston Institute for Race and Justice there. He was the author of several books and articles, and formerly served as the deputy director of the Public Defender Service for the District of Columbia.

ZACHARIAH OQUENDA is an attorney who lives in Sacramento, California.

TAYLOR PENDERGRASS was the director of advocacy and strategic alliances for the ACLU of Colorado. He was previously an ACLU national deputy director of campaigns.

JOHN F. PFAFF is a law professor at Fordham University and the author of *Locked In: The True Causes of Mass Incarceration and How to Achieve Real Reform.*

JESSICA PISHKO is an independent journalist, a lawyer, and the author of *The Highest Law in the Land: How the Growing Power of Sheriffs Threatens Democracy.* Since 2018, she has focused on American sheriffs.

LORI POMPA is the founder and executive director of The Inside-Out Prison Exchange Program.

DERECKA PURNELL is a human rights lawyer, a writer, and the author of *Becoming Abolitionists: Police, Protests, and the Pursuit of Freedom.*

THE REFLECTIVE DEMOCRACY CAMPAIGN, founded by the Women Donors Network, investigates and generates data on the demographics of American politics and confronts those demographics by catalyzing and supporting nationwide activism.

NATHAN J. ROBINSON is the editor-in-chief of *Current Affairs.*

SARAH A. SEO is a legal historian, a professor at Columbia University, and the author of *Policing the Open Road: How Cars Transformed American Freedom.*

ALEXANDER SHALOM is a lawyer and director of Supreme Court advocacy at the ACLU–NJ.

PATRICK SHARKEY is a sociologist, a professor at Princeton University, and the author of articles and books, including *Uneasy Peace: The Great Crime Decline, the Renewal of City Life, and the Next War on Violence.*

DASHKA SLATER is a journalist and the author of many books, including, most recently, *Accountable: The True Story of a Racist Social Media Account and the Teenagers Whose Lives It Changed.*

RAHSAAN SLOAN is a production coordinator for Dave's Killer Bread.

ABBE SMITH is the Scott K. Ginsburg Professor of Law at Georgetown University, where she is also the director of the Criminal Defense and Prisoner Advocacy Clinic and codirector of the E. Barrett Prettyman Fellowship Program. She was formerly a public defender at the Defender Association of Philadelphia. She is a member of the American Board of Criminal Lawyers and an author of numerous articles and multiple books.

CLINT SMITH is a poet and staff writer for *The Atlantic.* He is the author of *How the Word Is Passed: A Reckoning with the History of Slavery Across America.*

WILLIAM SNOWDEN is a professor at Loyola University New Orleans and a former public defender. He previously worked as the Louisiana director of the Vera Institute for Justice. He founded The Juror Project.

FORREST STUART is an ethnographer, a professor at Stanford University, and an author. His most recent book is titled *Ballad of the Bullet: Gangs, Drill Music, and the Power of Online Infamy*.

SOMIL TRIVEDI is the chief legal and advocacy director of Maryland Legal Aid. He was previously a senior staff attorney with the Criminal Law Reform Project of the ACLU.

IAN WARD is a journalist and a reporter for *Politico* and *Politico Magazine*.

Permissions Acknowledgments

Part I: Police

Derecka Purnell, "How I Became a Police Abolitionist." *The Atlantic*, July 6, 2020. Reprinted with permission of the author.

Jill Leovy, in Conversation with *The Marshall Project*'s Bill Keller, "*Ghettoside* Author Jill Leovy on What We Have Learned Since Rodney King: Not Nearly Enough, She Says." *The Marshall Project*, March 3, 2016. Reprinted with permission of the author.

Patrick Sharkey, in Conversation with Rogé Karma, "How Cities Can Tackle Violent Crime Without Relying on Police." *Vox*, August 7, 2020. Reprinted with permission of the author.

Editorial Board, "Whom Can We Call for Help? Police Should Not Always Be the Only Option." *The Washington Post*, March 16, 2021. Reprinted with permission of *The Washington Post*.

Katherine Beckett, Forrest Stuart, and Monica Bell, "From Crisis to Care." *Inquest*, September 2, 2021. Reprinted with permission of the authors.

Sarah A. Seo, "Police Officers Shouldn't Be the Ones to Enforce Traffic Laws." *The New York Times*, April 15, 2021. Reprinted with permission of the author.

Fines and Fees Justice Center, "Fines, Fees, and Police Divestment: Statement and Policy Recommendations." August 4, 2020. Reprinted with permission of the Fines and Fees Justice Center.

Jessica Pishko, "She Wants to Fix One of Louisiana's Deadliest Jails. She Needs to Beat the Sheriff First." *Politico*, November 10, 2021. Reprinted with permission of the author.

Marie Gottschalk, "Bring It On: The Future of Penal Reform, the Carceral State, and American Politics." *Ohio State Journal of Criminal Law* 12, no. 2 (Spring 2015): 559–603. Reprinted with permission of the author.

Part II: Prosecutors

John F. Pfaff, From *Locked In: The True Causes of Mass Incarceration and How to Achieve Real Reform*. New York: Basic Books, 2017. Reprinted with permission of the author.

Reflective Democracy Campaign, "Tipping the Scales: Challengers Take On the Old Boys' Club of Elected Prosecutors," October 2019. Reprinted with permission of the author.

Emily Bazelon, From *Charged: The New Movement to Transform American Prosecution and End Mass Incarceration*. New York: Random House, 2019. Excerpts from *Charged: The New Movement to Transform American Prosecution and End Mass Incarceration* by Emily Bazelon, copyright © 2019 by Emily Bazelon. Used by permission of Random House, an imprint and division of Penguin Random House LLC. All rights reserved.

Angela J. Davis, "Reimagining Prosecution: A Growing Progressive Movement." *UCLA Criminal Justice Law Review* 3, no. 1 (2019): 2–27. Reprinted with permission of the author.

Taylor Pendergrass and Somil Trivedi, "Beyond Reform: Four Virtues of a Transformational Prosecutor," *Stanford Journal of Civil Rights and Civil Liberties* 16, no. 3 (2021): 435–55. Reprinted with permission of the authors.

Rachel E. Barkow, "Can Prosecutors End Mass Incarceration?," *Michigan Law Review* 119, no. 6 (2021): 1365–97. Reprinted with permission of the author.

Community Justice Exchange, CourtWatch MA, Families for Justice as Healing, Project NIA, and Survived and Punished NY, "Abolitionist Principles and Campaign Strategies for Prosecutor Organizing." 2019. Updated January 22, 2020. Reprinted with permission of the authors.

Paul Butler, "Should Good People Be Prosecutors?," *Let's Get Free: A Hip-Hop Theory of Justice.* New York: The New Press, 2009. Reprinted with permission of the author.

Part III: Public Defenders

Charles J. Ogletree Jr., "An Essay on the New Public Defender for the 21st Century." *Law and Contemporary Problems* 58, no. 1 (1995): 812–85. Reprinted with permission of Pamela Ogletree.

Abbe Smith, "Defending Those People." *Ohio State Journal of Criminal Law* 10, no. 1 (2012): 277–302. Reprinted with permission of the author.

Noah Berlatsky, "Want to Reduce Mass Incarceration? Fund Public Defenders." *Medium*, September 11, 2018. Reprinted with permission of the author.

Paul D. Butler, "Poor People Lose: *Gideon* and the Critique of Rights." *The Yale Law Journal* 122, no. 8 (June 2013): 2176–2204. Reprinted with permission of the author.

Matthew Caldwell, "The End of Public Defenders." *Inquest*, February 22, 2022. Reprinted with permission of the author.

John F. Pfaff, "Why Public Defenders Matter More Than Ever in a Time of Reform." *The Appeal*, April 18, 2018. Reprinted with permission of the author.

Jeff Adachi, "Ten Things Public Defenders Can Do to Stand Up for Racial Justice," *Medium*, September 28, 2015. Reprinted with permission of Mutsuko Adachi.

Alexis Hoag-Fordjour, "Black on Black Representation." *New York University Law Review* 96 no. 5 (November 2021): 1493–1548. Reprinted with permission of the author.

Five Boro Defenders, *Manhattan DA Race 2021: A Voter Guide.* 2021. Reprinted with permission of the author.

Raj Jayadev, "1,862 Fewer Years in Prison." *PopTech*, October 23, 2015, 5:44 (video). Reprinted with permission of the author.

Interview with Raj Jayadev, Conducted by Premal Dharia. Reprinted with permission of the interviewee.

Part IV: Judges

Ally Jarmanning, "Mass. High Court Lowers Burden for Proving Racial Bias in Police Stops." WBUR News, September 17, 2020. Reprinted with permission of WBUR News.

Sam Mellins, "Judge Frees Man from Rikers in Exceptional Decision Citing Bail and

Jail Conditions." *The City*, September 21, 2022. Reprinted with permission of the author.

Alexander Shalom and Elie Honig, Interviewed by James Forman Jr., "New Jersey Bail Conversation." Original contribution. Printed with permission of the interviewees.

William Snowden, "How to Save a Life from the Jury Box." New Leaders Council Spark! Talk, YouTube, August 30, 2019, 5:10 (video). Reprinted with permission of the author.

Ian Ward, "How Progressives Are Knocking Out Local Judges Across the Country." *Politico*, September 3, 2021. Reprinted with permission of the author.

Nancy Gertner, "Reimagining Judging." The Square One Project, January 2021. Reprinted with permission of the author.

Part V: Prisons

Angela Y. Davis, From *Are Prisons Obsolete?* New York: Seven Stories Press, 2003. Reprinted with the permission of The Permissions Company, LLC on behalf of Seven Stories Press, sevenstories.com. All rights reserved.

Fay Honey Knopp, "Nine Perspectives for Prison Abolitionists." *Instead of Prisons: A Handbook for Abolitionists*, ed. Mark Morris. New York: Prison Action Research Project, 1976. Reprinted with permission of Alex Knopp.

Nathan J. Robinson, "Can Prison Abolition Ever Be Pragmatic?," *Current Affairs*, August 3, 2017. Reprinted with permission of the author.

Ruth Wilson Gilmore and James Kilgore, "The Case for Abolition." *The Marshall Project*, June 19, 2019. Reprinted with permission of the authors.

Reginald Dwayne Betts, "On Cages" Twitter Thread. October 22, 2019, 5:33 PM, https://twitter.com/dwaynebetts/status/1186757383361568770?s=20. Reprinted with permission of the author.

Dashka Slater, "North Dakota's Norway Experiment." *Mother Jones*, July/August 2017. Reprinted with permission of the author.

Clint Smith, "Restoring Pell Grants—and Possibilities—for Prisoners." *The Atlantic*, March 11, 2021. Reprinted with permission of *The Atlantic*.

Lori Pompa, "The Inside-Out Prison Exchange Program: Its Origin, Essence, and Global Reach." In *Giving Voice to Diversity in Criminological Research*, eds. Orla Lynch, James Windle, and Yasmine Ahmed. Bristol: Bristol University Press Digital, 2021, 253–56. Reprinted with permission of the author.

Adrian Horton, "'It Feels Like the Start of Something': Reginald Dwayne Betts on His Groundbreaking Prison Library Project." *The Guardian*, October 8, 2021. Reprinted with permission of the author.

Piper French, "A Future for Susanville." *Inquest* and *Bolts*, May 5, 2022. Reprinted with permission of the author.

Part VI: Aftermath

Lawrence Bartley, Crystal Mourlas-Jaun, and Rahsaan Sloan, "A Conversation About Second Chance Employment." 2023. Reprinted with permission of the authors.

Zachariah Oquenda, "The Case for a Fair Chance Housing Act: From a Brother's Perspective." *Medium*, July 20, 2021. Reprinted with permission of the author.

Kira Lerner, "D.C. Residents Are Voting from Prison This Week." *Bolts*, June 20, 2022. Reprinted with permission of the author.

James M. Binnall, "The Time I Was Called for Jury Duty . . . and What Happened Next." 2023. Original contribution. Printed with permission of the author.

Ben Fleury-Steiner, "Rights Restoration Success Stories." 2023. Original contribution. Printed with permission of the author.